NOTES
ON THE NEW TRANSLATION
OF THE TORAH

COMMITTEE OF TRANSLATORS OF The Torah

Editor-in-Chief	Harry M. Orlinsky
Fellow Editors	H. L. Ginsberg
	E. A. Speiser ז״ל
	Max Arzt
	Bernard J. Bamberger
	Harry Freedman
Secretary	Solomon Grayzel

Notes ON THE NEW TRANSLATION OF The Torah

Edited by HARRY M. ORLINSKY

for the Committee for the Translation of The Torah

THE JEWISH PUBLICATION SOCIETY OF AMERICA

PHILADELPHIA | 5731–1970

First edition, Second Impression

Library of Congress Catalog Card Number 69-19042
Manufactured in the United States of America
Designed by Sidney Feinberg

Contents

Introduction

The purpose of this volume of *Notes* is to account for the significant or interesting departures in the New Jewish Version (NJV) of the Torah from the older version of 1917. The *Notes* are intended primarily for the readers of the Torah translation and are based upon the Second Edition, First Impression of that translation. A projected Hebrew-English edition (to include the Torah, Haftaroth, and Megilloth) will be published in the next year or two. This edition will contain some variations which are intended to improve still further the translation found in the Second Edition. These variations are given in the *Notes* and are clearly indicated as belonging to the projected Hebrew-English edition.

This is the first time that a committee responsible for an official translation of the Bible has attempted a public and systematic exposition—in both the obsolete and the current meanings of the term—of its labors and reasoning. This unprecedented act is due in no small measure to the fact that there is now available, for the first time, a large knowledgeable and inquisitive audience for such *Notes.* A translation of the Bible in the vernacular for the Jewish community as a whole, or a commentary on the Bible, is one thing; an explanation of a translation is something else again. But mid-twentieth century America is not exactly a traditional time and clime for its Jewish community of over five and a half million souls. This sociological fact is evident from the new translation itself.

A *The Four Great Ages of Bible Translation*

The middle third of our twentieth century has witnessed the fourth great age of Bible translations. Back in the third and second centuries B.C.E., there lived in Alexandria, Egypt, a large and flourishing Jewish community that felt close attachment to its Judean homeland but had relatively little knowledge of its original Hebrew language. In consequence of its intimate contact with Hellenism, it had, among other things, begun to use Greek as its vernacular; Hebrew had literally become Greek to them. As a result of its desire to retain as much of Jewish tradition as possible, a Greek translation of its sacred Torah was made for the Jewish community; in time it came to be known as the Septuagint ("the Seventy").

At about the same time, there lived in western Asia, in Babylonia and Syria, another large Jewish community for whom Aramaic—long the diplomatic language and also the common language of the Near East—had become the vernacular. For them an Aramaic translation of the Torah was made; it came to be known as Targum Onkelos. (Subsequent Aramaic translations are the Jerusalem or Palestinian Targum—erroneously attributed to Jonathan ben Uzziel and hence also frequently referred to as [Pseudo-]Jonathan—and one that has been preserved only in fragmentary form.) The Septuagint and Targum constitute the first great age of Bible translation, and the former, for sundry reasons, has been the most influential translation down through the ages.

As the Christian sect began to grow within Judaism and then formed its own creed and institutions, it continued—in common with other Jewish communities—to regard and use the Septuagint as its Bible; but it also found it necessary to make translations of it available in the other languages which Christian communities employed. Thus there came into being several new versions of the Bible—a term which was meant to cover the Old Testament, Apocryphal additions to the Old Testament, and the New Testament—all of them translations of the Septuagint: Latin, Egyptian (dialects of Coptic), Armenian, Georgian, Gothic, Ethiopic, Arabic, and Slavonic. In addition, a Syriac translation, known (from the "Simple" or "Common" script) as the Peshitta, was made—perhaps from the Hebrew but under the influence of the Septuagint and Christian interpretation—and, above all, the Vulgate. Saint Jerome (Hieronymus; died in 420) made the last-named translation directly from the Hebrew text, aided not inconsiderably by Jewish tradition and teachers (he refers sometimes to *hebraeus meus,* "my Jewish teacher"). The Vulgate has long been the official Bible of the Roman Catholic Church; and official Catholic translations of the Scriptures into a vernacular language must be made from the Vulgate, unless special dispensation is given to translate directly from the Hebrew-Aramaic of the Old Testament and from the Greek of the New. The Vulgate is easily the most significant version of this second age of Bible translation.

For about a thousand years the Christian world was in the doldrums. In the flourishing Moslem world, on the other hand, from virtually one end of Asia-Africa-Spain to the other, economic, social, and cultural conditions were quite the opposite, and the various Jewish communities were among the beneficiaries from it all. In the tenth century, in the cosmopolitan and sophisticated region that was Babylonia, Saadia Gaon made for his fellow Jews an excellent translation of the Bible, accompanied by commentary, in Arabic. It is to this day the recognized Bible of Yemenite and other Arabic-speaking Jews.

In the sixteenth century, after about two centuries of Renaissance activity, the world of Christianity began to split wide open. Feudalism was being increasingly confronted by, and giving way to, commercial capitalism; in religious terms, Roman Catholic Christianity was being confronted by the Reformation, Protestant Christianity. One aspect of this religious confrontation revolved about the question of what really constituted the primary authority in Christendom: Was it the Roman Catholic Church with the Pope at the head, or was it rather God's own Word, that is, the Hebrew-Aramaic text of the Old Testament and the Greek of the New?

Asserting that it was the latter, Protestantism all over Europe set itself to making the Bible in its original languages available in the various vernaculars of the time. By 1525 the first part of two very notable versions appeared, William Tyndale's in English and Martin Luther's in German; the former, by way of several subsequent revisions, became the Authorized (or King [not Saint!] James) Version of 1611. These two translations stand out in the third great age of Bible translation.

The fourth great age was brought on by the deep and pervasive troubles that beset the capitalist system in Europe and America. With the rise of this system in its early and classical form—that is, in its most beneficial form, from the eighteenth to the earlier part of the twentieth century—the Christian nations on both sides of the Atlantic experienced a revival and extension of scholarly and cultural creativity unmatched in human history. Described by many as the Age of Reason, Enlightenment, Ideology, Analysis, and Science, this became the period in history that very many people were confident would see, to all intents and purposes, the end of group and national conflict; after all, man had finally come to realize that with proper planning and for self-interest, it was at long last possible, even necessary, to live and let live.

In this epoch, man began increasingly to question, then to

reject, and finally to ignore the Bible (the Hebrew Scriptures and the New Testament alike), the revealed Word of God for two thousand years and more, as the ultimate source of knowledge by which society could be comprehended and its manifold problems solved. Rationalists, political scientists, economists, historians, men of letters—all of them tended to believe, in this Age of Optimism, that if groups and nations learned to use the intelligence and knowledge which were men's inherently and by experience, then the kind of universal peace and personal contentment that religion had been promising humanity for the past two millennia would finally come to pass.

Alas, this has not come to pass. If anything, the opposite has prevailed. Ever since World War I, the world depression of the early thirties, the growth of various forms of totalitarianism in Europe and Asia, the horrors of World War II, the cold, hot, lukewarm, and warmed-over wars, domestic and international, of the past two decades, recessions and the fear of them, increasing automation and the specter of unemployment—all this and more have convinced many that reason and science alone are not able to bring our problems closer to solution. And so people have begun to come back to Holy Scripture, to the Bible.

But to what Bible? Since the seventeenth century, the English reader has known chiefly the Authorized (King James) Version (AV or KJ); more recently, since 1885, the British Revised Version (RV) has also become popular, more so than the American Standard Version (ASV) of 1901. But twentieth-century man is different from his counterpart of the three preceding centuries. For one thing the style, the words, the very atmosphere of King James and the Revised Version are utterly foreign to him. He was not raised in a Bible-reading home, and old-fashioned "Bible English" is not his literary meat. Moreover, the Bible frequently enough does not lend itself to "do-it-yourself" comprehension, and the modern would-be reader has found himself doubly frustrated in his attempt to understand what he was reading. As so often in other matters too, Benjamin Franklin knew what he was talking about when he said—about 1770, two centuries ago!—of the King James Version: "The language in that time is so much changed and the style, being obsolete and thence less agreeable, is perhaps one reason why the reading of that excellent book is of late so much neglected." Rendered in the idiom of our own time, Franklin said: "The Bible is not being read nowadays [1770!] because it is written in obsolete English."

There is, too, the matter of archeology. Ever since the tomb of the late King "Tut" (Tutankhamen; fourteenth century B.C.E.) of Egypt was cleared in 1922, the reader of the daily press and literary magazines has been told regularly and dramatically, if not always reliably, that excavation and discovery have brought to light many, very many documents and data of diverse kind, written and uninscribed, that enable—indeed, compel—the student of the Bible to translate and interpret the text quite differently from the traditional manner. Our understanding of the Bible has been revolutionized by the newly uncovered material from the Bible lands of the ancient Near East, and none of these data is to be found in the King James or the Revised Version.

For the modern reader of the Bible is not the naive believer that his ancestors were. He is, after all, the proud possessor of the knowledge and outlook that reason and science have made available to him. He is not coming to the Bible to discover the whole Truth; he is not ready by any means to give up the wisdom so brilliantly and laboriously gained in the past century. Rather, he is ready to approach the Bible as one source of information, along with several other sources, that may help him comprehend man and his universe. The Bible, to him, is now a guide to the truth, a repository of information of varying worth; but it is not the literal Truth itself.

Becoming aware of this new interest in the Bible, as groups and individuals clamored in increasing numbers and with ever greater intensity for the satisfaction of their biblical desires, all three major faiths, Protestant, Roman Catholic, and Jewish, embarked on new official versions of the Bible for their followers in Europe and America.

In 1937, the International Council of Religious Education authorized a new translation of the Bible. The council, consisting of the educational boards of forty major Protestant denominations of the United States and Canada and constituting the religious-educational arm of the National Council of the Churches of Christ, truly represented the enlightened element of American and Canadian Protestantism. The council appointed a committee of scholars to produce a version that would "embody the best results of modern scholarship as to the meaning of the Scriptures, and express this meaning in English diction which is designed for use in public and private worship and preserves those qualities which have given to the King James Version a supreme place in English literature." The Revised Standard Version (RSV) of the New Testament appeared in 1946, of the Old Testament in 1952, and of the Apocrypha in 1957.

In 1941, the Roman Catholic community of this country was presented with a revised New Testament. The Episcopal Committee of the Confraternity of Christian Doctrine then authorized a new translation of the Old Testament, to be done by members of the Catholic Biblical Association of America. "The supreme goal to be sought in rendering the word of God into the vernacular," said the letter of the Episcopal Committee, "is rigorous fidelity to the meaning of the original, expressed in simple and intelligible language." The fourth and last volume of *The Holy Bible Translated from the Original Languages* has just appeared (1969).

In 1917, the Jewish Publication Society of America (JPS) issued an English translation of the Hebrew Bible. For several decades this version satisfied the needs of the Jewish community in this country and abroad. But by the forties it had become apparent that a new version was needed; just as the Protestants had published RSV to "supplement" KJ, RV, and ASV, and the Roman Catholics had added the new Confraternity Version to the old Rheims-Douay Version (1582 and 1609–1610) revised by Bishop Challoner (1750), so too did the Jewish community demand a new translation to succeed the 1917 version. For, in truth, that version was essentially but a modest revision of the Revised Version of 1885, a revision that was only a small percentage of the whole.

In 1955 the Society appointed a committee of seven scholars to make a new translation. Late in 1962 the first part appeared, The Torah, *The Five Books of Moses: A New Translation of the Holy Scriptures according to the Masoretic Text.* When the remaining two divisions (the Prophets and the Writings) of this New Jewish Version of the Bible appear, the fourth great age of Bible translation will have come to a close. By that time, the writing of commentaries on each book of the Bible, with these translations as a basis, should be in full swing.

B (1) *The Philosophy of Bible Translation*

Since, as stated above, the older JPS version of 1917 was really only a relatively minor revision of the Revised Version, why couldn't the new JPS version have been but a modest revision of, say, the Revised Standard Version of 1952? In point of fact, there was strong sentiment among several important members of the Jewish Publication Society's Board of Trustees for precisely this kind of revision, namely, the updating of the language, the correction of serious errors, and the substitution of new interpretations for old when made necessary by the discovery of new data and analysis.

However, the Jewish community of the America of the mid-twentieth century was very considerably different from its ancestor of the beginning of the century, both in quantity and in quality. Half a century ago, the comparatively small and new Jewish community on this side of the Atlantic could justify an attitude toward an English version of the Bible for itself which, in effect, held that "what is good enough for the English Protestant world is good enough for us"; or as Max L. Margolis, editor-in-chief of the 1917 version put it, "No translation in the English tongue, however, can be anything but a revision of the English Bible of 1611, itself a revision. All attempts at modernizing the Bible English must necessarily fail. Once and for all time the revisers of 1611 fixed the model for all future undertakings . . ." (*The Story of Bible Translations,* 1917, pp. 104–5); yet in his unsigned essay of thirty-three pages on "The New English Translation of the Bible," reprinted in 1917 by JPS from *American Jewish Year Book,* vol. 19, 1917/18, pp. 164–193, Margolis wrote (p. 3), ". . . But it is impossible to stereotype a translation. There can be no doubt that the Revised Version is gradually becoming antiquated like the Authorized which it sought to supersede."

The world has changed, and changed very much, since World War I. And the English language has changed, and so too has the American Jewish community. Grown by 1950 to about five million souls, who were secure, mature, and optimistic in the continued opportunity to develop freely in every important aspect of its economic, political, cultural, and religious life, the American Jewish community was no longer content with an English Bible that had only undergone revision. In keeping with its new status and verve, unprecedented in the two and one-half millennia of Jewish Diaspora life, the Jewish community in the New World wanted a complete break with the past history of Bible translation.

This past history, interestingly, goes back to the first Bible translation ever made, the Septuagint. The Jewish translators of this version regarded the Hebrew text of the Torah as Sacred Scripture, every word of it revealed by God to Moses. They knew well the admonition in Deut. 4.2: "You shall not add anything to what I command you or take anything away from it . . ." (cf. 13.1). Indeed, the apocryphal work, the so-called *Letter of Aristeas,* after noting that the Septuagint translation had been officially adopted by the Jewish community of Alexandria (". . . Demetrius assembled the community of the Jews at the place where the translation was executed, and read it out to the entire gathering . . ."), proceeds with the statement that the leaders of the Jewish community and the translators ". . . bade that an imprecation be pronounced, according to their custom, upon any who should revise the text by adding or transposing anything whatever in what had been written down, or by making any excision. . . ."

Thus the Septuagint, an essentially word-for-word translation of Hebrew Scripture, became standard thereafter. Not many translators deviated from the norm as did Saadia (892–942) in his great Arabic translation of the Hebrew Bible, about which Margolis wrote *(The Story of Bible Translations,* pp. 53–4): "Though not a paraphrase, the version is by no means literal. Where necessary a word is added to bring out the sense clearly; several verses are frequently joined together in a syntactical nexus, and thus, though the original coloring is lost, the translation gains in lucidity. . . . What is principally aimed at is clarity and elegant diction. Ancient names of places are modernized. Though an upholder of tradition, Saadya emancipates himself from the forced interpretation of the rabbis, thus breaking ground for a rational exposition based on grammar and an adequate observation of the usage of words within the compass of the entire Scriptures. . . . Though naturally not free from faults, Saadya's version served as a mine in the hands of successive generations of Bible students; but it was intended in the first instance for the people, the Jews in the vast domain of Arabic culture. . . ."

The word-for-word procedure of the Septuagint was reinforced—as if reinforcement were needed—in the sixteenth and seventeenth centuries, when the rise of Protestantism gave impetus to new Bible translations in the vernaculars of Western Europe. For now, more than in the over one thousand years preceding, the Bible as the literal Word of God once again became preeminent. To such an extent was God's own Hebrew speech considered sacred that in the King James Version the words for which a direct equivalent was lacking in the Hebrew were italicized. Thus, while the predicate is clearly understood in the Hebrew, even though verbally absent, the King James Version, as is well known, italicized the English correspondents: ". . . and darkness *was* upon the face of the deep. . . . And God saw the light, that *it was* good. . . . And God made the firmament, and divided the waters which *were* under the firmament from the waters which *were* above . . . and let the dry *land* appear . . ." (Gen. 1.2 ff.)—as though God's Hebrew did not include "was," "it was," or "were," and as though *yabbasha* means "dry" rather than "dry land"!

It is precisely this philosophy of literal, mechanical translation which the New Jewish Version has set out to discard. It is generally agreed that the Jewish philosopher Philo, 1,900 years ago, laid the ideological foundation of Christianity; and it has recently been argued that it was another Jewish philosopher, Baruch Spinoza (1632–1677), some 1,600 years later, who was mainly responsible for destroying Philonism and for giving Christianity new direction. In Bible translation, it was the Jewish Septuagint version, some 2,200 years ago, that set the norm for a word-for-word reproduction of the Hebrew. The translation committee of the New Jewish Version, reflecting the verve, growing maturity, and optimism of today's great American Jewish community, would like to believe that its new version of the Torah, in its internal and external break with the past, has set a new pattern which authorized Protestant and Catholic translations of the future will tend to follow.

(2) *The Making of the Old (1917) and New (1962) JPS Versions of the Bible*

Rabbi Isaac Leeser (1806–1868) of Philadelphia was responsible for the first Jewish translation of the Bible made for American Jewry. Leeser's considerable learning in matters biblical and rabbinic derived in major measure from the fine research then flowering in Germany, and his translation of the Bible became in a short time the standard Bible for English-speaking Jews in America. First there appeared, in 1845 in Philadelphia, his version of the Pentateuch, *Torat ha-Elohim* ("The Torah of God"), in Hebrew and English (five volumes). This was followed eight years later by *The Twenty-Four Books of the Holy Scriptures . . . Carefully Translated According to the Masoretic Text on the Basis of the English Version,* the Hebrew text facing the English translation. Leeser's Bible, as it came to be known, had considerable merit, and it is useful even to this day. Its main fault lay in the style; too much of the Teutonic protruded in the translation. On the other hand, the grammatical niceties of biblical Hebrew frequently came through successfully, and the scholarship in general was on a consistently adequate level. Leeser's Bible would have retained much more of its deserved popularity well into the twentieth century—for it is generally superior even to such early twentieth-century authorized translations as the American Standard Version of 1901 (ASV)—had it not been for the appearance in 1917 of the translation sponsored by the Jewish Publication Society of America.

The Society had been formed in Philadelphia in 1888, and one of its first important projects was the launching of a new English version of the Bible. The British Revised Version had appeared only three years previously, and an American Revised Version had been promised by the end of the century. Furthermore, the officers of the Society were sensitive to the fact that Leeser's diction was hardly equal to that of the Authorized or Revised Version. The Jewish community was then small, and its leadership tended to conform to the Protestant majority; a Jewish variation on the theme of the Revised Version seemed the proper thing to do.

In 1894 a plan was adopted that called for a revision of Leeser. Several Jewish scholars were each assigned a book, their work to be reviewed by an editorial committee headed by Marcus Jastrow (author of the widely used *Dictionary of the Talmud,* 1886–1903). This procedure was less than successful; by 1903 only the translation of the Book of Psalms had made public appearance, and the project clearly lacked a future. Finally, in 1908, an entirely different procedure was worked out. A committee of seven scholars was set up, with Max L. Margolis of the Dropsie College—the only professional Bible scholar on the committee—as its editor-in-chief. As put by Margolis himself, in his usual forthright manner *(The Story of Bible Translations,* pp. 101–3):

> . . . the present writer . . . upon receiving his instructions from the Chairman of the Publication Committee of the Jewish Publication Society [Dr. Cyrus Adler, founder and President of Dropsie College], gave his entire time to the work for a space of eleven months, from September 1, 1908, to August 1, 1909, during which period he prepared a manuscript draft of the new

version. In addition to manuscripts prepared by the former Revision Committee, some of which had been revised by the old Editorial Committee and were accompanied by learned annotations chiefly from the pen of the late Dr. Jastrow, he had before him the two Anglican versions of 1611 and 1885, Leeser's work of 1853, other translations in various European languages done by Jews, and while he naturally surrounded himself with an apparatus including the best efforts, old and new, of biblical scholars, rejecting no help from whatever source it came, he made it his business to consult at first hand the ancient versions and the chief Jewish commentaries of medieval and modern times. When in December 1908 he met his colleagues on the Board . . . he set forth to them the principles which had guided him in the preparation of the draft, a transcript of which containing the Pentateuch had been forwarded to all of them in advance. The principles were discussed and somewhat modified by the whole Board. . . . Through sixteen sessions, each lasting ten days or more, from 1908–15, the body of scholars worked in conference upon the draft submitted to them. The mode of procedure was as follows: the propositions embodied in the manuscript draft, if unchallenged, were allowed to remain. When challenged, a new proposal was made and, if seconded, discussed. A vote was then taken, and if supported by majority, the proposal was entered. In the case of a tie, the Chairman [Adler] had the casting vote. The first proofs of the manuscript thus amended were sent out to all the seven members of the Board. The result was a mass of annotations returned by the Editors, infelicities of expression and imperfections of style being removed and good renderings excised that they might make room for better, and so many of them as were supported by a majority or could be disposed of by a general rule of the Board were immediately spread upon the proofs. There remained a small number, less than three hundred instances, which it was thought proper to reserve for discussion in a final meeting, the seventeenth, which took place in the autumn of 1915. On this occasion likewise the vote of the majority prevailed, the Chairman again being given the casting vote in the case of a tie. . . .

Later than the Catholic and Protestant communities in

America, but still better than never, the Jewish Publication Society of America initiated a new version of the Bible for the Jewish community of the United States and English-speaking Jews everywhere. The guidelines for this translation had been set forth by the writer at the annual meeting of the Society held in Philadelphia on May 10, 1953, in his address, "Wanted: A New Bible Translation in English for the Jewish People." After surveying something of the historical background and character of the more important Jewish and non-Jewish translations of the past, he placed special emphasis upon the two main elements that a new Jewish version should feature: (1) intelligibility in diction and (2) the fuller use both of the older commentaries—especially the Jewish but not at all excluding the Christian—and the recently discovered extrabiblical materials that had something really pertinent to offer the Bible translator.

Two years later, in 1955, after some six years of intensive discussion preceded by several years of desultory talk, the Society appointed a committee of seven scholars to prepare the new translation: Dr. H. M. Orlinsky as editor-in-chief, Dr. H. L. Ginsberg and (the recently lamented) Dr. E. A. Speiser as fellow editors, Rabbi M. Arzt (member of the Rabbinical Assembly—conservative), Rabbi B. J. Bamberger (member of the Central Conference of American Rabbis—reform), Rabbi H. Freedman (member of the Rabbinical Council of America—orthodox), and Dr. S. Grayzel (editor of the Jewish Publication Society)—the last-named also serving as secretary of the committee. Messrs. Louis E. Levinthal, Sol Satinsky, Edwin Wolf, 2nd, and Lesser Zussman, by virtue of their positions in the Society, participated in the solution of the committee's problems. Toward the end of 1962 the first part of the new Bible translation appeared: The Torah, *The Five Books of Moses: A New Translation of the Holy Scriptures According to the Masoretic Text.*

The members of the committee had been chosen for scholarly ability, broad outlook, and recognized status in the community at large. The Society itself is a purely cultural-educational organization with no specifically religious point of view and owing no theological allegiance to anyone; indeed, the American Jewish community as a whole, in its diversity, recognizes no single group or person as its religious authority. Consequently, if the new Jewish version manifests less eisegesis than either the new Protestant or the new Catholic version, one of the reasons is that the Society's committee of translators felt utterly free to render the Hebrew text as they believed the original author of that text meant it to be understood by his contemporaries.

The procedure was as follows. The editor-in-chief prepared a draft translation of the entire Torah for the committee. Submitted chapter by chapter with the draft was a considerable body of data consisting, when pertinent, of the renderings of such important older versions as the Septuagint, Targum, Vulgate, and Saadia, and of more recent translations such as Leeser, Revised Version, the 1917 Jewish version, Moffatt, the American (Chicago) Translation, Confraternity, Revised Standard Version, and La Sainte Bible; also the more pertinent comments of such notable exegetes of the Middle Ages as Rashi (d. 1105), his grandson, Samuel ben Meir (Rashbam; d. about 1174), Abraham ibn Ezra (d. 1167), David Kimhi (Radak; d. 1235), Moses ben Nahman (Ramban—Nahmanides; d. about 1270), Levi ben Gershom (Ralbag—Gersonides; d. 1344), and Obadiah Sforno (d. 1550), as well as the works of virtually every modern commentator of merit, Jewish (notably Samuel David Luzzatto—Shadal; d. 1865; and Meir Leib ben Jehiel Michael—Malbim; d. 1879) and Christian. Wherever the draft proposed a new rendering of import, some justification for it was offered. The editor-in-chief usually kept no more than ten or fifteen chapters ahead of the committee, so that he might benefit from the thinking and consensus of his colleagues.

Chapter by chapter the draft was sent to the main office of the Society in Philadelphia, where it was reproduced and copies sent out to each member of the committee. They in turn sent back to Philadelphia their reactions to the draft, including suggestions of their own, and these too were reproduced and distributed among all the members of the committee. On the average of once every two weeks the committee met for a full day at the New York school of Hebrew Union College–Jewish Institute of Religion, where every point in dispute was discussed, often at great length. Whenever a formal vote was necessary—usually a consensus was reached without the need to raise hands—a simple majority of those who voted decided the issue. Quite often the rendering agreed upon was different from anything proposed previously either in the original draft or in the responses.

C *The New Jewish Version (NJV)*

It has not always been easy to break with the more than two-thousand-year-old manner of translating the Hebrew Bible, the word-for-word manner. Thus in Gen. 14.1–2 (cf. vv. 8–9) ". . . Amraphel king of Shinar, Arioch king of Ellasar," etc., is but a mechanical rendering of the Hebrew order (X *mélekh* Y), when the natural order in English would be "King Amraphel of Shinar, King Arioch of Ellasar," etc.

The traditional translations of the Bible might well be designated "And" Bibles; hardly a sentence goes by without an "and" or two, sometimes more. The fact that English, unlike biblical Hebrew, is not coordinate in its sentence structure has been generally ignored by previous translators. So that rather than an automatic "And" for Hebrew *waw,* the context and the idiom ought to have led translators to employ "When," or "So," or "Then," or "Thus," or "Thereupon," or "Although," or "But," or "Yet," or "However," or the like. Traditional "And," precisely because it was mechanical, only succeeded in suppressing the full range of meaning of Hebrew *waw* and in preventing the translator from making clear to the reader the true meaning of the Hebrew verse. In addition, there are hundreds of instances when the *waw* ought not be translated at all, serving in the Hebrew only the function of introducing the verb. For instance, most traditional translations rendered initial *wa(-yómer elohim)* for each day of creation in Genesis 1 (vv. 3, 6, 9, 14, 20, and 24) by "And (God said)"; the new Jewish version reads simply "God said."

As a result of this overall view, the new version has tended to break up sentences and to combine sentences by subordinating clauses far more frequently than previous translations have done, where "and" mechanically joined clause to clause and sentence to sentence. Thus where the older Jewish version read (at Gen. 31.54; 32.1. It is 31.54–55 in the Christian versions), "And Jacob offered a sacrifice in the mountain, and called his brethren to eat bread; and they did eat bread, and tarried all night in the mountain. [1]And early in the morning Laban rose up, and kissed his sons and his daughters, and blessed them. And Laban departed, and returned unto his place," NJV reads, "Jacob then offered up a sacrifice on the Height, and invited his kinsmen to partake of the meal. After the meal, they spent the night on the Height. [1]Early in the morning, Laban kissed his sons and daughters and bade them good-by; then Laban left on his journey homeward."

It is not known as widely as it should be that the numbering of chapter and verse in the Bible was introduced for Christians (probably early in the thirteenth century) by Stephen Langton, Archbishop of Canterbury (naturally in the Latin, Vulgate Bible), who knew little or no Hebrew, so that when arguing with Jews they might more easily identify the passages that were cited; this procedure was first adopted by a Jew in the century following. The earliest division of the text of the Torah in Jewish circles was that of open and closed sections (respectively *pethuḥa* and *sethuma*) and of *sedarim* and pericopes (*parashiyoth*). As for verse division, in the days of the Talmud there were already occasional differences of opinion. Thus the word *we-hithgallaḥ* in Lev. 13.33 is cited in the Babylonian Talmud (Ḳiddushin 30a) as marking the middle verse of the Torah, whereas *wa-yásem alaw eth-* in Lev. 8.8 is thus designated in a massorah (and most printed editions), and *wa-yishḥaṭ* in Lev. 8.23 is given that distinction in still another rabbinic source. There is, further, the talmudic statement (Ḳiddushin 30a bottom; cf. Nedarim 38a top) that the Palestinians sometimes had shorter verses than the Babylonians (e.g., at Exod. 19.9, which was divided into three verses). All this information, and much more, may be found conveniently in G. F. Moore's article on "The Vulgate Chapters and Numbered Verses in the Hebrew Bible," *Journal of Biblical Literature,* 12 (1893), 73–78, and especially in C. D. Ginsburg's *Introduction to the Massoretico-Critical Edition of the Hebrew Bible* (1897; reissued 1966 by KTAV Publishing House), "The Sectional Divisions of the Text" (Chapter II, pp. 9–24), "The Division into Chapters" (Chap. III, pp. 25–31), "Sedarim" (Chap. IV, 32–65), and "The Division into Verses" (Chap. VI, 68–108).

And so this new version of the Torah has not hesitated at times (as put in the Preface to the Torah) "to follow . . . the logical units of meaning even when they do not coincide with the conventional chapters and verses." Thus the last verse of Gen. 7 and the first of Chapter 8 have been combined to form the beginning of a paragraph—as was done by Saadia Gaon a thousand years ago. As a matter of fact, Saadia even ran together the verses in Genesis 1 containing the phrase "And it was evening," etc., with those following: verses 4 and 5a; 5b and 6; 8 and 9; 13 and 14; 17 and 18; 23 and 24—not to mention 1.31 and 2.1. (See *Oeuvres Complètes de R. Saadia ben Iosef al-Fayyoûmî,* ed. J. Derenbourg, Vol. I: *Version Arabe du Pentateuque,* 1893, pp. 5–6.) A striking example of mid-verse division may be found at Gen. 2.4b (where further reference is made in the *Notes* to the parallel betwen *beyom asoth* and the "When" construction in *bereshith* in Gen. 1.1–3, § c); or see the *Notes* at 2.25; Exod. 22.1.

Like the *waw,* particles are the bane of the modern Bible translator who tries to reproduce for the reader the precise nuance of each occurrence. The older translators had no problem: simply and mechanically, without regard to idiom or context—sometimes even ungrammatically (e.g., at Gen. 3.22)—they turned every occurrence of *pen* into "lest," of *hinne* into "behold," of *lámma* into "why, wherefore," of *lakhen* into "therefore," and so on. Thus in Gen. 26.7, the older rendering was "(And the men of the place asked him of his wife; and he said: 'She is my sister'; for he feared to say: 'my wife';) 'lest (the men of the place should kill me for Rebekah, because she is fair to look upon.')"; contrast NJV: "(When the men of the place asked him about his wife, he said, 'She is my sister,' for he was afraid to say 'my wife,' thinking, 'The men of the place) might (kill me on account of Rebekah, for she is beautiful.')." In Num. 16.34, the older "(And all Israel that were round about them fled at the cry of them; for they said:) 'Lest (the earth swallow us up.')" has now become "(All Israel about them fled at their shrieks, for they said, 'The earth) might (swallow us!')." In Num. 20.18, traditional "(Thou shalt not pass through me,) lest (I come out with the sword against thee)" has given way to "else (we will come out against you with the sword)." And in Deut. 19.6, "Otherwise (. . . the blood-avenger . . . may overtake him and kill him)" has replaced the older "lest (the avenger of blood . . . overtake him . . . and smite him)."

Traditional "behold" for *hinne* is essentially a hebraism and would ordinarily be employed but rarely in English. Thus NJV at Gen. 1.29 reads "(God said,) 'See, (I give you . . .)' "; at 1.31: "(And God saw all that He had made,) and found (it very good)"; at 12.19: "(Now,) here is (your wife; take her and begone!)," against traditional "(now therefore) behold (thy wife . . .)"; at 28.15: "Remember, (I am with you . . .)" at Exod. 4.23: ". . . Now, (I will slay your first-born son)." At Exod. 16.14, Luzzatto already recognized the force of *hinne* as "then" (and he cited several instances of it); NJV reads "(When the fall of dew lifted), there [*we-hinne;* trad., "behold"], over the surface of the wilderness, lay a fine and flaky substance." In some instances, as with *waw,* it is best not to reproduce *hinne* at all, as in Gen. 12.11: "I know"—where an earlier rendering had "I am well aware" (for *hinne-na yadáti;* trad. "Behold now, I know").

Already the Old Greek (Septuagint) translation, and Saadia too, recognized the negative element in *lámma,* as well as the meaning "Why?" Thus in Gen. 27.45, *lama* (*eshkal gam-shenekhem yom eḥad*), traditionally rendered "why should I (be bereaved of you both in one day)," was translated "lest I should" in the Septuagint (*mḗ pote*) and Saadia (*li'alla*), and "Let me not (lose you both in one day!)" in NJV. Similarly in 47.19 (*lámma namuth;* cf. v. 15 and the reference there to Luzzatto), where the Septuagint (*ïna . . . mḕ*) and Saadia (*falam*) read "so that we do not die," and NJV has "Let us not perish"—as against traditional "Wherefore should we die . . . ?" Or see Exod. 32.12 (cf. v. 11 preceding), where NJV, following in the footsteps of the Septuagint (*mḗ pote*) and Saadia (*wala*) as well as being mindful of the context, reproduced *lámma* (*yomru miṣráyim*) by "Let not (the Egyptians say)," as against traditional "Wherefore should (the Egyptians speak?)." Further discussion of this problem may be found in S. R. Driver, *Notes on . . . Samuel* (2nd ed., 1913), at I Sam. 19.17 (p. 158 and nn. 1 and 2), and Brown-Driver-Briggs, *A Hebrew and English Lexicon,* p. 554a (§ D).

As for *lakhen* as an asseverative ("assuredly," "I swear," "I promise," "truly," and the like), mechanically rendered "therefore" in the older translations, see the *Notes* at Gen. 4.15 and 30.15—where reference is made to the Targum and early rabbinic literature.

The wide range of meanings commanded by the common conjunction *ki* has not been exploited fully in the traditional translations. Thus while it was long recognized that *ki* "often introduces the *direct* narration . . . in which case it cannot be represented in English (except by inverted commas)" (Brown-Driver-Briggs, *A Hebrew and English Lexicon,* pp. 471b–472a, § 1 B), the 1917 version (in keeping with older versions) reads at Gen. 21.30, "And he said: 'Verily [*ki*], these seven ewe-lambs shalt thou take of my hand . . .' " where NJV now reads, correctly: ". . . He replied, 'You are to accept these seven ewes from me. . . .' " Or see Exod. 3.12, where older "And He said: 'Certainly [*ki*] I will be with thee' " has given way in NJV to "And He said, 'I will be with you.' " Or see Exod. 17.14. In many other passages (as Brown-Driver-Briggs proceed to note), *ki* merely introduces the explanation of a proper name, so that traditional "(And he called the name of it Rehoboth) and he said: 'For [*ki*] now (the Lord hath made room for us . . .)' " at Gen. 26.22 is erroneous, as against NJV's "(so he called it Rehoboth,) saying, 'Now at last (the Lord has granted us ample space . . .).' " Or see Exod. 18.4, where NJV reads "(and the other was named Eliezer,) meaning [*ki*], ('The God of my father was my help . . .')," as against older "for." Among the scores of other examples (e.g., Gen. 4.25; 29.32; 41.51, 52), Exod. 2.10 may be cited: "She (named him Moses, explaining), 'I drew him out of the water' " (earlier printings read "She named him Moses, saying, 'It means: I drew him out of the water' "), as against traditional "(And she called his name Moses, and said:) 'Because [*ki*] I drew him out. . . .' "

Finally—since our word lends itself to almost limitless discussion in detail—the emphatic force of *ki* has often gone unrecognized, e.g., in Exod. 2.2, where NJV has "and when she saw how [*ki*] beautiful he was," where the older version read, "and when she saw him that [*ki*] he was a goodly child." Sometimes it is difficult to decide between the two; thus earlier printings read "(God saw) how [*ki*] good this was" at Gen. 1.10, 12, 18, 21, 25 (cf. v. 4), but this was given up in favor of traditional "that this was good."

There are numerous aspects to the new, nonmechanical manner of translating biblical Hebrew into English. A Hebrew term may have several nuances, depending on the context, and it is incorrect, if not misleading, to reproduce that term by a single English term throughout. Thus the word *báyith* may mean not only "house" but also "household" (Abraham's, Gen. 17.23) and "palace" (Pharaoh's, Gen. 12.15; Exod. 7.23), as well as "House" (God's, I Ki. 3.1; David's Dynasty, Isa. 7.13; or House of Jacob-Israel, Isa. 46.3). Biblical *shá'ar* denotes not only "gate" but also "court" (Deut. 17.8), "settlement" (Exod. 20.10; Deut. 12.15), and "public place" (Deut. 21.19). Hebrew *gevul,* the usual term for "border, boundary," represents also "territory" (Exod. 10.4, 19; Deut. 19.3) and "country" (Exod. 7.27), just as *éreṣ* denotes "territory" (Deut. 11.24) and "region" (Exod. 8.18; 9.26) as well as traditional "land, country." The word *sané* means not only traditional "hate" but also "be hostile to" (Gen. 26.27), "be unloved" (Gen. 29.31; Deut. 21.15), "reject" (Exod. 20.5), and "take an aversion to" (Deut. 22.13, 16); and by the same token its antonym *ahav* means to "favor" (Gen. 25.28), "befriend" (Deut. 10.19), and "to dote on" (Gen. 44.20) as well as traditional "love."

Along the same lines, *niḥam* has several nuances that traditional "repent" and "comfort" overlook. In Exod. 32.12, 14 (see the *Notes* there for the reference to Rashi) it is something like NJV's "renounce" that appears appropriate; in Gen. 6.6 "(And the Lord) regretted" (cf. v. 7 "for I regret") is more natural than Trad. "(And) it repented (the Lord)" (and in v. 7 "for it repenteth Me"). The same is true of NJV's "he reassured them" in Gen. 50.2 (for Trad. "comforted"), "have a change of heart" in Exod. 13.17 (Trad. "repent"), and "change His mind" in Num. 23.19 (Trad. "repent"). The root *naka* (hiphil *hikka),* traditionally and mechanically translated "smite," is more idiomatically and correctly rendered in NJV at Exod. 2.11–12: "(Moses . . . saw an Egyptian) beating (a Hebrew . . . he) struck down (the Egyptian)" (Trad., "smiting . . . smote"); or cf. NJV, "(Now the flax and barley were) ruined" as against the older "smitten" in Exod. 9.31; "(If he) knocks out (the tooth of his slave)" in Exod. 21.27 (Trad. "And if he smite out his bondman's tooth"); "(the land that the Lord has) conquered (for the community of Israel)" in Num. 32.4; and "(whom Moses and the Israelites) defeated" in Deut. 4.46.

It is still insufficiently recognized that such common words as *néfesh, shalom,* and *ṣadaq* are inadequately, where they are not incorrectly, comprehended traditionally. *Néfesh* has been generally rendered "soul" when "creature" (Gen. 1.20), "person" (Gen. 46.15), "desire" (Exod. 15.9), or even "corpse" (Num. 6.6; 19.13: *néfesh meth)* is the correct equivalent. In point of fact, "soul" is precisely the term that does not apply to *néfesh* in the Hebrew Bible; see the *Notes* at Gen. 2.7. Similarly, it is incorrect to withhold from *shalom* such meaning as "(Is he) well?" (Gen. 29.6: *hᵃshalom lo*) and

"(I grant him My pact of) friendship" (Num. 25.12); and see the *Notes* at Exod. 18.23 and Num. 6.26.

In dealing with forms of the root *ṣadaq,* the older versions have all too often overlooked some of its nuances, even its use as a legal, rather than an ethical term. Thus in Gen. 15.6, NJV has followed, e.g., the Targum, Rashi, and Radak in rendering *ṣedaqa* by "(He reckoned it to his) merit" instead of Trad. "(and He counted it to him for) righteousness"; and see, e.g., Deut. 6.25; 9.4. It is, however, chiefly as a legal term that our root—and its antonym *rasha*—is employed, which mechanically employed "righteous(ness)" fails to reproduce. Thus in Gen. 18.23, NJV has correctly rendered (*ha-af tispe*) *ṣaddiq im-rasha* by "(Will You sweep away) the innocent along with the guilty?" in place of the older "the righteous with the wicked." Similarly in Exod. 23.7, NJV has properly translated *ki lo aṣdiq rasha* "for I will not acquit the wrongdoer" (as against Trad. "for I will not justify the wicked"). Or see the new rendering of *we-hiṣdíqu eth-ha-saddiq we-hirshí'u eth-ha-rasha:* "and a decision is rendered declaring the one in the right and the other in the wrong," where the older version missed the force of *ṣadaq* and *rasha* altogether: "by justifying the righteous, and condemning the wicked" (Deut. 25.1). To its credit, the older version rendered *ṣédeq* in Deut. 16.20 correctly by "justice."

Other common words that have sometimes been denied a special meaning are *bo,* "enter," and *qarav,* "be near, approach." Thus in Num. 8.15 (cf. v. 22), NJV's "Thereafter the Levites shall be qualified [*yavó'u*] for the service of the Tent of Meeting" conveys more meaning than traditional "go in." In Exod. 12.48, NJV's "he shall be admitted" captures the force of *yiqrav* better than Trad. "and let him come near"; similarly in 22.7, "The owner of the house shall depose [*we-niqrav*] before God" (as against Trad. "shall come near unto God"), and Lev. 21.17, "shall be qualified [*yiqrav*] to offer the food of his God" (Trad., "let him . . . approach").

It is not always easy to capture the idiom in the Hebrew and at the same time reproduce it adequately in such an entirely different language as English; yet the modern translator may not shirk this task and—in the spirit of *lex talionis*—content himself with rendering a word for a word. The word *nasa,* "lift (up), carry (off), take (away)," is a good case in point. Thus *wa-yissa enaw wa-yar* in Gen. 18.2, rendered traditionally "and he lifted up his eyes and looked," is simply the biblical Hebrew manner of expressing the idiom "he looked up and saw." In 21.16 *wa-tissa eth-qolah wa-tevk,* previously translated "and she lifted up her voice, and wept," is only the way in which the ancient Israelite would express the English idiom "she burst into tears, she began to weep." However, the traditional versions were sometimes forced to avoid a word-for-word rendering because the result would appear ludicrous; thus in Gen. 39.1 *wa-yissa* (*ya'aqov*) *raglaw* was rendered "(Then Jacob) went on his journey" (NJV, "resumed his journey") instead of the mechanical "lifted up his feet." In Gen. 40.13,19 the play on *nasa rosh* (*me-al*) is brought out in NJV by rendering the first instance idiomatically "will pardon you" (with a note: *Lit. "lift up your head"*), and the second by "will lift off your head"; the older version read mechanically: "lift up thy head" and "lift up thy head from off thee."

The expression *maṣa* (or *nathan*) *ḥen be-ene-* is another good example. The traditional translation has been literal: "find (or give) favor (or grace) in the eyes (or sight) of." NJV, however, has made every effort to bring out the nuance of this phrase in the many occurrences of this expression: "But Noah found favor with the Lord" (Gen. 6.8); "if it please you" (18.3; Trad., "if now I have found favor in thy sight"); "You have been so gracious to your servant" (19.19); "in the hope of gaining your favor" (32.6; Trad., "that I may find favour in thy sight"); "if you would do me this favor" (33.10; Trad., "if now I have found favour in thy sight"); "and I will dispose the Egyptians favorably toward this people" (Exod. 3.21, cf. 11.3; as against Trad. "And I will give this people favour in the sight of the Egyptians"—*we-nathati eth-ḥen ha-am ha-ze be-ene miṣráyim*); "I beg you" (Num. 11.15); "It would be a favor to us" (32.5); and so on.

Along the same lines, an expression such as *wa-yiṭav ha-davar be-ene pharo* in Gen. 41.37 is rendered in NJV by "The plan pleased Pharaoh" in place of the older, mechanical "And the thing was good in the eyes of Pharaoh." A common expression such as *shama be-qol,* hitherto reproduced mechanically by "hearken to the voice of," is idiomatically and correctly rendered in NJV by "listen to" (Exod. 3.18), "pay heed to" (Exod. 4.8), "The Lord heeded Israel's plea" (Num. 21.3; traditionally, "And the Lord hearkened to the voice of Israel"), or simply by "heed" (Deut. 8.20; 13.19; 15.5; etc.) or "obey" (Deut. 26.14; 28.1, 15, 45). The phrase *laqaḥ be-yad,* traditionally rendered "take in one's hand," frequently connotes simply the idiom "take along, take with." Thus in Gen. 24.10, traditional and literal "(And the servant took ten camels, of the camels of his master, and departed;) having (all goodly things of his master's) in his hand" is manifestly incorrect for (*we-khol-ṭuv adonaw*) *be-yado*—that would be a handful indeed. Contrast the idiomatic, and correct, rendering in NJV: "(Then the servant took ten of his master's camels and set out,) taking with him (all the bounty of his master)." In Gen. 43.12 it is not literally "take in your hand" but "take with you (double the money)" that reproduces the force of *qeḥu ve-yedkhem*; or see Exod. 4.17; Deut. 1.25; 14.25. And it has long been recognized that *be-yad* alone can mean "in one's possession" rather than "in one's hand," as in Exod. 21.16 (see *be-yad* in Brown-Driver-Briggs, *Hebrew Lexicon,* pp. 390 f., §§ **b c d**). In some cases, the force of *laqaḥ be-yad* is elusive; thus at Exod. 4.20, the rendering "took . . . in his hand" (as in 4.17) is replaced in the projected Hebrew-English edition by "took . . . with him" (cf. Exod. 17.5, "take along").

The verb *shalaḥ* does not necessarily require an object to

denote "send a message or messenger." In Gen. 38.25, *we-hi shaleḥa (el-ḥamía) lemor* means "she sent this message (to her father-in-law), saying," rather than, as traditionally, "she sent (to her father-in-law), saying"—where "sent" is left lacking an object and the clause is grammatically incomplete. Similarly in Exod. 9.7, where NJV "(When Pharaoh) inquired," rather than traditional "sent," reproduces the force of *wa-yishlaḥ*; or Num. 22.10, where NJV "sent me this message," unlike older "sent unto me [saying]," does justice both to English and Hebrew idiom (*shalaḥ elay*).

Be-yom and *le-khol* are fine examples of what scholars have recognized as philologians but failed to make use of as translators. *Be-yom* (see Brown-Driver-Briggs, *Hebrew Lexicon,* p. 400a, § **d**), "in the day," is frequently used to denote simply "when, as soon as, at the time," for example, in Gen. 2.4; 3.5; Exod. 6.28; 10.28; Lev. 5.24; Num. 3.1. The term *le-khol* (see Brown-Driver-Briggs, p. 514b, § **d**) often serves to indicate a summing up, e.g., at Exod. 14.28: "(The waters turned back and covered the chariots and the horsemen)—Pharaoh's entire army," where *le-khol* (*ḥel paro*) has been traditionally rendered by the ubiquitous "even all (the host of Pharaoh)." As a matter of fact, Rashi has noted something of the kind on this very verse, and refers to *le-khol* in 27.3, 19, and Num. 4.32 in this connection. Or see NJV at Lev. 16.21: "(. . . all the iniquities and transgressions of the Israelites,) whatever [*le-khol*] their sins," as against traditional "even all (their sins)."

Similarly, it has long been known that the preposition *lifne* means more than "before (in time or in space), in front (or, in the presence) of"; but scholar-translators have not applied this knowledge. Thus Driver, *Notes on . . . Samuel* (1890; 2nd ed., 1913; followed by Brown-Driver-Briggs, *Hebrew Lexicon,* under *halakh,* p. 236a, § 2), had noted at I

Sam. 2.30 that *hith-hallekh lifne* in connection with God has the force of deserving or enjoying His approval and favor, citing in this connection Gen. 17.1; 21.40; and 48.15, and the Septuagint translation of these passages ("to be pleasing, or acceptable, to God"). The Targum rendered the three Genesis passages by "worship before," followed by Rashi (at Gen. 17.1, "attach yourself to My service"; cf. Sforno, "recognize My ways"). So that NJV's "walk in My/His ways" in these three passages in Genesis has good precedent and gives meaning to the Hebrew (contrast Trad. "walk before Me/Him"). Sometimes the force of *lifne* is elusive. Thus in Gen. 6.11 (also v. 13), it had been argued by Luzzatto (followed by Ehrlich) that *lifne* (*elohim*) meant here "in God's judgment"; but NJV followed tradition (e.g., Ibn Ezra) and was content with "before God." Similarly in Gen. 7.1, where Brown-Driver-Briggs (under *lifne,* p. 817a, § 4 *g*) had interpreted *lefanay* as "in My estimation," but where NJV followed Trad. "before Me." In 10.9, however, where Rashbam (see at 27.7) and Ramban, followed by Luzzatto and Jacob, understood *lifne Adonay* as "before the Lord" in the sense of "in the whole world," NJV has followed Ehrlich's interpretation of the phrase, "by the grace of the Lord" (Brown-Driver-Briggs, *"in the sight* [estimation] *of"*). In Gen. 27.7, NJV's "with the Lord's approval" (for *lifne Adonay;* as against Trad. "before the Lord") was anticipated by Rashi, Rashbam, Radak, Ramban, as well as Malbim and Driver (and see Brown-Driver-Briggs, p. 817a § 4 *h*). Other instances of this force of *lifne* may be found in Num. 3.4; 14.37; 20.3; and 32.20–32. Brown-Driver-Briggs (p. 817a § 4 *g*) has noted two additional passages where *lifne* denotes "in the estimation of (the Lord)," Deut. 24.4, 13, but where NJV has stayed close to Trad. "before." Similarly in Deut. 25.2, where NJV has rendered "in his presence" (Trad. "before his face"), though Brown-Driver-Briggs prefers "under the oversight of."

The exact nuance of the term *torah* as used in the Torah is not always easy to capture; see, e.g., the discussions in S. R. Driver, *The Book of Exodus* (1911; in *The Cambridge Bible* series), pp. 161–2 and 165–6 (on Exod. 18.16). Trad. "laws" is only mechanical. The renderings in NJV, deriving essentially from the specific context, range from "Teaching" (twenty-one instances, except for Exod. 13.9 all in Deut.—e.g., 1.5; 4.8, 44; 17.18, 19), "teachings" (for plural *toroth*: Gen. 26.5; Exod. 16.28; 18.16, 20), "instructions" (Exod. 16.4; Lev. 13.59; 14.54, 57; Num. 19.14; Deut. 17.11; 33.10), "ritual" (all in Lev. and Num.; e.g., Lev. 6.2, 7, 18; 7.1, 11, 37 ["rituals"]—thirteen instances in all; Num. 5.29; 6.13; 15.20; 19.2; 31.21), "directions" (plural *toroth,* Lev. 26.46), and "(one) law" (*tora aḥath*: Exod. 12.49; Num. 15.16), to "obligation" (of a Nazirite, Num. 6.21). While some of these renderings might have been eliminated and the total number reduced, the context of each occurrence of *torah* simply precludes any cut-and-dried translation.

In their pursuit of literal translation, translators have unnecessarily failed to do justice to numerous instances of the singular collective in biblical Hebrew. In Gen. 9.13 (cf. vv. 14 [twice] and 16), *anan* can only be rendered "(I have set My bow in the) clouds" (Trad., "cloud"); in Exod. 3.8, (*el-meqom*) *ha-kena'ani we-ha-ḥitti we-ha-emori we-ha-perizzi,* etc., rendered traditionally "(unto the place of) the Canaanite, and the Hittite, and the Amorite, and the Perizzite," etc., has become in NJV "(the home of the) Canaanites, the Hittites, the Amorites, the Perizzites," etc.; *binkha u-ven-binkha* in Exod. 10.2 is rendered in NJV, correctly, "(that you may recount in the hearing of) your sons and your sons' sons" (as against older ". . . in the ears of thy son, and of thy son's son"); in Exod. 25.2–3, *teruma* is properly reproduced in NJV by "(Tell the Israelite people to bring Me) gifts; (you shall accept) gifts (for Me from every person . . . [3]And these are the) gifts . . . ," in place of the older "(. . . that they take for Me) an offering . . . My offering. [3](And this is) the offering."

Biblical Hebrew sometimes expresses the idea of "(an)-other; rest of, remainder" merely by implication. Thus in Gen. 3.2 "(We may eat of the fruit of the) other trees (of the garden)," where traditional "(Of the fruit of the) trees (of the garden we may eat)" misses the point and is misleading; or see 41.22 ("In my other dream"). In 43.7, only "Have you another brother?" makes sense (recognized also in the older version). In Exod. 21.22 "(and a miscarriage results,) but no other misfortune ensues" is more meaningful than Trad. "(so that her fruit depart,) and yet no harm follow." In Lev. 7.10, NJV's "But every other meal offering" and in 7.19 "As for other flesh" are idiomatic, and make clear what is literal and misleading in traditional "And every meal-offering" and "And as for the flesh"; the same is true of NJV's "and of your other sacrifices" in Deut. 12.27, as against Trad. "and . . . of thy sacrifices." The phrase *yáyin we-shekhar,* traditionally rendered "wine and strong drink," is more correctly translated in NJV: "wine and any other intoxicant" (Num. 6.3; cf. Lev. 10.9; Deut. 14.26; 29.5); indeed, from the manner in which the two words are used—combined by "and" (as in the above passages; also Judg. 13.4, 7, 14; I Sam. 1.15; Mic. 2.11) and as parallels in poetry (Isa. 28.7; 29.9; 56.12; Prov. 20.1; 31.4, 6)—it would seem that our phrase means simply "any (or every) intoxicant." In Exod. 4.7, NJV's "like the rest of his body" (cf. the older "as his other flesh") is the only idiomatic way of reproducing *kivsaro*. In Lev. 8.17, *we-eth-ha-par* can only mean "the rest of the bull"; indeed, in Exod. 14.7 and Lev. 4.12 it is misleading even to translate *kol-* by "all"—only NJV's "(all) the rest of" (his chariots/bull) makes sense.

The wide range of nuances that the Hebrew verbal form can express is not apparent from the traditional, mechanical versions. Thus the inchoative or inceptive force ("begin to, become, come to") has been noted in NJV in such renderings as "the tops of the mountains became visible" (Gen. 8.5; Trad., "were seen"); "started digging a well" (Gen. 26.25; Trad., "digged"); "He fell asleep" (Gen. 41.5; Trad., "And he slept"); "so that the [Egyptians] came to dread the Israelites" (Exod. 1.12; Trad., "And they were adread because of the Israelites"); "stationed herself" (Exod. 2.4; Trad., "stood"); "and the altar shall become most holy" (Exod. 29.37; Trad., "shall . . . be"); "when the sin . . . becomes known (Lev. 4.14; Trad., "is known"); and "a fire of the Lord broke out against them" (Num. 11.1; Trad., "burnt among them"). Even when the Hebrew spells out the idea of "become," by the phrase *haya le-*, the older version will render mechanically; thus in Gen. 9.13 *we-hayetha le-oth berith* has been rendered literally "and it shall be for a token of a covenant" instead of "and it shall become" (NJV, "and it shall serve as a sign of a covenant"), and in Exod. 4.16 *hu yihyeh-lekha le-feh* has been reproduced traditionally as "he shall be to thee a mouth" as against NJV's idiomatic "Thus he shall serve (as your spokesman)."

A verb such as *qum* is sometimes used in biblical Hebrew merely as auxiliary to a main verb, so that in Gen. 23.7 *wa-yáqam (avraham) wa-yishtáḥu* is best rendered "Thereupon (Abraham) bowed low" (Trad., mechanically, "And Abraham rose up, and bowed down"); similarly in Gen. 31.17, "Thereupon Jacob put . . ." for *wa-yáqam ya'aqov wa-yissa* (Trad. "Then Jacob rose up, and set . . ."). In Exod. 2.17 NJV's "Moses rose to their defense" captures the idiom in *wa-yáqam moshe wa-yoshian* (as against Trad. "but Moses stood up and helped them"), as also in Num. 11.32, where the older mechanical, and even erroneous, rendering ("And the people rose up all that day, and all the night, and all the next day, and gathered the quails") has given way in NJV to "The people set to gathering quail all that day and night and all the next day" (for *wa-yáqam ha-am kol-ha-yom ha-hu . . . wa-ya'asfu*); the verb *qum* does not represent the main action at all. So too the verb *bo* ("enter") in Gen. 23.2, "and Abraham proceeded (to mourn for Sarah)," as against "And Abraham came," for *wa-yavo avraham* (*lispod le-sara*); this force of *wa-yavo* had been noted already by Rashbam (*afilu lo ba mi-maqom aḥer . . .*; cited favorably by *Perush al Ibn Ezra*) and Ramban (*she-nith'orer avraham . . .*), followed by Luzzatto. Ramban (followed by Luzzatto) has also noted, at Exod. 2.1 (with reference to Gen. 35.22; Hos. 1.3; etc.), this "auxiliary" use of *halakh,* "go," in *wa-yélekh* (*wa-yiqqaḥ*): *nizdarez* (*wa-yiqqaḥ*).

Since English idiom was of no greater concern for the older translation committee than the Hebrew idiom, it is not to be wondered at that both were not infrequently violated by "hebraisms." A common hebraism is one that involves the second of two nouns equally in construct to a third noun (see Gesenius-Kautzsch-Cowley, *Hebrew Grammar,* §128 **a,** p. 414). Thus in Gen. 40.1 the Hebrew phrase (*ḥaṭe'u*) *mashqe mélekh-miṣráyim we-ha-ofe* (*la-adonehem*) was rendered mechanically in the older version "the butler of the king of Egypt and his baker (offended their lord")—where "his" had to be added, although it is lacking in the Hebrew text, because the translation had to be literal (i.e., "hebraic"); yet it can only be rendered, as in NJV, "the cupbearer and the baker of the king of Egypt (gave offense to their lord)," if justice is to be done to both the Hebrew and the English idiom. Similarly in Exod. 3.8, where *éreṣ ṭova u-reḥava* appears in NJV as "a good and spacious land," in contrast to Trad. "a good land and a large"; or see in Exod. 5.10 "the taskmasters and foremen of the people went out" (for *wa-yeṣe'u nogese ha-am we-shoṭraw),* as against Trad. "the taskmasters of the people went out, and their officers"—

an awkward rendering. In Exod. 18.16, NJV's "and I make known the laws and teachings of God" succeeds where Trad. "and I make them know the statutes of God, and His laws" fails (and note that the Hebrew has no word for "them"); and similarly in Lev. 16.21, where NJV's "all the iniquities and transgressions of the Israelites" is to be contrasted with Trad. "all the iniquities of the children of Israel, and all their transgressions."

A figure of speech in biblical Hebrew that is well known to scholars but rarely recognized in the traditional translations is hendiadys (Greek for "one through two"), where essentially one thought is expressed by means of two words connected by "and." Thus in Gen. 3.16 the idea in *iṣṣevonekh we-heronekh* (Trad., literally, "thy pain and thy travail") is really NJV's "Your pangs in childbearing"; in Gen. 4.12, "a ceaseless wanderer" (as against Trad. "a fugitive and a wanderer") is what the expression *na wa-nad* denotes; in Gen. 12.1 (cf. 30.25; Num. 10.30), *me-arṣekha u-mi-moladtekha* (Trad. "out of thy country, and from thy kindred") is best rendered, as in NJV, "from your native land"; in Gen. 13.13, Trad. "wicked and sinners" does not reflect the hendiadys in *ra'im we-ḥaṭṭa'im* in the manner of NJV, "(Now the inhabitants of Sodom were very) wicked sinners"; in Gen. 23.4 NJV's "a resident alien" reproduces the hendiadys in *ger we-thoshav* that is missed in Trad. "a stranger and a sojourner"; in Gen. 47.29 NJV's "steadfast loyalty" (cf. "true kindness" in 24.49) brings out well the force of *ḥésed we-emeth* (Trad., "kindly and truly"). In Exod. 15.25 "a fixed rule" is closer than the older, mechanical "a statute and an ordinance" to the true meaning of *ḥoq u-mishpaṭ*; similarly in Deut. 3.24, where *ke-ma'asékha we-khigevurothékha* (Trad., "Thy works, and . . . Thy mighty acts") is well reproduced by NJV: "Your powerful deeds"; and so on (e.g., Gen. 1.14; 19.23; 45.6; Exod. 22.28; Deut. 5.24; 12.9, 12; 20.11). Sometimes it is difficult to decide; thus in Exod. 12.45, NJV's

"A resident hireling (shall not eat of it)," treating *toshav we-sakhir* as a case of hendiadys (Trad., "A sojourner and a hired servant") will be given up in the projected Hebrew-English edition for "No bound or hired laborer" (cf. Lev. 22.10); or see Deut. 21.5, where earlier "every disputed case of assault" was given up in favor of "every lawsuit and case of assault." For a detailed analysis of hendiadys, the reader may consult Joseph Hershberg's Hebrew study, *Pardes Ha-Lashon* (New York, 5710/1950), pp. 147 ff. (the whole study of 172 pp. is worth critical perusal), and especially E. Z. Melamed, "*Shnayim She-hem Eḥad* (*hen dià duoîn*) *Be-Miqra*," *Tarbiẕ*, 16 (5705/1945), 173–189, 242.

Another figure of speech in biblical Hebrew that has been insufficiently noted by translators is merismus (from a Greek word meaning "to divide into parts"), in which the totality of something is indicated in different ways, among them by the listing of the first and last of a series. Thus in Gen. 14.23, *mi-ḥuṭ we-ad serokh-náʻal* does not mean (Trad.) "a thread or a shoe-lachet" but (NJV) "so much as a thread or a sandal strap," i.e., no personal apparel at all. In Deut. 29.18, (*lemáʻan sefoth*) *ha-rawa eth-ha-ṣeme'a,* Trad. "(that) the watered (be swept away) with the dry," is rendered in NJV by "(to the utter ruin of) moist and dry alike," to bring out more clearly the idea of all vegetation. In Gen. 1.1, if (*bereshith bara elohim*) *eth ha-shamáyim we-eth ha-áreṣ* was meant to constitute merismus, then the translation should be "(When God began to create) heaven and earth," i.e., the universe, rather than (Trad. and NJV) "the heaven and the earth." See in general the article by A. M. Honeyman on "*Merismus* in Biblical Hebrew," *Journal of Biblical Literature,* 71 (1952), 11–18.

In keeping with the desire to reproduce the intent and character of the Hebrew, NJV has reproduced lists and series of numbers appropriately. Thus the numbers in the famous "begats" in Gen. 11.10–24 have been indicated by numerals:

"100 . . . 500 . . . 35 . . . 403 . . . ," etc., as against Trad. "a hundred . . . five hundred . . . five and thirty . . . four hundred and three . . . ," etc. Or compare the paragraphing of Numbers 1 (vv. 1–15) and 2 in NJV with that of the older version; the reader will not fail to observe how much more clarity and meaning the text acquires thereby. In the same spirit, when the plural form *bene,* "sons, descendants of," is employed in a list, although only one such is listed, NJV has rendered either "Dan's son: Hushim" (Gen. 46.23; Trad., "And the sons of Dan: Hushim") or "Born to Pallu: Eliab" (Num. 26.8; Trad., "And the sons of Pallu: Eliab"). In both passages a footnote tells the reader that the Hebrew reads the plural form.

Such expressions as *bene yisrael/moav/ḥeth,* etc., have usually been rendered by "the Israelites, Moabites, Hittites," etc., as against traditional "the children of Israel, Moab, Heth," etc. However, when God is the speaker, it was felt that the phrase "the Israelite people" or "the people of Israel" (or even "the children of Israel") was generally more idiomatic; see, e.g., Exod. 19.6; 25.2; 31.13, 17; Lev. 11.2; 15.2; Deut. 31.19. The older version rendered all these instances of *bene* mechanically by "the children of."

In this connection it should be noted that when the term *ben* denotes merely membership in a group or species, idiomatic rather than literal translation is in order. Thus *ben-adam* in Num. 23.19 is to be rendered something like "mortal" (in poetic context) rather than mechanically (Trad.) "son of man"; and "foreigner" (cf. Trad. "alien") reproduces *ben-nekhar* (Exod. 12.43) very adequately. *Bene ha-yona* appears in NJV as "pigeons" (Lev. 1.14; and elsewhere), as against Trad. "young pigeons" (for which there is no real authority); similarly, *bene-méri* in Num. 17.25 means simply "rebels," rather than Trad. "rebellious children."

The term *ré'a* has traditionally been rendered "neighbor," but this can sometimes be misleading. For the Hebrew term, strictly speaking, refers to any fellow Israelite rather than to a neighbor (who may or may not be an Israelite). Thus the section at Lev. 19.13–18 will be considerably clarified by giving up Trad. "neighbor" in the projected Hebrew-English edition in favor of "fellow," i.e., "fellow Israelite" (vv. 13, 16, 18). The projected rendering of *amith* (vv. 15, 17), hitherto rendered "neighbor," is "kinsman" (see, e.g., Snaith, *Leviticus and Numbers* in the new Century Bible series, 1967, at Lev. 6.2 [= Heb. 5.21]). And, finally, the term "countrymen" will replace "fellows" for *ammékha* (Trad., mechanically, "thy people") in v. 16 and "kinsfolk" for *bene ammékha* (Trad., mechanically, "the children of thy people") in v. 18. The reader will see clearly that this section deals with Israelites only. See also at Deut. 22.24, where Trad. "his neighbor's wife" (*ésheth re'éhu*) will be replaced in the projected edition, more correctly and clearly, by "another man's wife."

Starting out with traditional "Thou" ("Thy, Thine") in reference to God when He was addressed directly, NJV decided subsequently in favor of "You" ("Your"). The reasoning behind this decision was simple and forthright. First of all, and primarily, the Hebrew Bible itself never made any distinction between God and man or animal: whether it is God, or the serpent in the Garden of Eden, or Pharaoh who is addressed, the pronoun and the verbal form employed are always in the second singular (*atta; natháta*). This was recognized and followed faithfully by all the older translations, Jewish and Christian alike (e.g., Septuagint, Targum, Vulgate, Saadia). Indeed, the Authorized (King James) Version rendered all singulars by forms of "thou" and all plurals by forms of "ye." The Revised Standard Version, however, decided on "you" for both the singular and plural, but retained forms of "Thou" for God.

Not only does "thou" receive no support from the Bible, but this archaic word (and such corresponding verbal forms as "wast, art, shalt") have no place in a modern translation of the Bible: they are awkward and artificial in twentieth-century English. (The common assertion that the use of "thou" in a Bible translation makes for piety and awe is hardly pertinent to scholarship; the first and exclusive obligation of a translator is to the text. And who would certify that piety and awe have been maintained in recent centuries and decades as a consequence of the continued use of "thou"?)

A major consequence of NJV is the realization that Jewish interpretation of the Bible, beginning with the earliest rabbinic literature and extending through Saadia, Rashi, Rashbam, Ibn Ezra, Radak, Ramban, Ralbag, Sforno, and Abravanel, to Luzzatto (Shadal), Malbim, and others, should command in vastly increased measure the respect and gratitude of modern critical scholarship. The reader will not fail to note the frequency with which an older Jewish interpretation of a word or phrase or verse anticipated NJV or provided it with an important lead to a new interpretation. The Jewish commentators of ancient, medieval, and more recent times gain our scholarly respect not from a blind acceptance of their views but rather from a critical evaluation of their exposition in the manner that any modern commentator expects from his peers.

The New Jewish Version has benefited from the many criticisms, suggestions, and queries that were evoked by the draft versions and the first printings of the Torah. Out of the many correspondents, critics, and reviewers involved, two deserve public mention at this point, David S. Bamberger and Rabbi Ivan Caine.

ABBREVIATIONS AND TERMS EMPLOYED IN FOOTNOTES TO THE *TORAH*

Cf. A reference to another version, or to a cognate language, which justifies the translation adopted.

Heb The Hebrew word or phrase in transliteration, especially when necessary to point out a pun, homonym, or the like. *Heb* is also used to indicate the literal wording for which a superior rendering was employed; see Gen. 46.23 (note *d*) or 49.9 (note *a*). An example of a somewhat different type may be seen at Exod. 21.22, note *e*.

I.e. An explanation, to avoid adding words to the text, in order to clarify the translation; see Exod. 22.29, note *j*.

Lit. For the literal translation of a word or phrase that was given an idiomatic or somewhat free translation in the text; see Gen. 30.27, note *j* and 38, *k*; or 43.21 (note *b*), 34 (note *c*); or Deut. 18.1, note *a* (where the Hebrew and English cannot agree in number).

Meaning (or *Exact* or *Precise meaning* or *Nuance*) *of Heb uncertain*

Where the translation represents the best that the Committee could achieve with an elusive or difficult text. The term *Heb obscure* was sometimes employed to indicate that the text may be unintelligible because of corruption.

Moved up Where clarity required the shifting of a word or phrase within a verse or from one verse to another; see Gen. 10. 14, note *d*.

Or Indicates an alternative reading which the Committee found almost as acceptable as the one adopted for the text.

Others Indicates a well-known traditional translation, especially if it was used in the older (1917) JPS version, which the Committee does not find acceptable even as an alternate reading.

See Frequently used in place of *cf.*, but usually intended to begin a note attached to another passage in the Bible.

THE ENGLISH TRANSLITERATION OF THE HEBREW EMPLOYED IN THE *NOTES*

The system of reproducing the Hebrew into English has been simplified as much as possible; technical minutiae have been avoided. As for the consonants:

בּ = *b*	ח = *ḥ*	פּ = *p*	תּ = *t*
ב = *v*	ט = *ṭ*	פ = *f*	ת = *th*
ה = *h*	כּ = *k*	צ = *ṣ*	
ו = *w*	כ = *kh*	ק = *q*	

The letters א and ע (generally transliterated by ʾ and ʿ respectively) and final (silent) ה are not always represented, except where it is helpful to the reader.

The duplication of the consonant after the definite article or the *waw* consecutive is not indicated; thus *ha-shamáyim* and *wa-yómer* (instead of *hash-shamáyim* and *way-yómer*). Duplication of *sh* is avoided.

The accent always falls on the last syllable of the word unless indicated otherwise; thus *bereshith,* but *tóhu wa-vóhu.*

The shwa, generally represented by raised ᵉ (or ᵃ and ᵉ for *ḥataf-páthaḥ* and *-segol*), is indicated by simple *e* (or *a* and *e*); thus *bereshith* (instead of *bᵉreshith*), and *ḥamisha* and *elohim* (instead of *ḥᵃmishshah* and *ʾᵉlohim,* "five" and "God" respectively).

As for the vowels: both the *qámeṣ* (ָ) and the *pátaḥ* (ַ) are represented by *a,* and both the *ṣere* and the *segol* by *e.* The vowels *u, i,* and *o* present no problem. The length of the vowel has not been indicated.

It is assumed that the reader will have before him a Hebrew Bible if he wishes to follow the *Notes* fully.

A Bibliography and two detailed Indexes have been appended for the benefit of the reader; it is hoped that he will resort to these aids and find them useful enough to justify the effort devoted to their making.

KEY TO ABBREVIATIONS AND TERMS EMPLOYED IN THE *NOTES*

ASV: American Standard Version (American Revised Version of the Authorized [King James] Version), 1901. *See also* RV.

AV: Authorized (King James) Version, 1611

BASOR: *Bulletin of the American Schools of Oriental Research*

BDB: Brown-Driver-Briggs, *Hebrew Lexicon*

EBI: Kasher-Freedman, *Encyclopedia of Biblical Interpretation*

GKC: Gesenius-Kautzsch-Cowley, *Hebrew Grammar*

HUCA: *Hebrew Union College Annual*

IDB: *Interpreter's Dictionary of the Bible*

JAOS: *Journal of the American Oriental Society*

JBL: *Journal of Biblical Literature*

JQR: *Jewish Quarterly Review*

KJ: King James (Authorized) Version, 1611. *See also* AV.

LXX: Septuagint Translation of the Bible

NJV: New Jewish Version of the Torah (JPS, 1962). *See also* Trad.

Projected Reading: The projected Hebrew-English Edition of the Torah, Haftaroth, and Megilloth

RSV: Revised Standard Version of the Bible, 1952

RV: Revised Version (British Revision of Authorized Version), 1885

RVm:	Marginal readings in Revised Version
Trad.:	Traditional, JPS Version, 1917. *See also* NJV.
v., vv.:	Verse, verses
VT:	Vetus Testamentum

Genesis

בראשית

Chapter 1

Verse

1–3. When God began to create. For some 2,200 years—since the Septuagint version of the Torah was made by Jewish translators for the Jewish community of Alexandria, Egypt—all official translations of the Bible have rendered Hebrew *bereshith bara elohim* mechanically, "In the beginning God created." There are several cogent reasons, each independent of the others, for rejecting the traditional rendering as incorrect, and for accepting the temporal ("When . . .") construction.

(a) The first vowel in the first word, *be(reshith)*, as distinct from a form *ba(reshith)*, indicates that the word is in the construct (rather than in the absolute) state, and has the meaning "In the beginning of (God's creating . . .)" rather than "In the beginning (God created . . .)." Indeed, it is not even *bareshith* (the form doesn't happen to occur in the Bible) but *barishona* that one would have expected here for "In the beginning (God created . . .)."

This had already been noted by Rashi, who wrote: "But if you are going to interpret [this passage] in its plain sense, interpret it thus: At the beginning of the creation of heaven and earth, when the earth was (or the earth being) unformed and void . . . God said, 'Let there be light.' For the passage does not intend to teach the order of creation, to say that these [namely, heaven and earth] came first; because if it had intended to teach this, it would have been necessary to use the form *barishona* ('In the beginning' or 'At first) He created the heavens,' etc., since you have no instance of the form *reshith* in Scripture which is not in construct to the word following it, as for example 'In the beginning of the reign of Jehoiakim' (*bereshith mamlékheth yehoyaqim,* Jer. 27.1). . . . So here, too, you must say [that the phrase] *bereshith bara elohim,* etc., is equivalent to 'In the beginning of (God's) creating' (*bereshith bero).* Similar to this is the phrase *teḥillath dibber YHWH behoshé'a* (Hos. 1.1), that is to say, 'At the beginning of the Holy One Blessed be He's speaking (or 'When the Holy One Blessed be He began to speak) to Hosea, the Lord said to Hosea,' etc. And if you should say that the purpose of the text is to teach that these [namely, heaven and earth] were created first and that its meaning is 'In the beginning of everything (or 'First of all—*bereshith ha-kol*) He created these . . . ,' in fact the waters came first, since it is written 'And the *rúaḥ* of God was hovering over the waters,' yet Scripture had not yet revealed when the creation of the waters preceded the earth. . . ." (The reader should note here the reverse order. "When the LORD God made earth and *heaven,*" in 2.4.)

So that Rashi was right when he noted that the whole of verse 1 (N.B.: Rashi did not emend *bara* to *bero*!) was in construct to verse 3: [1]"In the beginning of God's creating (or "When God began to create) the heaven and the earth . . . [3]God said, 'Let there be light'; and there was light"—with verse 2 constituting a circumstantial clause, i.e., a clause which describes the circumstances under which the action in verses 1 and 3 took place: [2]". . . the earth being unformed and void," etc.

(b) When the story of creation is resumed later, in 2.4, it is, again, the temporal ("When") construction that is employed: "When the LORD God made earth and heaven" (*beyom asoth YHWH elohim éreṣ we-shamáyim*); and note how there also, as in 1.2, verses 5 and 6 constitute a circumstantial clause, with verse 7 being the fulfillment of verse 4 ("When the LORD God made heaven and earth . . . [7]the LORD God formed man from the dust of the earth . . .").

(c) The numerous ancient Near Eastern stories of creation nearly all begin with the "When" sentence structure, e.g., the Babylonian *Enuma Elish:*

> When above, the heavens had not been named,
> (And) below, the earth had not been called by name.

For further reading, see, e.g., A. Heidel, *The Babylonian Genesis: The Story of Creation,* 2nd edition (1951); N. Sarna, *Understanding Genesis* (1966), Chapter I, "Creation."

(d) Though verse 2 had traditionally been rendered as a separate sentence, "And the earth was (unformed and void . . .)," the relative order of the two words, *we-ha-áreṣ hayetha* (subject, verb)—apart from the arguments given above—points to the rendering "the earth being . . ."; Trad. "and the earth was" would have been expressed here by the usual order (verb, subject): *wa-tehi ha-áreṣ*. See, e.g., at Exod. 1.5 below, on *we-yosef haya* (as against *wayhi yosef*).

The implications of the new translation are clear. The Hebrew text tells us nothing about "creation out of nothing" (*creatio ex nihilo*), or about the beginning of time. What, then, according to our passage, constituted the first act of creation, if it was not heaven or earth or darkness or deep, etc.? The Hebrew text itself, once again, provides the answer directly, in verse 3: "(When God began to create the heaven and the earth . . .) God said, 'Let there be light'; and there was light." In other words—again as Rashi had already observed—the first thing that God did when He created the universe, as ancient man knew it, was to create light.

This conclusion is further supported by the fact that light (*'or*) was the first element to receive a name (that is, official existence) from God: "God called the light Day" (*wa-yiqra elohim la-or yom*, verse 5); the heaven and the earth, on the other hand, did not receive names until the second and third days respectively (v. 8, "Sky"; v.10, "Earth").

It may be observed here that "the heaven and the earth" in our verse 1 do not really denote heaven and earth as such, but simply "the universe, the whole world, the cosmos." (On merismus in the Bible, see Introduction, §c). Ready confirmation of this—as well as evidence that our verse was not understood in biblical times to indicate that God created the heaven and the earth in the beginning—may be found, e.g., in Exod. 31.17, ". . . For in six days the Lord made heaven and earth . . . ," i.e., it took God six days to make the whole world, the universe. See Yehoash, *Notes,* at Gen. 1.1.

1. **heaven.** The common rendering "heavens" has no authority. Hebrew *shamáyim* is plural (or dual) in form (a singular form does not exist in biblical Hebrew). Actually, *shamáyim* means nothing more than "sky," and this should perhaps have been the term employed here; cf. "expanse of the sky," (*reqí'a ha-shamáyim*) in vv. 14, 17, 20; "God called the expanse Sky" (*wa-yiqra elohim la-raqí'a shamáyim*) in v. 8; and "birds of the sky" (*of ha-shamáyim*) in vv. 26, 28, 30. It should be kept in mind that our notion of "heaven(s)," with its theological associations, is foreign to our verse; see, e.g., "Heaven" by T. H. Gaster in *Interpreter's Dictionary of the Bible,* II, pp. 351–2; "Kingdom of God of Heaven" by O. E. Evans, ibid., III, pp. 17–26.

2. **—the earth being,** etc. See on vv. 1–3 preceding, §d.

and a wind from[b] God (sweeping) ([b]*Others "the spirit of"*). The word *rúaḥ* occurs in the Bible some 380 times and has the meanings "wind, spirit, breath." Thus when Adam and Eve partook of the forbidden "fruit of the tree in the middle of the garden" and hid, God came into the garden "at the breezy time of the day" (*le-rúaḥ ha-yom,* Gen. 3.8). In 8.1 we are told that "God remembered Noah and all the beasts and all the cattle that were with him in the ark, and God caused a wind (*rúaḥ*) to blow across the earth, and the waters subsided." In 6.3, 17 and 7.15 *rúaḥ* means "breath," that which God blew into Adam's nostrils to bring him to life. And so on. Of course *rúaḥ* frequently has the meaning "spirit" elsewhere in the Bible, for example, in Isa. 11.2.

The evidence of the most ancient, primary versions of the Bible is further independent evidence for the meaning "wind" in our passage. The Septuagint translation of the Torah rendered our *rúaḥ* by "and a wind (of God was sweeping over the water)." And the Aramaic Targum of Onkelos reproduced our passage by "and a wind (from before God was blowing over the face of the waters)." The Targum was followed by Saadia, Rashbam, Ibn Ezra, Ramban, and others.

Even more. The Babylonian Talmud (Ḥagigah 12a) records a statement by Rab Judah (toward the end of the third century C.E.) in the name of his teacher, the noted Rab, that "Ten things were created (by God) on the first day (of Creation). These are: heaven and earth, *tóhu* and *bóhu* (traditional "unformed" and "void"), light and darkness, wind (*rúaḥ*) and water, and the duration of day and of night. . . ."

The wind also plays a significant role in the earlier, Mesopotamian version of creation. Thus in *Enuma Elish* (see §c at v. 1 above), the sky god Anu begot the four winds; and it is they, along with the seven additional winds that Marduk himself created, that later enabled mighty Marduk to slay terrible Tiamat and then introduce life and order in the world.

Finally, scholars have long been perturbed by the fact that if *rúaḥ* here in v. 2 was intended to mean "spirit," what then was the function of this living being when God began to create the universe? For in fact, the alleged "spirit of God" did nothing at all; it participated in no activity whatever, as if it were, like all the other elements contemporaneous with it, simply inanimate matter. Furthermore, unlike the other,

Near Eastern versions of creation, the biblical one is free of polytheism. The God of the Bible, unlike the male and female gods and their progeny elsewhere in the Fertile Crescent of old, had no sex and no mythology. He existed from time beyond comprehension, and He was alone among living beings when He began creation. Such inanimate elements as earth, water, sun, and darkness pose no problem for Hebraic monotheism. But what about the living being "spirit"? What was it doing alongside God Himself? Did it really coexist with God at creation, if not prior to it? And, finally, where in the Bible does the *rúaḥ* of God in the sense of "spirit" become associated with anything but a human being?

And so an unusually clear and consistent picture has emerged from the pertinent data available, one that begins in the second millennium B.C.E. and extends to the fourth century C.E., according to which *rúaḥ* in our verse was understood from the outset to mean "wind" and was so understood throughout the biblical period and well into the first millennium. Moreover, the rendering "spirit" in our verse creates difficulties where "wind" does not. Whence, then, "spirit" (or "Spirit")?

The noted Alexandrian Jewish philosopher Philo, in the first half of the first century C.E., was a firm believer in the literal truth of the Torah, and at the same time he was fully alive to the truth of Greek philosophical thought. He had developed a systematic comprehension of the Bible according to which the Jewish and Greek views of the universe—both ultimately deriving from God—complemented one another, to constitute the perfect explanation of the universe.

In the matter of creation, Philo naturally accepted the biblical account in Gen. 1: God, literally, created the universe and all that is in it. On the other hand, Philo recognized the truth of Plato's belief that before any concrete element could come into being, the idea or the concept of that element had to exist, that the spiritual counterpart of that physical element had to be conceived beforehand. Thus "earth" is explained as "invisible earth," i.e., the idea of the element earth; "water" is explained as "the incorporeal essence of water," i.e., the idea of water; and so on. Consequently, "wind" derived from the incorporeal essence or idea of wind, i.e., spirit.

But what began with Philo as a purely philosophical interpretation of our *rúaḥ* soon became something else altogether. For Christianity had begun to develop within Judaism, and then—after the Roman destruction of the Judean state and the Second Temple in 68–70 C.E.—increasingly outside of and in opposition to Judaism. And the more it found itself confronted by the Hellenistic-Roman world, the more it had to face the arguments and criticisms of the pagan philosophers. And since Philo the Jew had already done much in harmonizing biblical revelation with Greek reason, what was more natural than that Philo should become the main philosophical-theological source for Christian self-defense and countercriticism? When Christianity came to develop the concept of the Trinity—so that the Holy Spirit shared with the Father and the Son the unity of the Godhead—Philo's allegorizing idea of "spirit" for *rúaḥ* in our verse 2 was turned into "Spirit" (with capital "S") and, in time, pushed out altogether the original "wind." (For specific references and bibliography, see Orlinsky, "The New Jewish Version of the Torah: Toward a New Philosophy of Bible Translation," *Journal of Biblical Literature,* 82 [1963], 249–264.)

For those who would render "a mighty wind" (cf. "a tempestuous wind" in *An American Translation,* University of Chicago Press), let it be noted not only that there is no authority for this in any tradition but also that the word *elohim* does not have the meaning "mighty, tempestuous," or the like in a single one of the some 2,570 occurrences of the word in the Bible.

(and a wind from God) sweeping. Trad. "(and the

spirit of God) hovered." Heb. *meraḥéfeth* is somewhat elusive in meaning. In Deut. 32.11 it is used for an eagle in relation to its young: "(Like an eagle who rouses his nestlings,) Gliding down to his young" (*al-gozalaw yeraḥef*). Interestingly, it is used with the same subject (*nshrm*, "eagles") in the Ugaritic (Old Canaanite) texts of the fifteenth century B.C.E., where the most appropriate meaning is also something like "soar, sweep (over)"; and note above for Septuagint and Targum, "sweep (over), blow." The *qal* form *raḥafu* (*kol-aṣmotay*), Jer. 23.9, may harbor a root that is different from that preserved in the *piel* forms cited above and is of uncertain meaning.

water. Trad. "waters" is but a mechanical reproduction of the plural (or dual) form *máyim*. (Similarly *shamáyim* in v. 1 above.) There was at this time only one body of water (so the Septuagint); only during the second day (vv. 6–7) was there a separation of "water from water."

4. **(God saw) that the light was good.** (Also vv. 10, 12, 18, 21, 25.) In the earlier printings, Heb. (*wa-yar elohim et-ha-or*) *ki-ṭov* was rendered "how good (the light was)," as though *ki* were here a particle of emphasis (as in Gen. 49.7: *arur appam ki az*). However, it was realized subsequently that the text was simply asserting that God gave His formal approval to what He had brought into being. (See S. R. Driver, *The Book of Genesis,* 3rd ed., 1904, bottom of p. 5.) Trad. "And God saw the light, that it was good" is hardly acceptable English. See Introduction, §c.

5. **a first day**[c] ([c]*Others "one day"*). Trad. "one day" is, again, merely a mechanical reproduction of Heb. *yom eḥad*. For one thing, it will be noted at once that all the other days of creation are qualified not by the cardinal ("two," "three," "four," etc., "days") but by the ordinal: "a second," "a third," "a fourth," etc., "day" (*yom sheni*; *shelishi*; *revi'i*, etc.). It has, further, been generally overlooked that in enumeration, the cardinal will be employed for "first" and the ordinals for "second," "third," etc. Thus in Gen. 2.11, "(The

name of) the first ([river] is Pishon)" is expressed by (*shem*) *ha-eḥad* (not *ha-rishon*), with the ordinals *ha-sheni, ha-shelishi,* and *ha-revi'i,* "the second," "third," "fourth" (vv. 13–14) used thereafter. Finally, it may be observed here that the cardinal *be-eḥad* (*la-ḥódesh*), not the ordinal *ba-rishon,* is the regular term for "on the first day (of the month)"; as a matter of fact, the ordinal *ba-rishon* would have the meaning "in the first month," as in 8:13, *ba-rishon be-eḥad la-ḥódesh,* "in the first month, on the first (day) of the month." Some of this is discussed in Gesenius's *Hebrew Grammar,* 2nd English edition by E. Kautzsch-A. E. Cowley (1908), §98*a* (p. 292), §134*p* (pp. 435–6).

6. **expanse.** (also vv. 7, 8.) The vault stretched across the sky to separate the upper and lower waters. Heb. *raqí'a* denotes something (like metal) "beaten out," a strip of beaten metal, whence Septuagint *steréōma* and Latin *firmamentum,* "firmament"—a term generally used today for "sky." See T. H. Gaster, "Firmament," in *Interpreter's Dictionary of the Bible,* II, 270.

11. **(Let the earth sprout) vegetation: seed-bearing plants, fruit trees,** etc. (Also v. 12.) Understanding *ésev* and *eṣ peri* as explicating *déshe.* Trad. "(Let the earth put forth) grass, herb-yielding seed, and fruit trees," etc., construed the verse to refer to three different items: grass, herbs, and fruit trees.

of every kind. Compare Driver's comment on Trad. "after its kind": "Rather, *after its* KINDS (the word being collective). . . ." Such passages as 6.20 and Lev. 11.14, 15, 16, 19, 22 make it clear that *lemino/leminéhu* means here "all kinds of, every variety of."

14. **(they shall serve as signs for the set times—the days and the years.** Trad. "(and let them be) for signs, and for seasons, and for days and years" would make the lights (sun, moon, and stars) serve as signs and seasons—which they palpably did not; "signs" and "seasons" (or "set times; fixed occasions") are simply not comparable. Neither is it likely that "seasons," "set times" goes with following "days and

years," for the expected sequence would be "days and set times and years." Accordingly, it seems best to treat *le-othoth u-lemo'adim* as hendiadys (i.e., expressing one thought by means of two words), namely, "as signs for set times," the "set times" being "the days and years." The case for the traditional interpretation is well presented by Driver, *Genesis,* p. 10. On hendiadys, see Introduction, §c.

25. wild beasts (of every kind). Trad. "the beast of the earth (after its kind)" fails to distinguish *ḥayyath ha-áreṣ* from the domesticated beast (*ha-behema,* "cattle"). This occurs frequently (e.g., 3.14).

26. Let us (make man in) our (image, after) our (likeness). In the first printings, the rendering was "[d]I will . . . My . . . My. . . ." with note *d* reading: *Taking the Heb plural as plurals of majesty; cf. v. 27. Or lit. "Let us make man in our image, after our likeness."* The traditional rendering is now preferred, with the note entirely deleted. It may well be that the plurals here reflect ultimately an older Mesopotamian version of creation according to which a chief god and his assembly of gods took part in arriving at decisions. See 6.2 below on "the divine beings" (*bene elohim*), and cf. I Kings 22.19 ff. and Isa. 6.1 ff. In Jewish tradition, the phrase denoted God and His angels.

31. (And God saw . . .) and found it (very good). Trad. "and, behold, it was" is only a mechanical reproduction of Heb. *wehinne*—apart from the fact that "behold" is hardly used nowadays except as an interjection or when the listener is called upon to look at something exceptional. See further, Introduction, §c.

Chapter 2

2. ceased[a] ([a]*Or "rested"*). (Also v. 3.) The basic meaning of the root *shavath* is "cease, stop" (as in Gen. 8.22), and it is only in this sense that the *niphal* and *hiphil* forms are employed; "to rest" (Trad.) is a secondary meaning. See Driver, *Genesis,* p. 18 and n. 1.

4a. **Such is the story.** Nearly everywhere else, the formula *élle toledoth* is a superscription that points to what follows (5.1; 6.9; 10.1; 11.10, 27; 25.12, 19; 36.1, 9; [37.2 is difficult;] Num. 3.1; Ruth 4.18). But the present context (so also 37.2, and perhaps 10.32) demands that the formula refer to what precedes; thus Rashi: *élle* refers to those mentioned previously (*ha-amurim lemá'la*). On the composition of the text, see Driver, *Genesis,* p. 19 (at 2.4; with further reference to pp. II, VI, and VIII of his "Introduction") and note 1. See also at 37.2 below.

story. Trad., "generations." Heb. *toledoth,* etymologically "begettings, generations." But here, as noted by Driver, "the word is applied metaphorically to 'heaven and earth'; and it will denote . . . *particulars respecting heaven and earth. . . .*"

4b. On the division of the verse, see Introduction, §c.

When. Trad. "In the day" is mechanical and misleading. Driver (p. 37) put it well: *"in the day.* I.e., *at the time,* —Heb. usage compressing often what may have been actually a period of some length into a 'day,' for the purpose of presenting it vividly and forcibly: see e.g. Jer. xi.4. . . ." See Introduction, §c.

When, etc. For the temporal-circumstantial construction, see on "When God began," etc., at 1.1 above.

6. **flow.** Trad., "mist." Heb. *'ed* is to be connected with Akkadian Id or *edû,* subterranean source of fresh water; see "Mist" by G. B. Cooke in *Interpreter's Dictionary of the Bible,* III, p. 406.

7. **(a living) being.** It is now almost a commonplace among scholars that Heb. *néfesh* (*ḥayya*) does not mean "soul." Rather does *néfesh* connote approximately "being, person, self, creature," even "body," or whatever is needed to sustain life—in short, the life principle. Thus the identical expression *néfesh ḥayya* is used in 1.20, 21, and 24 with *shéreṣ, 'of,* and *behema* (i.e., the diverse creatures of sky, earth, and water; cf. 9.10 "every living thing on earth"—human beings and animals) and was rendered even traditionally "living creatures." Or see Num. 6.6, "(. . . he shall not go in where there is) a dead person" (*néfesh meth*), and 19.13, "(Whoever touches) a corpse (*be-meth*), the body of a person who dies" (*be-néfesh ha-adam asher yamuth*). It may also be noted that the verbal form of *néfesh* (all in the *niphal*) is found a total of three times in the Bible, and in every case it means something like "refresh oneself, catch one's breath" (not soul!): Exod. 23.12; 31.17; and II Sam. 16.14.

Actually, it is only after the idea of resurrection came into being (after 200 B.C.E., early in the Maccabean period; cf. Daniel 12.2–3) that the idea of a "soul" began to enter Jewish thought (see A. A. Neuman, *The Immortality of Man: A Jewish Viewpoint* [1949]; 26 pp.); and even then it is not *néfesh* but *neshama* ("breath" in biblical Hebrew) that becomes the term for "soul." Finally, if the present version of the Torah sometimes retained "soul" for *néfesh* (e.g., in the *Shema,* Deut. 6.5), it is only because of familiar English usage: "You shall love the LORD your God with all your heart and with all your soul and with all your mind"; more correctly, the rendering might have been: "with all your mind and with all your being and with all your might." See Introduction, §C.

9. (the tree of knowledge of good and) bad. The force of *ra* here is not that of a moral concept ("evil"); it is part of the expression *ṭov wa-ra,* "good and bad," and denotes *everything.* For other instances of merismus, see Introduction, §C.

10. (A river) issues (from Eden). Hebrew participle *yoṣe'* does not justify Trad. "went out" (past tense). On the implication of the text that the river actually "rose *in* Eden, outside the garden," see Driver, p. 39 and n. 2.

(and it) then (divides . . .). Trad., "(and) from thence (it was parted . . .)." The point seems to be that as the river issued from the garden (which was inside, and only a part of Eden, cf. v. 8), it divided and became four branches. See further, Driver, pp. 39, 58–59.

11. **(the one that) winds through.** (Also 13.) Trad. "compasseth," i.e., encircles, has unnecessarily limited the meaning of Heb. *sovev.* Thus already Luzzatto interpreted: it did not surround, but wound its way through the land (*lo maqqif, ella 'over we-sovev ha-áreṣ*); and J. A. Montgomery has noted at II Kings 3.9 (*International Critical Commentary on Kings* [1951], p. 360) that *wa-yasóbbu* (*dérekh shivath yamim*) means "and they went a roundabout (way of seven days in length)." However, until the geography of this section can be reconstructed with greater certainty it is best not to press either rendering. Thus already at the beginning of the century Driver noted (*Genesis,* p. 58; cf. Speiser, *Genesis,* pp. 19 f.), "Cush is generally Ethiopia, though it *might* (see on x.8) denote the Kasshites, a people dwelling in the mountainous region between Babylonia and the Caspian Sea . . . ," and he noted further (ibid., § 2) that in Friedrich Delitzsch's view ". . . Eden was the whole 'plain' . . . of Babylonia . . . Cush being a name of Babylonia (derived from the fact . . . that a Kasshite dynasty ruled in Babylonia for many centuries). . . ." No real progress has been made in the matter since Driver.

17. **(you) shall (die).** Trad. "(thou) shalt surely (die)" derives from the ancient tendency to reproduce the Hebrew text word for word, rather than idiomatically. Biblical Hebrew frequently varies the imperfect tense (e.g., *tamuth*), with the combination infinitive absolute-imperfect (*moth tamuth*), without intending any difference in meaning; here "(you) shall (die)" is emphatic enough. Our "you shall be doomed to die" (cf. Ehrlich) in the earlier printings was an attempt to avoid old-fashioned "surely die"; but "doomed to die by and by" is hardly the point here.

18. **a fitting helper.** (Also 20.) Driver commented on Trad. "a help meet" already in 1904 (*Genesis,* p. 41 and n. 2): " 'Meet' is of course an archaism, meaning *adapted, suitable.* . . . To speak of woman (as is sometimes done) as man's 'helpmeet' (absolutely) is an error implying strange ignorance of the English language." Heb. *kenegdo,* Driver notes further, means "**corresponding to** *him,* i.e. *adequate* to him . . . capable of satisfying his needs and instincts"—in short, fitting.

21. **(and closed up) the flesh at that spot.** Trad. "the place with flesh instead thereof" is unclear. The word *táḥath* means "under, at the spot" no less than "instead of"; thus in Josh. 6.20, (*wa-tippol ha-ḥoma*) *taḥtéha* means "(and the wall [of Jericho] fell) under itself, on the spot," i.e., collapsed. Already Rashi understood our word correctly; on *wa-yisgor* he comments: *meqom ha-ḥatakh,* "and He closed up the place of the cut."

23. **at last.** Trad. "now" is hardly correct for *ha-pá'am.* As put by Driver (p. 43), "*now at last,* in contrast to the animals which had before been brought to him. . . ." Similarly Ramban and Sforno.

25. The chapter division of the Hebrew text being relatively late and indecisive (see Introduction, §c), it seems reasonable to begin this new section-chapter with our verse, rather than to end the preceding section-chapter with it; note how vv. 7 and 21, dealing as they do with the theme of nakedness and clothing, constitute fitting endings to their respective sections. Rashi may have had something of this in mind when he asked at 3.1, on "Now the serpent was the shrewdest," etc.: "What does this subject have to do with the story of Adam and Eve? Scripture should have attached it to 'And He made for Adam and his wife garments of skin and He clothed them' (v.21). . . ."

Chapter 3

2. **of the other trees (of the garden).** Trad. "of the trees" not only makes no sense here—2.16–17 says distinctly that Adam was not permitted to eat of the "tree of knowledge"—but overlooks the fact that biblical Hebrew frequently implies "other, rest of" without a specific term being employed to express this concept. Note that Rashi understood the force of "*other* trees" in his comment: ". . . and even though he [the serpent] saw them eating of the *other* fruits [*mi-she'ar peroth*]. . . ." See also 41.22 below.

4. **(You are not) going to die.** On Trad. "(Ye shall not) surely die," involving the function of the infinitive absolute with the imperfect, see at 2.17 above.

5. **as soon as.** Trad. "in the day" does not do justice to the common use of *be-yom* as an adverb: "when, the moment that," or the like. See at 2.4 above and Introduction §c.

[a]-**divine beings who know**-[a] ([a-a]*Others "God, who knows"*). Earlier printings read the reverse: [a]-"God, who knows"-[a] with the note reading: *Or "divine beings, who know."* (Note the term *Others* in the present note, as against *Or* in the earlier printings.) There are two reasons for rejecting "like God, who knows": (1) although plural in form, the term *elohim* when it means "God" will regularly be associated with an adjective or verb in the singular; here participial *yode'e* is in the plural; (2) as noted, e.g. by Driver (*Genesis,* p. 45), "The distinction between God and divine beings was not so clearly drawn by the Hebrews as it is by us . . . angels are called sometimes the 'sons of God' (or 'of the gods'. . .)." Thus in our chapter, v. 22, God refers to Himself as "one of us" (*ke-aḥad mimménnu*), pointing clearly to a class of divine beings. There is also good Jewish tradition for our "divine beings": Targum Onkelos rendered our *elohim* by *ravrevin,* and Targum Jonathan by *malakhin*

ravrevin, "higher angels"; and Ibn Ezra interpreted our word *elohim* as *malakhim,* "angels, divine beings," as did earlier the Tractate Soferim (Chapter 4), when it cited *elohim* in our verse as an instance of the nonsacred use of the term (i.e., as distinct from the meaning "God"), and so subject to erasure if miswritten.

6. **(the tree was desirable) as a source of wisdom.** Trad. "(was to be desired) to make one wise" overlooks the fact that the *hiphil* conjugation in biblical Hebrew is readily intransitive-denominative no less than transitive-causative (see Gesenius-Kautzsch-Cowley, *Hebrew Grammar,* 28th ed., 1910, §53 *d e f g,* pp. 145–6). Thus Ps. 2.10: "(Therefore, O kings,) be(come) wise" (*haskílu*); or 94.8: "(Understand, O dullest of people! You fools, when) will you be(come) wise" (*taskílu*)?—in colloquial English: when will you wise up, get wise to yourselves? In our verse, "(the tree was desirable) as a source of wisdom" is another way of expressing the idea "for becoming wise, for gaining wisdom."

8. **the sound (of the Lord God moving about).** Trad. "the voice (of the LORD God walking)" not only creates some difficulty—we are not told that God had called to them, or that God was talking to Himself—but is simply mechanical for Heb. *qol,* as though this word does not mean also "sound" or (when used as an interjection) "Hark!" (as at 4.10 below). see F. Brown–S. R. Driver–C. A. Briggs, *A Hebrew and English Lexicon of the Old Testament* (1906), pp. 876–7.

moving about. See at v. 24 below.

at the breezy time (of day). Trad. "toward the cool" is unnecessarily free for Heb. *le-rúaḥ,* which means literally, as noted in Brown-Driver-Briggs, *Hebrew Lexicon,* under prep. *l* (pp. 516–7), §*6 a, "at* the breeze of the day." Many other examples are given there of *l* of time, e.g., *le-eth érev* in Gen. 8.11, "at the time of [i.e., toward] evening."

14. **More cursed (shall you be/Than all cattle).** Earlier printings read "Banned (shall you be from all cattle)." However, *arura ha-adama* in v. 17 below can only mean

"cursed be the ground," and it is to this that *arur átta min-ha-adama* ("you shall be more cursed than the ground") in 4.11 refers. This same meaning makes perfectly good sense here too: the cattle and beasts are cursed by the fact that they lack the reason and speech possessed by man, and the serpent was afflicted by an even greater curse, namely, he was forever to crawl on his belly and eat dirt. Biblical Hebrew uses *garash* or *shillaḥ* for "banish."

(shall you) crawl . . . dirt (shall you eat). Trad. "go . . . dust" is mechanical and does scant justice to the various nuances of Heb. *telekh . . . 'afar.* A rendering can be both literal and idiomatic, like "offspring" in the very next verse (15), in place of Trad. "seed," for Heb. *zéra.*

16. **Your pangs in childbearing.** Trad. "thy pains and and thy travail" has overlooked the structure of hendiadys (see at 1.14 above, and Introduction, §c).

17. The earlier printings read "In anguish," in deference to the meaning of Heb. *éṣev,* "pain" (cf. v. 16 preceding). However, not only is "By toil" (cf. Driver's comment on Trad. "in toil") just as acceptable here per se, but it serves as a better antecedent for v. 19 ("By the sweat of your brow . . ."; cf. Rashi: after you have wearied yourself in it greatly) and for 5.29, where Lamech says, in naming Noah, "This one will provide us relief from our work and from the toil of our hands" (*iṣṣevon yadénu*).

18. **(Thorns and thistles shall it sprout for you,) / But your food shall be the grasses of the field.** Earlier printings read "(Thorns and thistles/Shall it bring forth for you,) /And you shall feed on the grains of the field." The reading now adopted follows the interpretation of Ehrlich (*Mikra*).

19. **By the sweat of your brow.** More idiomatic, and not less correct, than Trad. "In the sweat of thy face" (*beze'ath appékha*).

Shall you get bread to eat. Trad. "shalt thou eat bread" (Heb. *tokhal léḥem*) is misleading. Cf. Rashi.

22. **Now that . . . what if.** Trad. "Behold, (the man is

become . . .); and now, lest (he put forth his hand . . .)" has incorrectly comprehended the force of Heb. *hen . . . we-atta pen* and so has misconstrued the syntax of the verse. These particles actually serve to introduce the protasis ("if" or "since, now that") and apodosis ("then" or [with *pen*] "what if, suppose"). In such instances, we are dealing with a single sentence, not with two independent sentences; see Brown-Driver-Briggs, *Hebrew Lexicon,* p. 243, II *hen,* §a.

24. **(the fiery) ever-turning (sword).** Trad. "(the flaming sword which) turned every way" has no authority. The *hithpael* conjugation, as long recognized, is sometimes used in biblical Hebrew to indicate repeated or frequentative or ongoing action; see Sforno's comment on *mith-hallekh* in 3.8: "walking hither and thither,"etc. (*áne wa-ána khefi takhlith ha-mekhawwen;* similarly *hith-hallekh ba-áreṣ* [Gen. 13.17] and *wa-yith-hallekhu mi-goy el-goy* [Ps. 105.13, I Chron. 16.20]). See also Ehrlich, *Mikra,* p. 18, at 5.28, followed more recently by Speiser, *Journal of the American Oriental Society,* 75 (1955), 117 ff.

Chapter 4

1. **knew.** On "experience" in the footnote, see Ehrlich, *Mikra,* p. 328 (at Deut. 11.28).

Cain . . . I have gained. An attempt to reproduce the word play in *qáyin . . . qaníthi,* cf. Moffat's attempt: "Cain (Got) . . . I have got." Trad. "[b]gotten ([b]Heb. *kanah,* to get)" has missed the word play.

2. **She then bore,** etc. Trad. "And again she bore his brother Abel" leads to the question: When had she borne him previously? The Heb. idiom *wa-tósef* (*lalédeth*) deserves a corresponding English idiom, such as "then" or "next" (so Moffat) or "later" (*An American Translation*) or "also" (*La Sainte Bible*; cf. *The Jerusalem Bible*: she gave birth to a second child).

4. **(and Abel, for his part,) brought the choicest of the firstlings of his flock.** Trad. "(And Abel, he also) brought of the firstlings of his flock and of the fat thereof" is misleading; in reproducing the Hebrew word for word, it indicates that Abel brought both "the firstlings of his flock" and "of the fat thereof." Actually, initial *u-(meḥelvehen)* is here the *waw* explicative: "namely, their *ḥalavim.*" See further immediately below.

choicest. The word *ḥélev* is used frequently in the Bible in the sense of "choicest, best part of" in reference to the land (Gen. 45.18: "you shall live off the fat [*ḥélev*] of the land"), to new oil and wine and grain (Num. 18.12, 27–29), and to wheat (Ps. 81.17; 147.14). At the same time it is not impossible that *ḥelvehen* here means "the fat parts," since it is the singular form (*ḥélev*) that connotes "choicest" as well as "fat," whereas the plural form elsewhere always means "fat pieces" (thirteen times: nine times in Leviticus, four times in II Chronicles)—and the fat pieces, as Driver has put it, constituted "a highly-prized portion of the animal, and so offered regularly upon the altar (Lev. i.8, iii.3 f.; in firstlings, Nu. xviii.17)."

paid heed to. (Also 5.) Trad., "had respect unto." The exact nuance of Heb. *sha'ah* is elusive here. All are agreed that the general idea is "turned to" (Rashi), "accepted" (Ibn Ezra; cf. Targum Onkelos); thus the Septuagint rendered "looked upon" in v. 4 and "He did not regard" in v. 5.

5. **distressed.** (Also 6.) Trad. "wroth" overlooks the fact that it is only when the word *af* is combined with it as its subject (*wa-yiḥar af . . .*) that the verb *ḥarah* means "his anger flared up, he became angry"; *ḥarah* by itself means "to be distressed" or the like.

7. The whole verse is admittedly difficult, and all translations are partially the result of learned guessing.

Sin couches at the door. The preserved text at *lapéthaḥ ḥaṭṭath roveṣ* is not in order when the feminine noun *ḥaṭṭath* has to serve as the subject of the masculine form of the participle, *roveṣ*; and even the conjectural emendation of the masculine *roveṣ* to the feminine *tirbaṣ* lacks meaning when it is remembered that the suffixes in the second half of our verse are both masculine: (*teshuqath*)*o*, "its/his (urge)" and (*timshal-b*)*o*, "(you shall rule over) it/him." Earlier printings read "Sin is the demon[d] at the door" ([d]*Cf. Akkadian* rabiṣu, *a type of demon*).

8. (Cain said to his brother Abel)[d] . . . (and when they were in the field . . .) ([d]*Ancient versions, including the Targum, read "Come, let us go out into the field"*). Trad. "And Cain spoke unto Abel his brother. And it came to pass, when they were in the field . . ." automatically leads to the question: Spoke about what? Or as put by Driver (*Genesis*, p. 65) on Revised Version "(And Cain) told (Abel his brother)"—and the same holds true for Trad. "Spoke unto": "The Heb. [*wa-yómer*] means, not 'told' [or 'spoke to'], but SAID UNTO, and the words said ought to follow. . . ." The words said—"Come, let us go out into the field" (*lekha weneṣe'a ha-sade*)—are found in such ancient versions as the Septuagint, Samaritan, and Targum Jonathan (whence, e.g., Ramban: *ki amar lo neṣe ha-sade*, "for he said to him, 'Let us go out into the field' "), not to mention the Peshitta and Vulgate. In all likelihood the three words fell out by accident as a result of the proximity of *ha-sade* and *ba-sade*. See the discussion by Orlinsky, *Journal of Biblical Literature*, 61 (1942), 91, n. 8, with further reference to 59 (1940), 515–517 and *Jewish Quarterly Review*, 32 (1941–42), 196, §4.

10. Hark, (your brother's blood cries out . . .). Trad., "The voice (of thy brother's blood . . .)." However, it is not the "voice" (*qol*) but the "blood" (*deme*) that cries out, if only because the latter, in the plural form, naturally serves as the subject of the participle (*ṣo'aqim*) in the plural; so already, e.g., Ibn Ezra; and see at 3.8 above. And on p. 155 of his English version (*Encyclopedia of Biblical Interpreta-*

tion, Vol. I, 1953) of Menahem Kasher's *Torah Shelemah,* Harry Freedman has noted the identical interpretation of RaLaSh (Rabbi Levi Shapiro, Frankfurt) in his commentary on the Bible, *Ha-rekhasim Le-viqa* (a clever use of Isa. 40.4; 1815): "Hark! the blood of thy brother," etc.

11. **more cursed than.** See at 3.14 above.

opened (its mouth). Earlier printings read "opened . . . wide"; but Heb. *paṣaḥ* (like *pathaḥ*) means simply "to open." For the contrary view, see Ehrlich (*Mikra* and *Randglossen*).

12. **(You shall become) a restless wanderer (on earth).** (Also v. 14.) Trad. "a fugitive and a wanderer (shalt thou be in the earth)" has overlooked the presence of hendiadys in Heb. *na wa-nad*: Cain was to be not both "a fugitive" (more literally "a totterer") and "a wanderer," but "a wanderer ever on the move," i.e., a restless (or ceaseless) wanderer. On hendiadys, see at 1.14 above and Introduction, §c.

14. **(anyone who) meets (me).** Trad. "(whosoever) findeth (me)" has failed to note that Heb. *maṣa* means not only to "find" but also to "meet, come across or upon, encounter."

15. **I promise.** Heb. *lakhen* has traditionally been rendered "therefore." But already the *Mechilta de-Rabbi Simeon ben Johai* (ed. J. N. Epstein–E. Z. Melamed), top of p. 6, noted the meaning of *lakhen* as "I swear, assuredly" in Num. 20.12 (*we-en lakhen ella shevu'a*), citing *lakhen* in conjunction with *nishbáti* in I Sam. 3.14; and M. Margulies has cited several other instances (e.g., Exodus Rabbah, Deuteronomy Rabbah, Tanḥuma—and the note by M. Zulay) in his edition of *Midrash Wayyikra Rabbah* (part III, 1956, p. 528, line 4) in connection with *lakhen* in Exod. 6.6; and cf. Targum Jonathan at Num. 25.12. See the recent discussion by F. J. Goldbaum in *Journal of Near Eastern Studies,* 23 (1964), 132–135.

17. **and named the city after his son Enoch.** This is not only idiomatic English but also the correct transla-

tion of the Hebrew. The traditional, word-for-word rendering, "and he called the name of the city," etc., is hardly good English.

20. (he was the ancestor of those who dwell in tents) and amidst herds. That is, Jabal was the first nomad. Trad., "and have cattle." The Hebrew reads literally "(who dwell in tents) and herds," and some such word as "who own, breed, raise, pasture" is expected before *miqneh,* "herds"; as put succinctly by Benno Jacob, *Genesis,* p. 148, "Die Konstruktion . . . ist hart." The ancient versions (Septuagint, the Targums Onkelos and Jonathan, Vulgate) introduced some such word; cf. Rashi: he was the first to pasture animals in uncultivated places.

21. lyre. Trad. "harp" is hardly correct for Heb. *kinnor* (which serves in Modern Hebrew for "violin"); see E. Werner's article on "Musical Instruments" in *Interpreter's Dictionary of the Bible,* III (1962), 474–5; and on "pipe" (or flute) for *ugav,* see p. 471.

22. copper. Trad. "brass," which is the Old English equivalent of our bronze (an alloy of copper and tin), has come to denote another alloy, that of copper and zinc. It is worth noting here (with Driver) that the writer of our verse had no knowledge of the long Stone Age that preceded the Chalcolithic (Copper/Bronze-Stone) and Bronze Ages.

25. (and named him Seth,) meaning, "God has. . . ." Trad. "for God has . . ." overlooks the fact that Heb. *ki* sometimes has the force of "that is, namely," as in Gen. 41.51, 52. This has been noted by Ehrlich, *Randglossen,* vol. I (1908), p. 25, with reference to Num. 11.16 and Isa. 5.7.

26. invoke the Lord by name. That is, to employ the name of God in prayer, vow, sacrifice, etc. Trad. "call upon the name of the LORD" is unclear.

Chapter 5

1. **record.** Trad. "book" is misleading; the "book" as now understood is postbiblical in origin. Heb. *séfer* denotes simply a written account, record, document.

line. Heb. *toledoth* here serves to introduce, as put by Driver (p. 74), "*The line of Seth from Adam to Noah*: In the form of a genealogy of ten generations. . . ." See at 2.4a above.

When. On *be-yom* as a temporal particle, see above at 2.4. Note that the "When" construction resembles 1.1 and 2.4; all three passages are attributed by scholars to the same literary source (see Driver).

22. **walked.** (Also v. 24.) In such pasages as this—so also Noah at 6.9—Heb. *hith-hallekh* means "to conduct one's life." Since God is involved here, such interpretations as Sforno's *hith-hallekh bidrakhaw* ("he walked in His ways") and Rashi's *ṣaddiq haya* ("he was righteous")—followed, e.g., by Ehrlich, Driver, and Jacob—are correct.

29. **will provide us relief (from our work).** So the Septuagint (*dianapaúsei hēmâs*). Heb. *niḥam* has a range of nuances that is suppressed by traditional-literal "comfort."

Chapter 6

2. **divine beings.** In line with the use of the plurals—with God Himself as the speaker!—in 1.26 ("Let *us* make man in *our* image, after *our* likeness"), it is clear that Heb. *bene elohim* means "divine beings" rather than traditional "sons of God." It had already been noted, e.g., by Driver (p. 82, n. 1)—though this had been generally overlooked until recognized and argued more fully by Isaac Mendelsohn in the

forties—that "'sons of *gods,*' meaning (cf. 'sons of the prophets' = members of the guild of prophets) members of the class of divine beings, to which . . . Jehovah Himself also belongs. . . ." On *ben* (lit., "son") as "member (of a guild)," see Mendelsohn, *Bulletin of the American Schools of Oriental Research,* No. 80 (1940), pp. 17–21; *Journal of the American Oriental Society,* 60 (1944), 68–72; G. Brin, *Leshonenu,* 31 (1966/5727), 5–20, 85–96. Jewish tradition (cf. e.g., Targum, *bene ravrevayya,* "sons of nobles," and Rashi, *bene ha-sarim we-ha-shofeṭim,* "sons of princes and judges"), no less than Christian, tended to avoid the mythological-anthropological in our expression. See the discussions in Driver and Jacob (pp. 170–172).

3. **My breath shall not abide[b] in man.** Trad. "My spirit shall not abide in man." The earlier printings read "(My spirit shall not) shield[b] (man)"; however, it was realized that there is insufficient basis for associating Hebrew *yadon* with Akkadian (Babylonian-Assyrian) *dinānu* either in morphology or in meaning. Trad. "abide" derives directly from Septuagint (*oủ mḕ*) *katameínē* and Targum *yithqayyem;* yet it must be put forthrightly, as Driver did (pp. 83–4), ". . . It is wisest to acknowledge the simple truth, which is that both textually and exegetically the verse is very uncertain, and that it is impossible to feel any confidence as to its meaning." Hence our footnote on "abide": *meaning of Heb uncertain.*

4. **cohabited.** Earlier printings had "consorted with." Trad. "came in unto," while literal for Heb. *ba el,* is hardly idiomatic.

5. **every plan devised by his mind.** (Cf. also 8.21.) Trad. "every imagination of the thoughts of his heart" is a wholly unimaginative, word-for-word reproduction of the Hebrew (Do thoughts have imagination? Does the heart have thoughts?), and does scant justice to the meaning "mind" that Heb. *leb* so frequently has. The ancient Semites recog-

nized the "heart" (Akkadian *libbu*) as the seat of thought, with the bowels or liver as the seat of the emotions.

nothing but (evil). Bringing out more fully the force of *raq* (*ra'*), Trad. "only (evil)," on which Driver had commented: i.e., nothing but evil.

6. **And the Lord regretted that.** More idiomatic, and correct, than Trad. "And it repented the Lord that."

7. **(I will blot out) from the earth the men whom I created.** In reproducing the Hebrew word order mechanically, Trad. "(I will blot out) man whom I have created from the face of the earth" has ignored the simple fact that whereas the word order in Hebrew prefers the object immediately after the verb (*emḥe eth-ha-adam*) and the relative clause immediately after the object (*asher baráthi*), the word order in English does not. The clause "whom I have created" should at least have had the help of commas.

8. **(found) favor (with).** The traditional term "(found) grace (in the eyes of)" is hardly modern in the sense of "found favor with, pleased"; furthermore, it has theological overtones altogether lacking in the Hebrew Bible.

9. **(Noah was) a righteous man; he was blameless in his age.** Trad. "(Noah was) in his generations a man righteous and whole-hearted" barely does justice to the Hebrew: (a) the connective "and" is lacking in the Hebrew, so that the syntax of the original has been distorted; (b) by placing "in his generations" in a position of emphasis, it has also distorted the significance of Heb. *be-dorothaw*. It is true that some rabbis of old made of Noah a righteous man only in relation to the extreme lawlessness of his contemporaries; but this is not the intent of the Hebrew text. See Rashi's comment on this, and Jacob's (*Genesis*, pp. 183–4).

age. Heb. *dor(oth)* denotes "age(s)" rather than "generations" in the literal sense. Thus in Ugaritic (Old Canaanite) *dr dr* means "eternity, forever," exactly like *ledor dor* (parallel to *le-olam*) in Exod. 3.15; so that whereas "throughout the generations" is acceptable for *mi-dor dor* (Exod. 17.16), Trad. "in his generations" is hardly acceptable for *be-dorothaw* in our verse.

walked. See at 5.22 above.

11. **lawlessness.** (Also v. 13.) Earlier printings read "injustice," but it was felt that a more "active" noun was needed. Trad. "violence" unnecessarily limits Heb. *ḥamas* to physical force.

13. **I have decided to put an end to all flesh.** Understanding the expression *ba lefanay* to indicate judgment. So Ramban: "their verdict of guilty was sealed," followed, e.g., by Cassuto (p. 31). Cf. Driver (p. 87), in commenting on Revised Version *is come* IN *before me*: I.e. "before my mind; it is resolved upon by me."

I am about to (destroy them). Trad. "and, behold, I will" does injustice to the several idiomatic nuances of Heb. *hinne*. See Introduction, §c.

14. **compartments.** So already Targum *medorim,* whence, e.g., Rashi: *medorim medorim lekhol behema we-ḥayya,* "separate compartments for every domesticated and undomesticated animal." Trad. "rooms" attempts to convey the same idea, as does, e.g., the term "cells" (cf. Driver, p. 87: "*rooms*. More exactly . . . *cells* [lit. *nests*] . . .").

16. **Make an opening for daylight (in the ark).** On the assumption that Heb. *ṣóhar* (a word that occurs only here in the Bible) is related to the dual form *ṣaharáyim* ("noon"). As to the common rendering "roof," Driver has commented (p. 88), ". . . *roof* is doubtful: it is based upon the meaning of the corresponding word in Arabic, *back*."

17. **For My part, I am about to bring.** Trad. "And I, behold, I do bring" (cf. v. 13 above) is mechanical, and suppresses the force of Heb. *wa-ani hineni*. Sforno has caught the Hebrew perfectly: "*You* (for your part) finish the ark, and *I* (for My part) will immediately afterwards bring the Flood."

the Flood—waters upon the earth—(to destroy). Trad. "the flood of waters upon the earth" has obscured the fact that the Hebrew reads *eth-ha-mabbul máyim,* lit., "the Flood, waters." (Similarly 7.6.)

18. (and you shall enter the ark), with your sons, (your wife, and your sons' wives). Earlier printings read "—you, your sons," etc., following in part Trad. "thou, and thou sons, and thy wife, and thy sons' wives with thee"; but this failed to do justice to the Hebrew (as well as to the English) idiom, for whereas biblical Hebrew requires *atta* ("you") and *ittakh* ("with you"), English does not. (See also 7.7.)

19. And of all that lives, of all flesh. Trad. "And of every living thing of all flesh" has unnecessarily—as well as incorrectly—turned *u-mi-kol-ha-ḥay,* which stands in apposition to *mi-kol-basar* (both being the objects of the verb *tavi,* "you shall take into"), into the construct of *mi-kol-basar* (". . . living thing of all flesh").

20. to stay alive. Trad. "to keep them alive" (for *le-haḥayoth*) not only supplies unnecessarily an object ("them") that is lacking in the Hebrew but overlooks one of the various nuances of the *hiphil* of *ḥaya,* namely, "to remain alive." (Contrast v. 19, where *le-haḥayoth* does have an object.) For the nuance "let live," see at Exod. 1.17, 18 below.

21. For your part, take. As in v. 17 above, Trad. "And take thou unto thee" has suppressed the force of initial *we-atta* (*qaḥ lekha*) in the Hebrew. Once again, Sforno has comprehended the Hebrew: "And as for you, now (or, next) take all food. . . ."

Chapter 7

1. Then. Trad. "And (the LORD said unto Noah)" does scant justice to the wide range of meanings possessed by Hebrew conjunctive *waw.* See Introduction, §c.

(Go into the ark) with all your household). On Trad. "(Come) thou and (all thy house into the ark)," see at 6.18 above.

for you alone (have I found righteous). Trad. "for thee" has not realized the full force of Heb. (*ki-*)*othekha* (*ra'íthi*), which is placed in an emphatic position: "for it is *you* that . . ." etc.

2. **seven pairs.** (Also v. 3.) Trad. "seven and seven" has not only unnecessarily added an "and" where the Hebrew lacks it, but has missed the idiom in Heb. *shiva shiva;* similarly *shenáyim shenáyim* "two (of) each"—not Trad. "two and two"—in vv. 9, 15 below.

4. **For in seven days' time (I will make it rain).** Trad. "For yet seven days, (and I will cause it to rain)" is hardly English, and has failed to express the idiom in the Hebrew (*ki leyamim od shiva*).

6. **the Flood came, waters (upon the earth).** On Trad. "the flood of water was"—in violation of *we-ha-mabbul haya máyim* (*al-ha-áreṣ*)—see at 6.17 above.

9. **two of each.** See at v. 2 above.

11. **All the fountains,** etc. Some scholars recognize two lines of poetry in the second half of the verse (note the parallelism and the inversion):

nivqe'u *kol-ma'yenoth* *tehom rabba*

wa-arubboth *ha-shamáyim* *niftáḥu*

Cf. Jacob, pp. 205–6. It may be observed that the supplement to our passage is expressed in 8.2, in prose.

12. This verse is placed within parentheses to indicate that vv. 13–16 follow immediately upon v. 11, with our v. 12 being resumed by v. 17.

19–20. When the waters had swelled much more . . . all the highest mountains . . . were covered. [20]Fifteen cubits higher did the waters swell, etc. Compare Rashi at v. 20,

"Fifteen cubits above (*lemá'la*): above the peaks of all the mountains, after the waters had reached to the tops of the mountains." Trad. "And the waters prevailed exceedingly . . . and all the high mountains . . . were covered. Fifteen cubits upward did the waters prevail" does not bring out the force of *gaveru* ("swell"), *gevohim* ("highest"), and *milmá'lah* ("higher").

22. **the merest breath of life.** An attempt to reproduce the nuance of the Hebrew. Trad., "with breath of the spirit of life." This is the only instance in the Bible where *neshama* and *rúaḥ* are used in combination; thus it is *nishmath ḥayyim* in 2.7, and *rúaḥ ḥayyim* in 6.17 and 7.15.

24. **And when the waters had swelled . . . (8.1) God remembered Noah,** etc. The syntactical construction of the Hebrew is not comprehended in Trad. "And the waters prevailed . . . (8.1) And God remembered Noah," etc. For 7.24 is actually the protasis ("when . . .") of which 8.1 is the apodosis (= then), as already recognized by Saadia in his Judeo-Arabic translation of the Torah: "And when (*wa-lammā*) the waters . . . God remembered (*dhakara allahu*) Noah . . ."—the whole (7.24 and 8.1) constituting a single sentence. On the late chapter-verse division of the Hebrew text of the Bible, see Introduction. §c.

Chapter 8

4. **the mountains of Ararat.** So Trad. This expression may be understood as either "the mountains of the *land* Ararat" or "the Ararat mountain range." It has been insufficiently recognized that (as put by Driver, p. 93, n. 1), "there is no 'Mount Ararat' in the Old Testament." It should be kept in mind that even in the singular, *har* often means "massif" (e.g., *har* Sinai) or "hill country" (e.g., *har* Ephraim; *har* Judah).

5. **became visible.** Trad. "were seen" suppresses one of the nuances of the Hebrew verb, the inchoative or inceptive. Compare "may appear, become visible" (not "be seen") for *tera'e ha-yabbasha* in 1.9 above. See Introduction, §c.

11. **plucked-off.** Trad. "freshly (plucked)" for Heb. *ṭaraf* lacks justification in biblical Hebrew usage; it is based on the idea that it was a fresh leaf that had been plucked from an olive tree—rather than an old leaf that had been picked up somewhere—and brought back by the dove (thus Radak; Cassuto, p. 62 of his Hebrew commentary, *From Noah to Abraham*). Jewish tradition generally has recognized in our *ṭaraf* simply "torn, broken off, plucked"; cf., e.g., Targum Onkelos, Rashi.

13. **began to dry . . . was drying.** On the assumption that Heb. *ḥarav* denotes the process of drying up, as against *yavesh* which denotes the completed process (as in v. 14), namely, "was dry"; thus Sforno: "the surface of the ground was *ḥarav,* but it had not become *yavesh* enough for him to be able to go out." On the other hand, it may be that both words, *ḥarav* and *yavesh,* really have the same meaning, namely, "be(come) dry," and that one author employed *ḥarav* for the ground (8.13b) and *yavesh* for the water (8.7), whereas another did the opposite (using *ḥarav* for the water in 8.13a and *yavesh* for the ground in 8.14). Elsewhere the two words are used interchangeably, as in Isa. 44.27; Jer. 51.36; and Nahum 1.4; thus *go'er ba-yam wa-yabbeshéhu* in Nahum 1.4 (parallel to *we-khol-ha-neharoth heḥeriv*) is expressed in Ps. 106.9 by *wa-yig'ar beyam-suf wa-yeḥerav*).

21. **Never again (will I).** Trad. "I will not again . . . any more," being literal, fails to bring out the force of the Hebrew idiom (*lo osif . . . od*).

devisings of man's mind. See at 6.5 above.

22. Many scholars now recognize the Hebrew verse as poetry, consisting of a series of lines of two beats each: *zéra we-qaṣir / we-qor wa-ḥom / we-qáyiṣ wa-ḥóref,* etc.

Chapter 9

4–6. While the construction and meaning of some parts of these verses are elusive (e.g., the preposition in *be-nafsho*; the construction of *be-nafsho damo* in v. 4; the particle *we-akh* and the preposition in *le-nafshothekhem* in v. 5), the force of the passage is clear enough: "Man may eat flesh, but only flesh which no longer has blood in it. . . . Man may slay animals; but the blood of man is not to be shed with impunity, either by man or by beast. The life of man is to be inviolably sacred" (Driver, p. 96).

6. For in His image / Did God make man. Treating this verse as poetry. Trad. (as prose), "for in the image of God made He man."

11. (I will maintain) My covenant with you: never again shall all flesh be cut off, etc. Trad. "(And I will establish) My covenant with you; neither shall all flesh be cut off any more" has missed the explicative force of *we-(lo yikkareth kol-basar od)*—"namely, that is," represented in the new version by the colon—thus misleading the reader into thinking that not only will God establish His covenant with Noah and his offspring but, in addition ("neither," etc.), He will never again cut off all flesh. Rashi understood the construction correctly; on *wa-haqimothi* he comments: *e'eseh qiyyum livrithi* ("I will make a confirmation of My covenant"); *u-máhu qiyyumo* ("And what is its confirmation?"), *oth ha-qésheth* ("the sign of the rainbow"), *kemo she-mesayyem we-holekh* ("as [Scripture] concludes farther on" [v. 13]).

12. (for all) ages (to come). On "ages" (for *doroth*) as against Trad. "(for perpetual) generations," see at 6.9 above.

13. (I have set My bow in the) clouds. (Also v. 14.) Heb. *anan,* contrary to Trad. "cloud," is singular collective; cf. Driver (p. 98) on v. 14.

(and it shall) serve as (a sign). Trad. "be for," being literal, has suppressed the idiom in Heb. *haya le-*, which means "become, serve as." Compare "become" in v. 15 below.

18. —Ham being (the father of Canaan). Trad. "; and Ham is" overlooks the circumstantial force of Heb. *we-ḥam hu* (*avi khenáʻan*) "now Ham is," "Ham being." The pedigree is introduced here in this manner because Canaan will shortly be cursed (vv. 25–27); cf. Rashi's admirable comment on this passage: Why was it necessary to state here the genealogy of Ham? Since this section goes on to deal with the drunkenness of Noah, in which Ham disgraced himself, and through him Canaan was cursed, and since the text had not yet recorded the genealogy of Ham, so that we should not know that Canaan is his son, it was necessary to state here, "Now Ham is the father of Canaan."

20. (Noah . . .) was the first to plant (a vineyard). In being literal, Trad. "(And Noah . . .) began, and planted (a vineyard)" fails to comprehend the close association of the two verbs for "began" and "planted" (*wa-yáḥel . . . wa-yiṭṭa*). Thus already Sforno commented on *wa-yáḥel*: *hith-ḥil be-phóʻal bilti na'uth,* etc., "he began with an improper activity"; and Driver noted (p. 109, at v. 21; cf. Cassuto, p. 89), "Noah, it is implied, was the *first* to plant a vineyard."

21. and he uncovered himself. Trad. "and he was uncovered" has done scant justice to the reflexive function of the *hithpael* form of Heb. *wa-yithgal.* So already Rashi.

23. placed it against both their backs. This is what already Ibn Ezra seems to have had in mind (see also the *Perush al Ibn Ezra*). Trad. "and laid it upon both their shoulders" does not present a clear picture of the action. The term "backs" not only clarifies the picture but also reproduces Heb. *shekhem* correctly.

(their faces) were turned the other way. So already Ibn Ezra (see the *Perush al Ibn Ezra*: *we-gam penehem haya beṣad aḥor,* "their faces too were turned the other way") and Sforno. Trad. "and their faces were backward" is not as clear as the Hebrew text.

25. The lowest of slaves. Trad. "a servant of servants," because it is literal, has failed to express the superlative function of the Hebrew construction; as put by Luzzatto (p. 51): *hap-paḥoth she-ba'avadim,* "the least of slaves"; and cf. Driver (p. 110), *"servant of servants.* I.e. the very lowest of servants."

27. And let him dwell. Trad. "And he shall dwell" has missed the optative ("wish") force of Heb. *we-(yishkon)*, parallel to *yaft* ("May [God] enlarge") and *wihi* ("And let [Canaan] be").

Chapter 10

1. For the ethnic list as a whole in this chapter, see Driver, *Genesis,* 112–119; Cassuto, pp. 96 ff.; Speiser, "Man, Ethnic Divisions of," *Interpreter's Dictionary of the Bible,* III (1962), 235–242.

2. descendants. (And frequently.) Not only is this term frequently correct for Heb. *banim,* but in this very chapter several of the *banim* are manifestly not "sons" (so Trad. mechanically throughout); thus the Kittim and the Dodanim (for which the Septuagint here and the parallel passage in I Chron. 1.7 reads correctly "Rodanim," i.e., the Rhodians) in v. 4 are strictly ethnic terms. Luzzatto (p. 52) emphasizes this point.

5. From the structure of the list as a whole—see especially vv. 20 and 31—scholars agree that the summing-up clause, "these are the descendants of Japheth . . . ," accidentally fell out of the original text; for a contrary view, see Cassuto pp. 109 f.

8. (who was) the first (man of might). This is probably what was intended by Trad. "he began to be (a mighty one)."

man of might. This phrase goes with *gibbor ṣáyid* ("a mighty hunter") in v. 9. Earlier printings read "man of power," which went with v. 10 ("The mainstays of his kingdom . . ."), pointing to Nimrod's "power of governing men and organizing a kingdom" (Driver, p. 120). Luzzatto (pp. 53–4) may be right: first he became famous as a man of might (*mefursam bi-gevuratho*) and consequently he brought his fellow men under his domination (*we-al yede khakh hevi bene-adam táḥath memshalto*); and see Cassuto, pp. 111–113, for the epic background.

9. **by the grace (of the Lord).** The preposition *lifne* (especially in combination with God) has long been felt to have a meaning beyond simple "before, in front of." Thus in 6.11 (also in v. 13), Luzzatto had interpreted *lifne YHWH* as "(And the earth became corrupt) in God's judgment [*bemaḥashéveth ha-el*] (for He knew that human society could not continue amidst lawlessness . . .)"; in this he was followed, e.g., by Ehrlich (*Mikra,* p. 19, "in the sight of God, i.e., in the view of God and in His opinion"; *Randglossen,* p. 31, "vom Standpunkt Gottes, wie Gott die Sachen ansah; vgl. V. 13") and Speiser (*Genesis,* p. 51," [in the view of God,] according to God's [regretful] conclusion"). Ibn Ezra, on the other hand, in his discussion of our expression in 6.11, arrives at the conclusion that the meaning is: God was fully aware of the lawlessness; and Cassuto comes close to this in his comment: in full view of God. See also Sforno.

In our verse, however, Luzzatto—like Rashbam (see at 27.7) and Ramban before him, and Jacob (p. 281) after him—understood *lifne YHWH* to mean simply "in the whole world." Ehrlich (*Mikra,* p. 29; *Randglossen,* p. 43), followed by the present rendering ("by the grace of the Lord") and Speiser ("by the will of Yahweh"), interpreted *lifne YHWH* as "with the Lord's approval and consent" (*birṣon YHWH we-haskamatho*)—but only after emending (*gibbor*) *ṣáyid* to *ṣur* and rendering it approximately "a protective overlord" and "ein schützender Held." Brown-Driver-Briggs,

Hebrew Lexicon, under *lifne* (p. 817a, § 4 a *g*), interpret "*in the sight* (estimation) *of* (the Lord)." In sum then: the final word has by no means been said on the precise meaning of *lifne* in these various passages. See also at 27.7 below and Introduction, §c.

10. The mainstays (of his kingdom). Heb. *reshith,* usually meaning "beginning" (so Trad. here), also means "chief, choice, best" (as in Deut. 33.21; Amos 6.6), and hence "mainstay" (Jer. 49.35; so also Moffat, *An American Translation,* Revised Standard Version). But see immediately below, on Calneh.

Calneh.[c] Described long ago as "uncertain" (Driver, p. 121), a city in southern Babylonia by this name is still unknown, after the discovery of so many Mesopotamian and related documents since the beginning of the century. Hence it has been suggested (originally by A. Poebel, and later more fully by W. F. Albright, *Journal of Near Eastern Studies,* 3 [1944], 254–5) that the consonants of preserved *we-khalneh* ("and Calneh") were originally pronounced *we-khullánah,* "and all of them." (Our traditional system of vowels did not come into being until after the period of the Babylonian Talmud, i.e., until after the sixth century C.E.) Thus our verse would read (with our note *c*), "The mainstays of his kingdom were Babylon, Erech, and Accad, all of them being in the land of Shinar." But Shinar—even if it is to be associated with Sumer (as proposed, e.g., by S. N. Kramer, followed by Speiser, *Genesis,* p. 67)—is itself an elusive entity (see, e.g., T. Jacobsen's article on "Shinar" in *Interpreter's Dictionary of the Bible,* IV [1962], 332; also S. N. Kramer's article on "Sumer," pp. 454–463). C. H. Gordon has proposed a city Calneh in southern Babylonia as the original mother city of Calneh in the north (just as Ur in the south was the mother city of Abraham's Ur, a commercial colony in the north); see his article on "Calneh" in vol. I of *Interpreter's Dictionary,* p. 490. The problem of "and Calneh" has hardly been solved.

14. **the Caphtorim.**[d] Within the Bible it is clear from Jer. 47.4, as well as from Amos 9.7, that the Philistines derive from Caphtorim; see J. C. Greenfield's articles on "Caphtor" and "Philistines" in *Interpreter's Dictionary of the Bible,* respectively vols. I (p. 534) and III (pp. 791–795).

19. **territory.** Heb. *gevul* means "territory, country," as well as "boundary, border." Trad. and earlier printings, "border."

30. **as far as.** Lit., "as you come," i.e., as one comes. See, however, Jacob's observation (p. 294) on the lack of *ad* before *bo'akha.*

32. **These are,** etc. On *élle . . . le-toledotham,* see at 2.4a above.

Chapter 11

2. **came upon.** As against Trad. (mechanically) "found" for *maṣa.* Similarly at 37.15 and elsewhere.

6. **(nothing . . . will be) out of their reach.** Trad. "withholden from them." As put by Driver (p. 136), "If this great work is the beginning of their ambition, what will be the end of it, nothing soon will be beyond their reach. . . ."

7. **Let us.** On "Let Me" in earlier printings, see at 1.26 above.

(Let us,) then, (go down). Trad. "Come, (let us go down)" has treated Heb. *háva* here as though it had the force of a verb in the imperative, instead of a particle (interjection); see Gesenius-Kautzsch-Cowley, *Hebrew Grammar,* 28th ed., § 105*b* (p. 307).

28. **in the lifetime of.** So Rashi (*beḥayye*), followed by Luzzatto, Ehrlich, Driver, Jacob (p. 324), Cassuto, and many others. Trad., "in the presence of."

31. **(Ur of the) Chaldeans.** Trad. "Chaldees" is a less modern form.

Chapter 12

1. **(Go forth) from your native land.** Heb. (*lekh-lekha*) *me-'arṣekha u-mi-moladtekha* (Trad., "out of thy country, and from thy kindred") is a classic instance of hendiadys (cf. at 1.14 above, and Introduction, §c); note the more usual manner of expressing our concept just a few verses back, in 11.28: *be-éreṣ moladto,* "in his native land," or in 24.7: *me-éreṣ moladti,* "from my native land."

3. **Shall bless themselves by you.** Understanding the Heb. *niphal* form *we-nivrekhu vekha* as reflexive (see note *a* in the Torah at end of v. 1 preceding), rather than passive (Trad., "in you . . . shall be blessed"); cf. Rashi (followed, e.g., by Luzzatto, p. 61; Ehrlich, *Mikra,* p. 32; Jacob, pp. 337–9), "There are many Aggadic interpretations, but its plain meaning is this: A man says to his son, 'May you be like Abraham.' . . ." A more detailed argument (including a discussion of the *hithpael* form where only the reflexive force is possible, in the identical context, in 22.18 and 26.4—*we-hithbarakhu bezarakha kol goye ha-áreṣ*) may be found in Driver, p. 145.

8. **the hill country.** Trad. "the mountain" restricts the force of Heb. *ha-har* unnecessarily, and overlooks its use as a technical geographical term. See above at 8.4.

invoked, etc. See at 4.26 above.

9. **journeyed by stages (toward the Negeb).** So already Rashi, followed by Luzzatto; cf. Driver (p. 148); "*journeyed,* viz. by stages, as is customary in the East." See also 13.3 below. Trad. "(And Abraham) journeyed, going on still (toward the South)" has missed the force of *nasa'*.

11. **(As) he was about (to enter Egypt).** Trad. "And it came to pass, when) he was come near (to enter into Egypt)," because it is literal, has failed to reproduce the idiomatic force of *hiqriv* (*lavo*).

(I know) what a beautiful woman you are. Trad. "that thou art a fair woman to look upon" is more mechanical than idiomatic. Earlier printings read "I am well aware" (for "I know").

13. (and that) I (may remain alive). Trad. "(and that) my soul (may live)" has overlooked the common use of Heb. *néfesh* as a personal pronoun; cf. Driver (p. 149), and see at 2.7 above.

Chapter 13

9. north . . . south. In translating literally, Trad. "the left hand . . . the right hand" has suppressed the idiomatic use of Heb. *semol* and *yamin* as terms for "north" and "south." Thus in Old Semitic (Mari Texts), *banu-yamina,* "the sons of the right" (cf. the biblical name Benjamin: *bin-yamin*), i.e., facing east, means "southerners." Cf. "north" at 14.15 below, for Trad. "on the left hand" (*mi-semol*).

10. all the way to (Zoar). Lit., "as you come to, reach"; see at 10.30 above.

12. near (Sodom). For this force of Heb. *ad,* in addition to the usual meaning "as far as, until," see Luzzatto (though rejected by Jacob, p. 363) and H. L. Ginsberg (*Bulletin of the American Schools of Oriental Research,* 122 [1951], 12–14).

13. (were very) wicked sinners. Treating lit. (and Trad.) "wicked and sinners" as hendiadys. See at 1.14 above, and Introduction, §c.

Chapter 14

1–3. Now, when . . . all the latter. The syntax of the passage and the alignment of the military forces are not clear. Thus if *bime* in v. 1 is to be taken with the four kings that follow (Trad., "And it came to pass in the days of Amraphel," etc.), there is no subject for the verb *asu* at the beginning of v. 2. Sforno got around this difficulty by taking *bime* only with Amraphel, with the remaining three kings serving as the subject of *asu*: ". . . In his days (i.e., of King Amraphel of Shinar), Arioch, Chedorlaomer, and Tidal rose and made war against Bera and his comrades. . . ." Note also the presence of the particle *eth-* in v. 2 before Kings Bera and Birsha, but its absence before the three kings that follow (Shinab, Shemeber, and the king of Bela); in this connection, it has long been noted that the names Bera and Birsha may have been intended to be associated with the Hebrew words *ra'*, "evil" and *résha*, "wickedness." A recent attempt to shed light on this perplexing problem as a whole may be found in N. Sarna, *Understanding Genesis* (1966), Chap. VI, "The Battle of the Kings," pp. 110–115.

10. **threw themselves.** Cf. Ibn Ezra *birṣonam lehim-maleṭ*, "in their desire (i.e., purposely) to escape," quoting the expression *wa-yippol al-panaw*, "and he threw himself on his face" (cf. 17.3); see also the *Perush al Ibn Ezra.* Luzzatto follows Ibn Ezra and quotes 24.64. Trad. "fell" is misleading here.

14. **mustered.** Trad., "led forth." Heb. *wa-yáreq* is uncertain and its meaning is uncertain; see Driver (p. 163) and Jacob (374–5).

retainers. Based on a suggestion by W. F. Albright that was developed by his student T. O. Lambdin, in *Journal of the American Oriental Society*, 73 (1953), 160. Trad. "trained men" derives from the root *ḥanakh*, "to train."

15. **north.** Trad., "on the left hand." See at 13.9 above.

17. **defeating (Chedorlaomer).** Trad. "the slaughter of" is misleading (see Driver, p. 164); Trad. usually rendered Heb. *hikka* by "smote."

19. **Creator.** (Also v. 22.) As noted already by Driver (pp. 165 f.; cf. Mandelkern, *Veteris Testamenti Concordantia,* under *qanah*), on Revised Version "possessor" and marginal "maker" (so Trad.), Heb. *qoneh* "applied to God . . . denotes Him as the *author*—here and *v.* 22 of nature, Dt. xxxii.6 of Israel's national existence. . . ." Ugaritic has now confirmed this interpretation; cf., e.g., the expression *qn 'rṣ*, "creator of the earth."

24. used up. Trad. "eaten" limits the scope of Heb. *akhal* to the "provisions" in v. 11; the "wealth" (*rekhush*) there mentioned was not used up but, according to v. 16, returned.

Chapter 15

1. Some time later. Trad. "After these things," while literal, hides the fact that Heb. *aḥar ha-devarim ha-élle* is really "a loose formula of connexion: xxii.1, 20, xxxix.7, xl.1" (Driver, p. 174).

2. die (childless). As noted by others (e.g., Ramban—except that he rejects the interpretation; Luzzatto; Driver, p. 175), Heb. *holekh* "sometimes has the force of *go away, vanish* (Job vii. 9), *depart* (from life). . . . Cf. the corresponding Arab. *halaka,* to perish. LXX. *apolúomai.* . . ." See Brown-Driver-Briggs, *Hebrew Lexicon,* p. 234a, § II.

3. steward. Understanding the expression *ben-bethi* (lit., "a son of my house") as a technical term; cf. *bene-váyith* in Eccles. 2.7. Earlier printings read "one of my household" (cf. Trad., "one born in my house"), i.e., a member of my household. But the Hebrew term, like the term *ben-mésheq bethi* in v. 2 (usually rendered approximately "the one in charge of my household") remains elusive.

6. merit. So Targum, Rashi, Radak, and several others for *ṣedaqa* (see Luzzatto, who rejects this meaning, pp. 68–69); see also Deut. 6.25; 9.4. Trad., mechanically, "righteousness."

9. **(a young) bird.** Heb., *gozal.* But Trad. "pigeon" (Septuagint *peristerán*; Targum *yona*; Midrashim; Rashi; etc.) may be correct, since (as noted, e.g., by Ibn Ezra) all the animals involved here are associated elsewhere in the Bible with sacrifice, and it is not just any young bird in general but a pigeon that is there specified. Cf. Lev. 1.14.
14. **go free.** Heb. *yaṣa* may be used as a technical term for liberation from slavery, as at Exod. 21.3–4 (alongside the fuller expression, *yaṣa laḥofshi* in vv. 2 and 5).
17. **oven.** Heb. *tannur* is simply an earthenware stove (sometimes portable); see G. A. Barrois's article on "Oven" in *Interpreter's Dictionary of the Bible,* III (1962), 612–3. Trad. "furnace" points to too formidable a structure.

Chapter 16

1. **an Egyptian maidservant.** Trad. "a handmaid, an Egyptian" (for *shifḥa miṣrith*) violates the Hebrew (as well as the English) idiom by being literal.
3. **concubine.** Trad. "wife" overlooks the fact that Heb. *isha* denotes a secondary as well as a principal wife. So also 30.4 below.
5. **(The wrong done me) is your fault.** Cf. Rashi, "The wrong done me—upon you I place the punishment"; Driver, "the wrong done to me by Hagar: may the responsibility for it rest upon thee!" Trad. "(My wrong) be upon thee" is less than clear.

between you and me. Idiomatic English, for the natural Hebrew order, "between me and you."
6. **as you think right.** Idiomatic for what is literally in Hebrew "that which is good in your eyes."

(and she ran away) from her. Trad. "from her face," in rendering literally, has hardly done justice to the Hebrew idiom ([*wa-tivraḥ*] *mi-panéha*). Similarly in v. 8, "(I am running away) from (my mistress Sarai)," in place of Trad. "from the face of."

12. **He shall dwell alongside of all his kinsmen.** Earlier printings read, "And in defiance[c] of all his kinsmen he shall camp" (with note *c* reading: *Precise nuance of Heb uncertain*). It is true that many scholars have interpreted Heb. *al-pene* to connote hostility or defiance, citing such passages as 25.18; Deut. 21.16; Job. 1.11; 6.28; and 21.31 as cases in point (cf. Driver, pp. 182–3; Speiser, 118). However, it is not certain that the Hebrew expression does point to defiance. Perhaps the original note *c* should have been retained.

Chapter 17

1. **El Shaddai.** Since the origin and meaning of Heb. *shaddai* are uncertain, it is best to transliterate the Hebrew; see Jacob on "El Schaddaj" (pp. 420–1). Trad. "God Almighty" derives from a popular etymology which has no basis in fact (*she-dai*). W. F. Albright has proposed the meaning "The Mountain One" (*Journal of Biblical Literature*, 54 [1935], 180 ff.), after Akkadian *shadû*.

Walk in My ways. Something of this significance of *hith-hallekh lefanay* was recognized already by the Septuagint ("be acceptable to Me") and Targum ("worship before Me"), followed by Rashi ("attach yourself to My worship") and Sforno ("recognize My ways"). See 24.40 and 48.15 below and Introduction, §c. Trad., mechanically, "before Me."

2. **between Me and you.** The Hebrew word order was retained here, contrary to English idiom (see 16.5 above), in deference to God's precedence.

7. **ages.** See at 6.9 above.

9–10. **As for you, you and your offspring to come,** etc. This order does greater justice to the Hebrew than our earlier reading: "As for you, you shall keep My covenant, you and your offspring to come, throughout the ages. [10]Such shall be the covenant, which you shall keep, between Me and you and your offspring to follow: every male among you. . . ."

12–14. and throughout the generations, etc. This order (as in vv. 9–10 above) brings out the force of the Hebrew more effectively than the reading in earlier printings: "At the age of eight days, every male among you throughout the generations shall be circumcised, even the homeborn slave and the one bought from an outsider who is not of your seed.—[13] The slave that is born in your household or bought with your money must be circumcised!—Thus shall My covenant be marked in your flesh as an everlasting pact. [14]An uncircumcised male who does not circumcise the flesh of his foreskin—such a person shall be cut off from his kin; he has broken My covenant."

14. (from his) kin. Cf. Driver (pp. 188, 189), "father's kin." For a recent study of the terms *am* and *goy* in biblical Hebrew, see Speiser, *Journal of Biblical Literature,* 79 (1960), 157–163. And see Driver at 25.8 below.

18. by Your favor. So Ehrlich, Driver (p. 188, "I.e. under the eye and care; cf. Hos. vi.2; also Jer. xxx.20; Is. liii.2"), and see at 10.9 above. Ramban interprets as "forever." Trad., mechanically, "before Thee."

19. Nevertheless. So Ehrlich (*Mikra,* p. 45: *adrabba*). This is probably the force intended by Trad. "Nay."

Chapter 18

2. Looking up. Trad. "And he lifted up his eyes" does not bring out the idiom in *wa-yissa enaw.* See Introduction, §c.

3. if it please you. Trad. "if now I have found favor in thy sight" is mechanical rather than idiomatic. See 6.8, and Introduction, §c.

6. **choice flour.** As against Trad. "fine flour" (Septuagint *semídalis*), Heb. *sóleth* denotes not fine (i.e., finely ground) flour but choice flour—only the inner kernels of the wheat—that is ground. See "Flour" by J. F. Ross, *Interpreter's Dictionary of the Bible*, II, 302; Snaith, *Leviticus and Numbers* (*Century Bible,* 1967), p. 34, at Lev. 2.1.

15. **lied.** Earlier printings read "dissembled." Trad. "denied" is not borne out by the use of Heb. *kiḥesh* in the Bible ("to deceive, deal falsely").

18. **populous.** It is generally overlooked that Heb. *aṣum* means "numerous" (parallel to *rav,* "many") no less than "mighty"; see Brown-Driver-Briggs, *Hebrew Lexicon,* p. 783a.

bless themselves. See at 12.3 above.

19. **I have singled him out.** Trad. "I have known him" has overlooked one of the numerous meanings and nuances of Heb. *yada.* Here the word has the force of "recognized, acknowledged"; cf. Driver (p. 195): "*known,* in a practical sense, = *noticed, regarded, cared for. . . .*"

what is just and right. It has been insufficiently noted that Heb. *ṣedaqa*—no less than *mishpaṭ* and the like—is really a legal rather than a moral-ethical term, i.e., "justice" rather than Trad. "righteousness." Cf. v. 23 below, and 38.26.

20–21. outrage (of Sodom and Gomorrah) . . . outcry. Trad. "cry . . . cry" has not done justice to the Hebrew variants *za('aqath) . . . ṣa('aqath*). Of course, "outrage" and "outcry" could be reversed; thus Ibn Ezra (cf. Ramban) offers both interpretations: on *za'aqath* (v. 20) he comments: they spoke rebelliously against God; or else the outcry of the victims. Similarly, in 19.13, *ṣa'aqatham* could be rendered either "their outrage" or "the outcry against them."

23. **innocent . . . guilty.** As in v. 19 above, the Hebrew words *ṣaddiq* and *rasha* are legal rather than moral-ethical terms (Trad., "righteous . . . wicked"). Cf., e.g., Driver on Revised Version's "do right" in v. 25 ("deal justly" in our Torah translation): "in a forensic sense."

27. my Lord. (Also vv. 30, 31, 32; and frequently elsewhere.) As against Trad. "the Lord," it would seem that *adonay* also has the meaning "my Lord," with final *qameṣ* construed as the possessive pronoun.

Chapter 19

2. early. Understanding the *hiphil* form *hishkim* not as a verb with the meaning "to rise early" but as used adverbially in association with the accompanying verb (Ehrlich, *Mikra,* at v. 27; Speiser, p. 138). Consequently, it has to be assumed that a verb is lacking in v. 27 below, where *wa-yashkem avraham ba-bóqer el-ha-maqom* is rendered "Next morning, Abraham hurried to the place . . ." (cf., e.g., Luzzatto).

4. gathered about. Heb. *savav* need not always mean "surround" (as in earlier printings). See Luzzatto, and 2.11 above. Trad., "compass . . . about."

8. shelter. This meaning suits Heb. *ṣel* better than Trad. "shadow."

9. (and already he acts the) ruler! Trad. "(and he will needs play the) judge" is mechanical for *shafaṭ*. See Jud. 2.16 and Ruth 1.1 ("chieftains" for *shofeṭim*).

11. blinding light. Trad. "blindness" derives from Septuagint *aorasía* (so also in II Kings 6.18), the same word used elsewhere (Deut. 28.28) for the usual Hebrew word for "blindness," namely, *iwwaron*. However, it has long been noted (cf., e.g., Driver, p. 199; Jacob, 456–7, ". . . nicht Blindheit, sondern ein Irresehen") that the blindness in *sanwerim* differed from ordinary blindness. Already the Midrash Ha-

Gadol (see M. M. Kasher, *Encyclopedia of Biblical Interpretation,* vol. III of English version by H. Freedman, bottom of p. 63): "with dazzling brightness." This insight has gained support from recent studies by B. Landsberger and E. A. Speiser of Akkadian *shunwurum,* "give light, dazzle."

helpless. Trad., "wearied themselves." Heb. *wa-yil'u* is sometimes elusive in meaning; but Rashbam's argument seems cogent enough: "*wa-yil'u* means they were unable (*lo yakhelu*) again to find the entrance. . . . Similarly *wenil'u miṣráyim lishtoth máyim min ha-ye'or* [Exod. 7.18], they [the Egyptians] could not drink water from the Nile. . . ." As his clinching argument, Rashbam has noted, correctly, Exod. 7.21, where the very words *welo yakhelu* ("and they could not") correspond to *wenil'u* in v. 18.

13. **the outcry against them.** See above at 18.20–21.

14–15. **(Lot spoke to his sons-in-law,) who had married (his daughters) . . . your two remaining daughters.** This rendering understands participial (*ḥathanaw*) *loqeḥe* (*benothaw*) in v. 14 as referring to sons-in-law who had married his daughters, whereas participial *ha-nimṣa'oth* in v. 15 has reference to two unmarried daughters still living in Lot's house; cf. Ibn Ezra (and see the *Perush al Ibn Ezra,* note *nun*), to whom participial *ha-nimṣa'oth* in v. 15 points to the fact that v. 14 speaks of two sons-in-law whose wives (i.e., daughters of Lot) had died (i.e., "Lot spoke to his sons-in-law who had been married to his daughters"). Rashi separates *ḥathanaw* from immediately following *loqeḥe benothaw*: as to the former—Rashi comments—Lot "had two married daughters in the city"; as to the latter, "those daughters who were in the house were betrothed" (interpreting participial *loqeḥe* to mean "those who were to marry them"). Others (e.g., Driver) interpret both participles in the same way: Lot spoke to his sons-in-law, who were to marry his daughters . . . take your wife and your two remaining daughters who are present (as opposed to the prospective sons-in-law who—v. 14—were not in Lot's house). S. Iwry, in *Textus*, 5 (1966), 34–43, has suggested (n. 9, pp. 39–40) that our *ha-nimṣa'oth* has the technical meaning "detained, held." All in all, the precise meaning of vv. 14–15 is still elusive.

17. to the hills. (Also v. 19.) Trad., "to the mountain"; but the Hebrew (*ha-hára*) is generally understood here to denote "mountainous country" (Driver, p. 200).

19. You have been so gracious, etc. Earlier printings read, "Please, if you favor your servant, having already shown me so much kindness by saving my life—I cannot flee to the hills, lest disaster overtake me and I die." On "You have been so gracious," see 6.8 above.

20. —it is (such a little place)—. Trad. "—is it not (a little one)?—," in reproducing *halo* literally, has overlooked the fact that this particle frequently expresses "(but, indeed) it is"; in other words, it serves to introduce a rhetorical question (with which cf., e.g., Latin *nonne*).

23. sulfurous fire. Taking the two Hebrew words *gafrith* and *esh* not as two separate items (Trad., "brimstone and fire") but as an instance of hendiadys (cf. at 1.14 above and Introduction, §c).

26. (Lot's wife looked) back[c] ([c]*Lit. "behind him"*). Rendering Heb. *me-aḥaraw* (lit., "behind him") neutrally ("back"). Trad. "(looked back) behind him" takes no cognizance of the difficulty in placing Lot's wife in front of her husband (see the comments by Rashi, Ibn Ezra, Ramban)—though her position with relation to Lot was hardly in the author's mind. Since v. 17 reads (God to Lot): "Do not look behind you" (*aḥarékha*), *aḥaréha,* "behind her," is what might have been expected in our verse (cf. *Perush al Ibn Ezra*).

27. Next morning, Abraham hurried to the place. A verb of some sort (e.g., *wa-yélekh,* "he went") would normally be expected here, between *wa-yashkem* and *el-ha-maqom* (on the adverbial force of *wa-yashkem,* see at v. 2 above). In translating literally, Trad. "And Abraham got up early in the morning to the place" merely points up this lack. Our "hurried (to the place)," just like Luzzatto's *halakh behashkama (el ha-maqom),* has supplied the verb; cf. Ehrlich (*Mikra,* p. 51).

Next morning. See at 21.14 below.

34. **Father.** Treating *avi* as a form of direct address rather than as the possessive (Trad., "my father").

Chapter 20

10. **(What . . .) was your purpose.** Lit., "(What . . .) did you see" (Trad., "sawest thou"). As put by Driver (p. 207), "*hadst in view;* what was thy object in making this false statement?" Similarly Luzzatto: What was your purpose?

16. **vindication**[a] ([a]*Lit. "a covering of the eyes"*). However the Hebrew expression (*kesuth enáyim*) is explained—see, e.g., the various interpretations listed in Kasher's *Encyclopedia of Biblical Interpretation,* ed. H. Freedman, vol. III, pp. 96–7, and on pp. 473–4 of Jacob's *Genesis*—the force of it seems to be "vindication, justification" (Hertz).

Chapter 21

12. **do as she says.** Trad. "hearken unto her voice" is a hebraism.

14. **(Early) next (morning).** Idiomatic for *ba-bóqer,* lit. (and Trad.), "in the morning." Cf. Driver (p. 211), "Abraham obeys at once; and next morning. . . ."

16. **she burst into tears.** Trad. "she . . . lifted up her voice, and wept" is a hebraism; see Introduction, §c.

17. **has heeded (the cry).** Note the preposition: (*shama*)

. . . *el-(qol)*. Trad. "hath heard (the voice)" would do justice to *eth* in the first part of the verse.

23. **kith and kin.** Reproducing the alliterative character of the Hebrew idiom *nin . . . nékhed.* Trad. "my son . . . my son's son" is less than certain.

33. **[Abraham] planted.** Trad. "And Abraham planted" does not inform the reader that the word for "Abraham" is actually lacking in the Hebrew. (It is present in the Septuagint, Samaritan, Peshitta, and Vulgate.)

invoked . . . the name of the Lord. See at 4.26 above.

Chapter 22

1. **put . . . to the test.** Trad. "prove" in the sense of "test" was already sufficiently obsolescent in 1904 for Driver to explain it (pp. 216–7): "I.e. put to the test. . . ."

2. **(your) favored one.** (Also v. 12.) Following the interpretation of *yaḥid* in the Septuagint (*tòn agapētón,* "the beloved one") and in line with the fact that (as against Trad. "thine only son") Isaac was not Abraham's only son.

4. **looked up.** See at 18.2 above.

6. **firestone.** On the assumption that by Heb. *esh* (Trad., "fire") the writer meant the tools (in addition to the wood, mentioned separately) needed to kindle the fire; it is less likely that the flame itself had been carried throughout the journey.

7. **Father.** See at 19.34 above.

Yes, (my son). Trad. "Here am I" fails to do justice to the sundry nuances of *hinne* in dialogue. After walking side by side for two days and more, Abraham would hardly have responded to his son's opening remark by "Here am I."

8. **will see (to the sheep).** Trad. "will [a]provide Himself" ([a]Heb. *jireh*; that is, *see for Himself*) has unnecessarily departed from the literal translation of Heb. *yireh,* especially since the site involved, Adonai-yireh ("the Lord will see") is explained in v. 14: "That is, *The Lord seeth.*" Cf. also *Behar YHWH yera'eh* ("On the mount of the Lord there is vision") at the end of v. 14.

13. a[b] ram ([b]*Reading* 'eḥad *with many Heb mss. and ancient versions; text* 'aḥar "*after*"). Trad. "and behind him a ram" is misleading in that (a) there is nothing in the Hebrew for "him" and (b) *áyil aḥar* (lit., "a ram behind") is impossible Hebrew. Actually, while the printed editions of the Hebrew Bible read *aḥar* (as do Symmachus and the Vulgate), many Hebrew manuscripts, the quotation of our phrase in the book of Jubilees (18.12), and such ancient translations as the Septuagint, Targum, Samaritan, and Peshitta read *eḥad.* On balance, there can be little doubt that the latter is original, and that the *d* in the Old Hebrew script was accidentally misread as *r,* to become *aḥar.* (The letters *d* and *r* looked very much alike in several ancient Hebrew scripts.) It is hardly necessary to add that no emendation is involved here, and that *aḥar* in the printed editions has absolutely no more authority than *eḥad.* (See Orlinsky, "The Masoretic Text: A Critical Evaluation," Prolegomenon to KTAV reissue of C. D. Ginsburg, *Introduction to the Massoretico-Critical Edition of the Hebrew Bible* [1966], pp. XVIII ff.) On the Targum (ed. A. Sperber [1959], bottom of p. 31), see S. B. Schefftel, *Biure Onkelos,* ed. J. Perles (1888), p. 38. It may be noted here that Rashbam attempted valiantly to prove that *aḥar* here means "afterward" (*aḥare ken*); so Luzzatto.

Chapter 23

2. (Abraham) proceeded. Already Rashbam (followed by the *Perush al Ibn Ezra,* as against Ibn Ezra) noted that Heb. *wa-yavo* is not to be understood here literally (Trad.), "came"; similarly Ramban (end of his long discussion; followed by Luzzatto). See also Ramban on *wa-yélekh* in Exod. 2.1 (followed by Luzzatto) and Introduction §c.

bewail. As against Trad. "weep" for Heb. *bakha,* the combination *lispod . . . welivkothah* is technical for "mourn . . . and bewail her."

4. **a resident alien.** Heb. *ger-wethoshav* is treated here as hendiadys; so Ehrlich (*Mikra*), and see Introduction, §c. Trad., "a stranger and a sojourner."

6. **the elect of God.** Understanding Heb. *nesi elohim* as an honorific title; so Ibn Ezra (and cf. the *Perush al Ibn Ezra*: *ki huqam me'eth Ha-Shem,* "for he was designated by God"). Trad., "a mighty prince," on which Driver commented (p. 275), "i.e. a prince worthy to belong to God, mighty or noble."

the choicest of our burial places. I.e., in our choicest burial place. Trad. "the choice of our sepulchres," in reproducing *mivḥar qevarénu* literally, has neglected the Hebrew idiom, for this is one way of expressing the superlative in biblical Hebrew; cf., e.g., Jud. 5.29 *ḥakhmoth sarothéha* ("the wisest of her ladies," lit., "the wise ones of her ladies"). See Gesenius-Kautzsch-Cowley, *Hebrew Grammar,* p. 431, §133 *h.*

7. **Thereupon (Abraham) bowed low.** Construing *wa-yáqam* (with *wa-yishtáḥu*) in the same manner as *wa-yavo* in v. 2 above (with *lispod* and *livkothah*), namely, as an auxiliary verb: He proceeded to bow low = Thereupon he bowed low. So Luzzatto, and cf. *wa-yáqam* (with *wa-yélekh*) in 24.10; Num. 11.32; and Gen. 31.17 below.

8. **you must agree.** Heb. *shema'úni* stands here for *shim'u li,* "listen to me, heed me," rather than Trad. "hear me."

9. **sell.** So already Targum Jonathan and especially Ramban (on v. 8), as against Trad. "give," for Heb. *nathan.* Cf. "pay the price" for *nathan késef* in v. 13.

10. all who entered the gate of his town[a] ([a]*I.e. all his fellow townsmen*). (Also v. 18.) Actually the force of the Hebrew is not certain. Earlier printings read "all who sat on the council of his town," on the supposition that this was the force of "all who entered the gate of his town" in Akkadian (E. A. Speiser, *Bulletin of the American Schools of Oriental Research,* 144 [Dec. 1956], pp. 20–23); the discussions by G. Evans (*Bulletin of the American Schools of Oriental Research,* 150 [1958], 28–33; *Journal of the American Oriental Society,* 78 [1958], 1–11) indicate otherwise.

13. that I may bury. The cohortive form *we'eqbera* following the imperative form *qaḥ* clearly indicates purpose ("that I may . . ."); cf. Orlinsky, *Jewish Quarterly Review,* 31 (1940–41), p. 374, § I *A*. Trad. "and I will bury" would represent *weqavarti.*

16. at the going merchants' rate. Lit., "passing over to the merchant" (Trad., "current money with the merchant"), i.e., at the rate acceptable and current among merchants.

17. passed. (also v. 20.) Understanding *qum* here as a technical term for transfer of ownership; see Brown-Driver-Briggs, *Hebrew Lexicon,* p. 878, 7B (with reference also to Lev. 25.30; 27.19; and perhaps I Sam. 24.21). Trad., "was made sure."

Chapter 24

4. native land. Projected version. See at 12.1 above (and cf. *éreṣ moladti* in v. 7 below); Driver: "native country."

8. this oath to me. Trad. "this my oath" does not bring out clearly enough the objective genitive in Heb. *shevu'athi.*

10. taking with him. Trad. "having . . . in his hand" misses the Hebrew idiom in *beyado,* and also creates an impossible picture of the servant carrying in his hand all his master's goods. Ramban and Sforno, e.g., interpret *beyado* as "in his authority, charge"; note especially that Ramban construes the phrase *wekhol-ṭuv adonaw beyado* with *wa-yiqqaḥ,* comparing II Kings 8.9. See also 43.12 below, and Introduction, §c.

12. **grant me good fortune.** (Also 27.20.) An attempt to reproduce the idiom in Heb. *haqre . . . lefanay,* lit., "cause to meet . . . before me" (Trad., "send me . . . good speed"); cf. Luzzatto, Driver.

17. **let me sip.** Cf. Rashi, Luzzatto. Trad. "give me to drink" has overlooked the distinction between the usual Hebrew words for "drink" (*shathah* and *shaqah*; cf. vv. 14, 18–19) and the word used here, *hagmi'íni.*

18. **and she quickly lowered (her jar).** Trad. "and she hastened, and let down (her pitcher)" misses the idiomatic use of *wa-temaher* with the verb (*wa-tóred*) following. Similarly in v. 20 below, where Heb. *wa-temaher wa-te'ar* (lit. and Trad., "And she hastened, and emptied") is idiomatic for "She quickly emptied."

20. **Quickly emptying.** See at v. 18 above.

21. **silently wondering (whether the Lord).** Cf. Driver (on Trad., "holding his peace, to know"): I.e., reflecting silently.

22. **nose-ring.** Trad. "ring" is unnecessarily imprecise for *nézem* here, in light of v. 47. So Brown-Driver-Briggs, *Hebrew Lexicon,* p. 633b.

35. **(and he has become) rich.** Trad. "(and he is become) great" is mechanical, and limits the nuance of Heb. *wa-yigdal.* Similarly in 26.13.

40. **whose ways (I have followed).** For this force of (*hith-hallekh*) *lifne* in connection with God, see at 17.1 above and Introduction, §c.

45. **praying in my heart.** Trad. "speaking to my heart" is a mechanical rendering of the idiom in Heb. *dabber el-libbi.*

48. I bowed low in homage. Both Hebrew terms, *wa-eqqod wa-eshtaḥaweh* (the second now known from Ugaritic to derive from the root *ḥwh*), mean approximately "to bow low" in homage (see Brown-Driver-Briggs, *Hebrew Lexicon,* under *qdd* on p. 869a and under *sh-ḥ-h* on p. 1005); Driver, *Exodus* (at 4.31), "in reverence." Trad., "I bowed my head, and prostrated myself."

49. true kindness. On the hendiadys involved, see at 1.14 above and Introduction, §c. The same expression, *hésed we-emeth* is employed at 47.29 below.

55. [d]**some ten days**[d] ([d-d] *Lit. "days or ten"*). Our translation is only a guess at what may not be the original Hebrew text. Trad. "a few days, at the least ten," with no note, is hardly a translation of Heb. *yamim o asor.*

57. and ask for her reply. Trad. "and inquire at her mouth" is mechanical for Heb. *wenishala eth-píha.*

58. I will. Biblical Hebrew idiom, unlike English, simply repeats in the reply the words employed in the question (*hathelekhi . . . elekh,* Trad., "Wilt thou go? . . . I will go."). See also at 29.5–6 below.

Chapter 25

4. Enoch. Trad. has reproduced here the Hebrew name *ḥanokh* by "Hanoch," as distinct from "Enoch" in 4.17 and 5.18 ff. (Similarly "Shaul" instead of "Saul" for *sha'ul* in 36.37.) But this distinction is arbitrary.

5. willed. Trad. "gave" not only restricts the force of Heb. *nathan* but misleads the reader into believing that Abraham gave away his property while he was still alive; v. 6 immediately following indicates the contrary, namely, that v. 5 deals with a bequest.

8. to his kin. See Driver (p. 241) on Trad. "to his people": *to his father's kin.* See also Driver (*Exodus*) at Exod. 30.33.

18. they camped alongside (all their kinsmen). So already Ibn Janaḥ (and cf. Luzzatto). Earlier printings read "[b-]they made raids[-b] against" ([b-b]*Exact force of last part of v. uncertain*), on the supposition that *al-pene* indicated hostility ("against"); but see at 16.12 above.

23. Two separate peoples shall issue from your body. Earlier printings read, "Two peoples apart while still in your body," which is hardly what the Hebrew says.

28. favored. Trad. "loved" (so also earlier printings) misses the nuance in Heb. *ahav.* Similarly "unloved" (as against Trad. "hated") for *sane'* in 29.31 below. See also at 26.27 below.

29. famished. (Also v. 30.) So Ibn Ezra on *ayef*: "hungry and thirsty" (with the *Perush al Ibn Ezra* comparing Ps. 143.6; see also Isa. 32.2). Trad., "faint."

30. gulp down. So Driver (on Trad. "swallow"): ". . . or, *eat quickly*. The word (*haliṭéni*) occurs only here, and implies voracity." See also Luzzatto (with reference to talmudic usage).

Chapter 26

1. previous. Heb. *rishon* means "former, preceding" as well as (Trad.) "first." Cf. the comment of Bahya ben Asher ben Halawa of Spain (13th–14th century; on p. 21 of M. Kasher, *Encyclopedia of Biblical Interpretation,* ed. H. Freedman, IV, p. 21): "the earlier; not the first since the world began."

5. kept My charge. Earlier printings had "followed My mandate," which was unnecessarily free for Heb. *shamar mishméreth.*

7. thinking, "The men . . . might kill me. . . ." Heb. *pen* followed by direct speech; cf. Ibn Ezra (and the *Perush al Ibn Ezra*). Trad., mechanically, "lest." See Introduction, §c.

10. **What (have you done . . .).** Earlier printings had "See, what (you have done . . .)"; but initial "See" (cf. such parallel passages as 12.18 and 20.9) was superfluous.

13. **richer,** etc. See at 24:35 above.

25. **started digging.** The dig was not completed until v. 32. Trad. "digged," in overlooking the inchoative force of the imperfect, is misleading. Cf. 8.5 above, and 27.34 below.

26. **councilor.** Heb. *meré'a* is a technical term, approximately a "confidential adviser" (Driver). Trad. "friend" is too bland.

27. **you have been hostile to me.** Trad. "ye hate me" misses the nuance of Heb. *sane'* (and the force of vv. 12–17 above, where Abimelech's envy of Isaac's success turned into hostility). See at 29.31 below on "unloved" (rather than "hated") for *sane'*, and at 25.28 above for "favored" (rather than "loved") for *ahav.*

28. **a sworn treaty.** Trad., "oath." But the Heb. *alah* involves more directly the oath in the covenant; thus *alathi* in 24.41 corresponds to *shevu'athi* in 24.8, and the *alah* in our verse is complemented by the verb *wa-yishshave'u* in v. 31 below (and cf. the name Shibah = "oath" in v. 33).

between our two parties. Ibn Ezra (and especially the *Perush al Ibn Ezra*), followed by Luzzatto (see note* on p. 109) and Ehrlich, bring out the point of "two parties" very well. Trad. "betwixt us" fails to do justice to the form *benothénu* (as distinct from *benénu* immediately following—which Trad. renders, with no support from the Hebrew, "even [!] betwixt us"). Interestingly, the Targum renders our *benothénu* by *ben-avahathana,* "between our fathers" (i.e., involving Abraham); and see Rashi and Rashbam. See also 42.23 below.

31. **(Isaac then) bade them farewell.** Trad. "(and Isaac) sent them away," rendering mechanically, has missed the idiom in Heb. *wayshalleḥem.*

Chapter 27

3. **and hunt me some game.** Trad. "and take me venison" hardly conveys the Hebrew idiom.

4. **(prepare) a dish (for me).** (Also vv. 7, 14, 17.) Earlier printings read "a tasty dish" (cf. Trad., "a savoury food"). However, there is no justification for the adjective, and the Septuagint and Targum (also Ibn Janaḥ) were quite right in rendering Heb. *mat'ammim* simply by "food, dish."

so that I may give you my innermost blessing. (Also vv. 19, 25, 31.) This is an attempt to represent something of the force of *nafshi* in Heb. *ba'avur tevarekhekha nafshi* (Trad., "that my soul may bless thee"; on *néfesh* not meaning "soul," see at 2.7 and 12.13 above). It may well be, however, that *nafshi* here, as elsewhere, is nothing more than (as put by Driver, p. 256) "A pathetic periphrasis for the pers[onal] pron[oun] (which is used in v. 7) . . ."; in vv. 7 and 33 our *tevarekhekha nafshi* (cf. vv. 4 and 31) is reproduced by nothing more than *wa-avarekhekha*, "that I may bless you," and note in this connection simple *wa-yevarakhehu* ("and he blessed him") in vv. 23 and 27.

5. **(Rebekah) had been listening.** So Ibn Ezra (*hayetha shomá'ath*). Trad. "heard" fails to do justice to participial *shomá'ath*. And in v. 6, "I overheard" (cf. Driver's comment, p. 256) brings out the full nuance of *shamá'ti* that Trad. "I heard" does not.

7. **with the Lord's approval.** As noted by Driver (p. 256) on Trad. "before the Lord": "With a solemn sense of His presence, often . . . though not necessarily . . . at a sanctuary." Already some medieval Jewish commentators recognized *lifne* here as having the force of approximately "God willing; with God's approval." Thus Rashi interpreted: "With His permission, that He should approve my action"; Rashbam commented: "in the name of the Lord . . ."; and the Ramban

wrote: The expression *lifne Adonay* occurs only here in the entire section because Rebekah intended this blessing to be made "in the Holy Spirit" (cf. Radak, "prophetically"). Similarly Malbim: the prophet does not himself create the prophecy; he is merely the tool for the expression of God's will. See also at 10.9 above and Introduction, §c.

11. smooth-skinned. Trad. "a smooth man" (*ish ḥalaq*) is now a misleading expression.

15. the best clothes. So Driver (on Trad. "the choicest garments"): I.e., as we should say, his best suit.

18. which of my sons are you? Trad. "who art thou, my son?" is literal and pointless, and hardly represents the intent of the Hebrew. Thus Radak noted that Isaac was uncertain whether it was Jacob or Esau who was standing before him.

20. granted me good fortune. See at 24.12 above.

28. new grain and wine. It would seem that, as distinct from *yáyin* and *shémen* ("wine" and "oil" respectively), the terms *dagan, tirosh,* and *yiṣhar* (especially in combination), usually employed in ritual and poetical texts, indicate "fresh (or new) grain, wine, and oil." See Driver, p. 258.

34. he burst into (wild and bitter) sobbing. Trad. "he cried (with an exceeding great and bitter cry)" overlooks the inchoative force: he began to cry. See at 8.5 and 26.25 above, and 41.5 below.

36. Was he, then, named Jacob that he might supplant me these two times? Cf. Sforno: Just because he happened to be called Jacob (*ya'aqov*) did he have to supplant me (*ya'aqevéni*) . . . ? Or see Rashbam: Just because he was named Jacob (*ya'aqov*) and, as the younger brother, is entitled to but one share, should he now receive twice the portion that I, the older brother, am entitled to? Trad. "Is not he rightly named Jacob? for he hath supplanted me these two times" is, on closer scrutiny, actually pointless.

40. grow restive. See the argument in Driver (p. 261) for "grow restless," as against Trad. "break loose." Jacob (pp. 570–1) offers much data, and ends up with "wenn du recht hast (?)."

41. harbored a grudge against. So Targum and Ibn Ezra.

44. a while. Trad. "a few days," in reproducing Heb. *yamim aḥadim* literally, is misleading.

45. Let me not. So Luzzatto. Heb. *lama,* (traditionally rendered "why?") frequently has the meaning "no(t)," as indicated by the Septuagint. See Introduction, §c.

Chapter 28

3. El Shaddai. See at 17.1 above.

4. to you (and your offspring). Trad. "(and give) thee . . . to thee (and to thy seed)" is really a hebraism *(lekha . . . lekha)*; English idiom does without the repetition of "to you."

8. Esau realized. So Radak, Sforno. Trad. "and Esau saw" misses the force of *wa-yar.*

10. and set out for. Cf. Saadia (also quoted by Ibn Ezra) and Rashi: *wa-yélekh* (Trad., "and went") has the force here of infinitive *lalékheth,* "to go."

11. a certain place. So Rashbam: *bemaqom eḥad.*

12. a stairway[b] ([b] *Or "ramp"*). It has long been recognized (see Driver, pp. 264 ff., "a flight of stone steps") that Heb. *sullam* indicates a stairway or ramp of the kind employed, e.g., in the ziggurats of Mesopotamia, as against Trad. "ladder" (with rungs).

14. shall bless themselves. See at 12.3 above (as against Trad. "shall . . . be blessed").

15. Remember. An attempt to reproduce something of the force of Heb. *hinne*; see Introduction, §c. Trad., mechanically, "And, behold."

20. made a vow. Trad. "vowed a vow" is a pure hebraism (*wa-yiddar . . . néder*).

Chapter 29

1. **resumed his journey.** This is a rare instance where a literal translation of the Hebrew ("And Jacob lifted up his feet and went") would have been so absurd that even Trad. had to avoid it, rendering instead, "(Then Jacob) went on his journey." See also v. 11 below on *nasa,* and Introduction, §c.

Easterners. Just as "Israelites" (or Ammonites, Moabites, Hittites, etc.) is idiomatic for *bene yisra'el,* as against literal and Trad. "children of Israel," so is "Easterners" as against Trad. "children of the east." On the expression *bene-qédem,* see Driver (p. 268; also p. 241, at 25.6). Another possible rendering is "Kedemites" (as at Judges 6.3, 33; etc.).

3. **be rolled . . . watered . . . be put back.** Trad. "they rolled . . . watered . . . put back" has failed to do justice to the indefinite subject in Heb. *wegalelu . . . wehishqu . . . weheshívu,* properly reproduced in English by the passive.

5–6. **Yes, we do . . . Yes, he is.** Lacking as it does a particle for "yes," biblical Hebrew expresses a reply in the affirmative by repeating the words of the question assertively: Do you know? We know. Is he well? He is well. See at 24.58 above.

8. **is rolled.** Trad., "they roll"; see at v. 3 above.

10. **uncle.** Biblical Hebrew has no other way of expressing the concept "uncle" than by "mother's (or father's) brother."

11. **broke into tears.** Trad. "and (he) lifted up his voice and wept"—precisely because it reproduces the Hebrew mechanically—fails to do justice to the idiomatic use of *nasa eth-qolo* (*wa-yevk*). Cf. at v. 1 above on *nasa,* and Introduction, §c.

12. **kinsman.** So already Rashi: *qarov,* "relative." Trad. "brother," a mechanical rendering of Heb *aḥi,* is misleading

here. As noted by Driver (p. 270), "*brother.* I.e. *relation*; here, *nephew,* as xiv, 14, xxiv, 48. So v. 15."

13. **all that had happened.** Trad. "all these things" hardly brings out the idiom in Heb. *eth kol-ha-devarim ha-élle.*

19. **outsider.** By *ish aḥer* the author meant not (Trad.) "another man" but one who was not a relative, i.e., an outsider. Driver has noted (p. 271), ". . . Marriages tending to break down the family connexion . . . were viewed with disfavour."

27. **bridal week.** (Also v. 28.) Trad. "week" is unclear ("Fulfil the week of this one"). What was meant, clearly, was the week of wedding festivities, as explained by Rashi, Ibn Ezra, Rashbam, and others, with Judges 14.12 in mind.

31. **unloved.** One of the nuances of Heb. *sane'* (cf. at 26.27 above, "to be hostile to"); so already Ramban (at the end of his comment; followed by Luzzatto): "Some assert that in the case of two wives, when one is loved very much the other is said, in contrast, to be *senu'ah,* as it is stated (v. 30), 'indeed, he loved Rachel more than Leah,' not that he hated her. . . ." Or see Driver (p. 272), "*hated.* The word is to be understood in a relative sense = *less loved* (cf. v. 30). . . ."

32. **It means.** Heb. *ki* is hardly causal here (Trad., "because"), but rather introduces the explanation of the name. So frequently in the verses that follow, and elsewhere. See Introduction, §c.

Chapter 30

4. **as concubine.** Cf. 16.3 above.

6. **vindicated me.** As noted by Driver (p. 224) on Trad. "judged me": "And (as is implied) given me my due. A common usage. . . ." Similarly Radak and the Malbim (in part).

15. **I promise.** Cf. Targum Jonathan *bishvu'ah*. For the meaning of Heb. *lakhen,* see at 4.15 above, and Introduction, §c. Note that Trad. "therefore" is a non sequitur here: to what would "therefore" be the sequel?

20. **will exalt me.** So, e.g., Brown-Driver-Briggs, *Hebrew Lexicon,* p. 259a; cf. *zevul* "lofty, exalted place," and Ugaritic *zbl,* "prince." And see now M. Held (following W. F. Albright), *Journal of the American Oriental Society,* 88 (1968), 90–96. Trad. "will dwell with me" (going back to Targum, Aquila, Vulgate, etc.) has no known etymology and can scarcely be gotten out of the Hebrew construction *yizbeléni.*

21. **Lastly.** Seems more appropriate a rendering for Heb. *we-aḥar* than Trad. "and afterwards."

25. **my own homeland.** Understanding Heb. "my place and my land" as hendiadys; see at 12.1 above, and Introduction, §c.

32. **animal.** Heb. *se,* contrary to general belief, is a generic term that denotes the goat as well as the sheep; see v. 38 below. Trad., "sheep."

33. **In the future.** So Malbim *bizman he-athid.* Also Luzzatto.

34. **Very well.** So Targum Jonathan (followed by Radak) *ya'uth;* Rashi: *"hen* denotes here acceptance of the terms" (*leshon qabbalath devarim*); Malbim: "He agreed to these conditions. . . ." Trad. "Behold" is meaningless here.

35. **But.** Thus Malbim: Laban immediately altered the agreement. Trad. "And" fails to do justice to the force of the *waw* in *wa-yásar.* In commenting on *wa-yásar* ("namely: Laban"), Rashi and Ibn Ezra may have been indicating the adversative; for it is Jacob, according to v. 32, who should have been "removing" the animals.

38. **goats**[k] ([k]*Lit. "flocks"*). Heb. *son,* "flocks," can consist of sheep and/or goats. See comment on *se* ("sheep" or "goat") at v. 32 above.

40. **But Jacob dealt separately with the sheep; he made**

these animals face, etc. Earlier printings read, "The ewes, on the other hand, Jacob kept apart and made these animals face," etc.

Chapter 31

1. he heard the things that Laban's sons were saying. Trad. "he heard the words of Laban's sons, saying:" is hardly English.

7. cheated. So Targum *shaqar.* Trad. "mocked" hardly does justice to the Hebrew (*héthel be-*) here. Thus Driver (on Revised Version, "deceived"): "Lit. *mocked*: viz. by taking advantage of me (Jer. ix.5)."

time and again[a] ([a]*Lit. "ten times"*). (Also v. 41.) Trad. "ten times" has overlooked the long-recognized idiomatic use of such numbers as "ten" and "seven" and "five" for "several; many." So Ibn Ezra (and the *Perush al Ibn Ezra*); Rashbam, ". . . namely, many (*harbeh*) . . ."; followed, e.g., by Luzzatto, Driver ("repeatedly").

15. used up our purchase price. The Hebrew expression *akhal késef* accords with ancient Near Eastern technical terminology; the present translation is an attempt to bring out the idiom, as against Trad. "devoured our price."

17. Thereupon (Jacob put . . .). As elsewhere (cf. 23.7 above), Heb. *wa-yáqam* is employed here not as an independent verb (Trad., "Then Jacob rose up, and set . . .") but in conjunction with the verb (*wa-yissa*) that follows: "Jacob proceeded to put. . . ." The same usage of *wa-yáqam* is to be found in v. 21 below: *wa-yaqam wa-ya'avor,* "He proceeded to cross; soon he was across." And note the similar use of *maher* with a verb in 24.18, 20 above.

19. Meanwhile Laban had gone. An attempt to convey the force of Heb. *we-lavan halakh* (not *wa-yélekh lavan*!). Trad. attempted similarly with its "now Laban was gone."

household idols. (Also v. 34.) Trad., "teraphim." It has long been recognized (so Driver, p. 283) that Heb. *terafim* denotes household gods; their precise function, however, is not yet known, as can be seen in the recent discussion by M. Greenberg, "Another Look at Rachel's Theft of the Teraphim," *Journal of Biblical Literature,* 81 (1962), 239–248.

stole. (Also v. 32.) Earlier printings read "appropriated," an evasion of the plain meaning of Heb. *ganav.*

20. [c]**kept Laban the Aramean in the dark**[c] ([c-c] *Lit. "stole the mind of Laban the Aramean"*). (Also v. 26.) An attempt to reproduce the idiom of the Hebrew; cf. Trad. "outwitted" and Driver's "duped" in his comment (p. 283) on Revised Version, "stole away unawares."

21. **Soon.** See at v. 17 above.

24. **Beware of attempting anything with Jacob.** (Also v. 29.) Trad. "speak not (to Jacob)," while literal, can hardly represent the force of Heb. *dabber* here; that would mean that Laban is not even permitted to greet Jacob. Our idiom may be found also in 24.50, where Driver (p. 237) calls it "A proverbial expression."

25. **on the Height.** (Also v. 54.) Trad., "in the mountain." It has been generally recognized that a specific height (as against Laban's "hill country of Gilead") was intended; see the discussion in Driver, p. 284.

30. **Very well, you had to leave (because . . .).** An attempt to convey the force of the Hebrew *(we-atta halokh halákhta),* hardly reproduced in Trad. "And now that thou art surely gone."

38 ff. On this section see now J. J. Finkelstein, *Journal of the American Oriental Society,* 88, (1968), 30–36.

40. **Often.** Understanding Heb. *hayíthi* (lit., "I was; I had been") as idiomatic for "often, in the past." Trad. has attempted this with "Thus I was."

41. **time and again**[e] ([e]*Lit. "Ten times"*). See at v. 7 above.

50. **(though no one else be about), remember, God**

Himself will be witness. Trad. "(no man being with us); see, God is witness" has missed the syntax of the Hebrew; thus Driver has noted (p. 288), "the second clause (*re'e elohim* . . .) is the apodosis of the first clause (*en ish immánu*): '*no man* BEING *with us.*' "

Chapter 32

1. **bade them good-by.** *Heb. barakh* (Trad., "blessed") frequently means no more than "greet; bid farewell," and the like; cf. v. 30 below and 47.10. (It may be noted here that in some printed editions, our verse constitutes the final verse, v. 55, of preceding chapter 31.)

(left) on his journey homeward. Trad. "(departed) and returned to his place" is not only misleading—for what transpires at this point preceded his return home—but does not do justice to the force of *wa-yélekh wa-yáshav . . . limqomo,* which denotes "set out to return. . . ."

4. **(sent . . .) ahead.** Trad. "before him," while literal, hardly conveys the idiom. Similarly at v. 17 below.

5. [b]-**Thus shall you say. . . .**"-[b] On the syntax adopted in this translation (so Radak), the phrase "To my lord Esau," etc., is part of the message. The alternate rendering, according to which the phrase "Thus says your servant Jacob," etc., begins the message, is favored, e.g., by Ibn Ezra (see the *Perush al Ibn Ezra*) and Ramban.

6. **(in the hope of) gaining your favor.** Trad. "(that I might) find favor in thy sight" is a hebraism.

10. **(and I will) deal bountifully with you.** Trad. "do thee good" hardly brings out the meaning of *we-eṭíva immakh.*

17. **ahead.** (Also vv. 18, 22.) As at v. 4 above.

20. **He gave similar instructions to.** Idiomatic for "And he instructed also."

reach him. Trad. "find him" hardly conveys the nuance of Heb. *maṣa.*

26. **he wrenched (Jacob's) hip at its socket.** Lit., "the hollow of his thigh." The reader will be interested to know that the editor engaged in correspondence on this section with the late Dr. I. William Nachlas, noted orthopedist of Baltimore, Maryland.

30. **You must not (ask my name!).** Trad. "Wherefore is it that thou dost (ask after my name?)" does not recognize the meaning "Do not" for *lámma;* similarly at 27.45 above, and see Introduction §c.

And he took leave of him there. One of the nuances of *barakh;* cf. "bade good-by" at v. 1 above. Trad. "blessed" is not only mechanical but may even be misleading here, in that he had already blessed Jacob by virtue of the change of name to "Israel." (In 33.11 below, the word *berakha* will have the meaning "present, gift.")

31. **a divine being.** The first part of note [d-d] on "being divine" at v. 29 (*Or "God"*) applies here too.

Chapter 33

8. **To gain my lord's favor.** See at 32.6 above.

10. **if you would do me this favor.** See at 32.6 above.

from me. Idiomatic for Heb. *mi-yadi,* overlooked by Trad. "from my hand." Similarly at 24.10 above.

12. **at your pace.** So Rashi, and compare Ibn Ezra and Luzzatto. Trad. "before thee" would have been expressed not by present *lenegdékha* but by *lefanékha;* it is precisely thus (*lifne avdo*) that Jacob expresses his counterproposal to Esau in the very next verse.

13. **are a care to me.** See Driver, p. 299; and under *al* in Brown-Driver-Briggs, *Hebrew Lexicon,* p. 753a, §*b.*

18. **safe.** Trad. "in peace" fails to convey the idiom in Heb. *shalem*; thus Driver (p. 300): *safe and sound.*

Chapter 34

1. **to visit.** Trad. "to see" does not bring out the force of the preposition *be-* in Heb. (*liroth*) *bi*(*venoth*), as against *eth-*. See Luzzatto, Jacob (p. 649, "besuchen").
2. **(and lay with her) by force.** So Luzzatto, Ramban (*hayetha anusa,* "she was forced"). Trad. "(and lay with her,) and humbled her" does not bring out the force of the Hebrew idiom.
3. **he spoke (to the maiden) tenderly.** Trad., "comfortingly." Heb. *dabber al-lev* (lit., "speak on the heart") is sometimes an elusive idiom. Ibn Ezra (followed by Luzzatto) interprets: *divre rakkim weniḥumim,* "tender and comforting words." Others render "persuasively."
10. **move about.** Trad., "trade." The precise meaning of *saḥar* (and the historical implications) have been much discussed recently; see C. H. Gordon, *Journal of Near Eastern Studies,* 17 (1958), 28 ff.; W. F. Albright, *Bulletin of the American Schools of Oriental Research,* 163 (Oct. 1961), 44 ff.; E. A. Speiser, 164 (Dec. 1961), 23 ff. Cf. our "traveling man" = salesman.
12. **bride price.** Heb. *móhar* is the price paid by the groom to the bride's father for the purchase of the bride (see Driver, p. 304). Hence Trad. "dowry"—what the bride brings to the groom at marriage—is erroneous.
16. **kindred.** (Also v. 22.) See at 17.14 above.
24. **All who went out,** etc. See at 23.10 above.
25. **unmolested.** This refers to the attackers, Simeon and Levi; so Rashi (following Bereshith Rabba). In favor of Trad. "unawares," Rashbam (followed by Luzzatto; and see the Targumim) has noted that *béṭaḥ* regularly refers to the inhabitants of a place.
31. **(Should our sister) be treated.** Idiomatic for the indefinite subject in the Hebrew (*ya'aseh*), overlooked in Trad. "Should one deal (with our sister)."

Chapter 35

3. **when.** Heb. *be-yom* serves often simply as a temporal conjunction; see at 2.4 and 3.5 above, and Introduction, §c. Trad., "in the day."
6. **Luz—that is, Bethel—in the land of Canaan.** In following the Hebrew word order, Trad. "Luz, which is in the land of Canaan—the same is Beth-el—" misleadingly makes Bethel synonymous with Canaan rather than with Luz.
10–12. **You whose name is Jacob,** etc. The Hebrew of these verses shows all the earmarks of poetry; note, also, that they constitute a blessing.
16–17. **she had hard labor . . . her labor was at its hardest.** On the assumption that the force of the *piel* (*wa-teqash*) is different from that of the *hiphil* (*behaqshothah*). This is the only instance of the *piel* of this verb in the Bible.
28. **(Isaac) was . . . old.** In rendering Heb. *wa-yihyu yeme* mechanically, Trad. "And the days (of Isaac) were . . ." has missed the idiom.

Chapter 36

9. **This, then, (is the line of Esau).** Understanding our verse as summing up what preceded. See 37.2 below.
12. **descendants.** (Also v. 13, and *passim.*) Trad. "sons" does not do justice to the range of meanings in Heb. *bene.*
15. **clans.** (And *passim* in this chapter.) It has long been recognized that the "sons" (*bene*) in the section preceding (vv. 9–14) are really clans; thus Driver (p. 314), "The tribes or clans of Edom, reckoned as descended from Esau's three wives. The names are not those of individuals, but merely *represent* tribes or clans (cf. ch. x.). . . ." It has further been recognized that the names of the *allufim* in vv. 15–19 are

all but identical with those of the clans in vv. 9–14 (see Driver, p. 315). So that the *allufim* here are really "clans" rather than Trad. "chiefs." Further, the terms "families" (*mishpaḥoth*), "localities" (*meqomoth*), "names" (*shemoth*), and "settlements" (*moshavoth*) of the *allufim* in vv. 40–43 are to be associated with "clans" rather than with "chiefs"; one hardly speaks of a chief's locality or settlement ("chiefs . . . in the land of Edom," vv. 16, 17; or "chiefs . . . in the land of Seir," v. 30), or lists chiefs "name by name" (*bishmotham*)—it is, rather, clans that are so listed. Note, too, that in v. 19, Trad. "These are the sons of Esau, and these are their chiefs" makes little sense, whereas ". . . the sons of Esau, and . . . their clans" is quite meaningful. Finally, one of the *allufim* is named Oholibamah (v. 41), which is also the name of one of Esau's wives (vv. 2, 5, 14, 18, 25); now whereas Oholibamah could readily serve as the name of a clan, this is hardly possible in the case of a chief.

In his comment on vv. 22–28, Driver (p. 316) speaks not of (Trad.) "the children" but of "The sub-clans, or families, of the native Horites, regarded as subdivisions of the seven larger groups enumerated in v. 20." And in v. 30, Driver (p. 317), noting the reading of the Septuagint (*hēgemoníais*) would emend *le'allufehem*—unnecessarily, in our interpretation—to *le'alfehem* and render "according to their clans."

In may be noted that *élef,* (lit., "thousand" and deriving from the same root as *alluf*) also means "a company, group, contingent, clan"; see Num. 1.16 (where *alfe* is parallel to *maṭṭoth,* "tribes"); 10.4; Josh. 22.21, 30; Jud. 6.15; I Sam. 10.19 (used with *shéveṭ,* "tribe," and note *mishpaḥah* in v. 21). Finally, it seems likely that related *'alp* in Ugaritic likewise has the force of "clan"; see H. L. Ginsberg–B. Maisler, *Journal of the Palestine Oriental Society*, 14 (1934), 259; Ginsberg, *The Ugarit Texts* (in Hebrew, 1936), pp. 91–92. Others, however, reject "clan" for "chief(tain)," e.g., U. Cassuto (*Encyclopediah Miqra'ith,* vol. I, 1950, column 332) and C. H. Gordon, *Ugaritic Handbook* (Glossary).

37. **Saul.** In reproducing Heb. *sha'ul* here by "Shaul" instead of by "Saul" (the king, I Sam. 9.2 and *passim*), Trad. has been arbitrary. Similarly Trad. "Hanoch" (instead of "Enoch") at 25.4 above.

Chapter 37

2. **This, then, is the line of Jacob.** As in the case of 2.4 and 36.9 (and perhaps also 10.32) above, the Hebrew formula *élle toledoth* sums up what precedes. As put by Driver (p. 321), "P's [The Priestly Code's] introduction to the history of Jacob, so far as it belongs to the period after Isaac's death (xxxv. 29)"; see also his comments at 2.4 above (*Genesis,* p. 19 and n.1, with his further references to pp. ii, vi, and viii of the "Introduction"). Perhaps "story," rather than "line," would be clearer. Rashbam has an interesting statement at this point in connection with the two kinds of biblical interpretation, the *peshaṭ* (exegesis) and the *derash* (eisegesis).

as a helper to (the sons of . . . Bilhah . . .). So Ibn Ezra (*shimmesh lahem;* followed by Luzzatto) and Malbim (*she-hayah meshareth otham*). In rendering Heb. *ná'ar* mechanically, Trad. "being still a lad, even with (the sons of Bilhah . . .)" has not been very helpful.

3. **an ornamented tunic**[a] ([a]*Or "a coat of many colors"; meaning of Heb uncertain*). (Also vv. 23, 32.) In earlier printings, the footnote read: *Others "a coat of many colors,"* in the belief that the meaning of Heb. (*kethóneth*) *passim* was certain and that Trad. "(coat of) many colors" was erroneous. As for the terms "coat, tunic," already Driver had observed (p. 322): "A coat,—or, more strictly, *a tunic.*" The problem of "ornamented, many colors" is something else again; the etymology and meaning of Heb. *passim* are unknown, and all renderings are but guesses. In addition to "many colors" and "ornamented," other renderings have been proposed, such as "with sleeves" and "a long garment with sleeves" (the "long" deriving from an assumed etymology of root *pss,* the flat of the hand or foot, and hence "of, or reaching palms and soles"; see W. F. Albright, *Journal of Biblical Literature,* 37 [1918], 116). Ibn Ezra's comment is as good as any: *passim* means "ornamented" (*meruqémeth*; and see the *Perush al Ibn Ezra*); and Radak explained our term as a garment "made up of multi-colored strips." In II Sam. 13.18–19, our *kethóneth passim* is worn by daughters of royal birth. Perhaps one day the wall paintings in the 19th century B.C.E. tomb at Beni-ḥasan in Egypt, depicting richly colored, striped garments, may shed some specific light on our *passim.*

4. **him.** English idiom makes it difficult to indicate the emphatic position of Heb. *otho*: "(And when his brothers saw) that it was him that (his father loved more than . . .)."

(speak) a friendly word. Trad. "peaceably," a purely mechanical rendering, does not do justice to the considerable range of meanings in Heb. *shalom*: "peace; welfare; friendship; vindication; victory," and the like (cf. v. 14 below). Thus Sforno: ". . . they could not speak with him in a friendly way (*leshalom were'uth*), as is customary with brothers (*keminhag aḥim*)." See Introduction, §c.

7. **(when suddenly my sheaf) stood up and remained upright.** Trad. "arose, and also stood upright" hardly reproduces the picture intended by Heb. (*wehinne*) *qáma* (*alummathi*) *wegam-niṣṣáva*—which is not that the sheaf arose and, in addition, stood upright, but rather that it stood up and remained standing.

8. **for his talk about his dreams.** Sforno comes close to this understanding of Heb. *al-ḥalomothaw we'al-devaraw,* lit. (and Trad.), "for his dreams and for his words," in his

comment: "because he said to them, 'Hear,' to alert them to concentrate on understanding the significance of his dreams."

11. **(his brothers) were wrought up at him.** Trad. "envied him" not only is pointless here but shows unawareness of the nuance of Heb. *qinne,* which denotes deep emotion (jealousy, anger, zealousness, and the like). See at Num. 5.14.

(kept) the matter (in mind). Trad. "the saying" reproduces Heb. *davar* mechanically.

13. **(Your brothers) are (pasturing).** Trad. "Do not (thy brethren feed) . . . ?" is not only out of place here—did Jacob ask Joseph a question?—but overlooks the fact that Heb. *halo* is frequently only a synonym of *hinne.* See Introduction, §c.

I am ready. Cf. Ibn Ezra, "I will do as you say."

15. **came upon (him).** As against Trad. "found" for Heb. *maṣa,* see at 11.2 above.

16. **Could you tell me where they are pasturing?** This is how Heb. *haggída-na li* would be expressed here in idiomatic English, as against Trad. "(I seek my brethren.) Tell me, I pray thee, where they are feeding the flock."

20. **A savage (beast).** (Also v. 33.) Trad. "an evil (beast)" repeats mechanically the equation *ra'ah*="evil." Earlier printings read "a wild (beast)"; but this would more likely have been represented in Hebrew by (*ḥayyath*) *ha-sadeh.*

21. **tried to save him.** So already Alshech (in Kasher's *Encyclopedia of Biblical Interpretation,* ed. H. Freedman, vol. V, 1962, p. 23): "He is praised for his good intentions as though he had really delivered him"; and see Luzzatto and Malbim (. . . *she-hishtaddel lehaṣṣilo,* ". . . that he tried to rescue him"). Trad. "delivered him" is misleading.

25. **to a meal.** Trad. "to eat bread," in being literal, fails to reproduce the idiom in Heb. *akhal léḥem.*

gum. Trad., "spicery." Cf. Driver (p. 324), "Most

probably, *gum tragacanth*: certainly, nothing so general as 'spicery.' "

27. agreed. Trad. "hearkened unto him" has added the prepositional phrase where there is none in the Hebrew (simply *wa-yishme'u*). So Joseph Bechor Shor (in *Encyclopedia of Biblical Interpretation* [see at v. 21 above], p. 29): "They approved of his proposal."

30. Now, what am I to do? Trad. "and as for me, whither shall I go?" in being literal (except for "go" in place of "come," for *ba*) has missed the intent of the Hebrew idiom. Rashi caught the spirit of it: "Where shall I flee from the grief of father?" and so did Luzzatto (even though he criticizes Rashi). On the double use of the pronoun, *wa'ani* (*ána*) *ani* (*va*), Ibn Ezra comments that that is but Hebrew style (*raq dérekh ha-lashon kakh*) and that a single *ani* would have sufficed (see also *Perush al Ibn Ezra*); hence only one "I" in our translation.

32–33. examine it . . . He recognized it. Though the same root (*nkr*) is used in both instances (*hakker . . . wa-yakkirah*), English idiom requires two different verbs. Trad. "Know now . . . And he knew it" is mechanical.

35. sought (to comfort him). Trad. "rose up" conceals the true force of Heb. *wa-yaqúmu* (. . . *lenaḥamo*); see Torah Temimah 37:38 (in *Encyclopedia of Biblical Interpretation* [see at v. 21 above], 40): ". . . his family attempted to comfort him."

36. courtier. (Also 39.1; 40.2, 7.) Understanding *saris*, lit., "eunuch," in the "generalized sense of *court-official* . . ." (Driver, p. 326).

chief steward. Lit., "chief of the cooks (or slaughterers, butchers)," *sar ha-tabbaḥim*. The precise title and function in Egypt is not known.

Chapter 38

1. **About that time.** Trad. "at that time" does not do justice to the idiom in Heb. *wa-yehi ba-eth ha-hi,* as though the event involved took place at precisely the time that Joseph was sold to Potiphar. See Ibn Ezra: "this is not the time when Joseph was sold, but before he was sold"; Ralbag (in *Encyclopedia of Biblical Interpretation,* vol. V, p. 87), "Part of the narrative that follows took place about the time of the sale of Joseph"; Ibn Caspi (ibid.): "The phrase is elastic, and may mean before or after the events just narrated." Luzzatto follows Ibn Ezra and Ralbag.

camped. Understanding *wa-yeṭ* as elliptical for *wa-yeṭ oholo* (see Jud. 4.11; also Gen. 12.8; 26.25; 35.21); so Radak, followed by Jacob (p. 711). Trad. "and turned into" lacks justification for both "turned in" and "to" (Heb. *ad*).

near. On *ad* in the sense of "near," see Ginsberg, *Bulletin of the American Schools of Oriental Research,* 122 April 1951), 12–13.

8. **do your duty (by her) as a brother-in-law.** Our Western society lacks the institution—and so also the technical terminology—of levirate marriage. Hence the Hebrew verb *yabbem* (cf. the noun *yavam* "levir") must be rendered in somewhat roundabout fashion; cf. Trad. "and perform the duty of a husband's brother (unto her)."

12. **(When) [c]his period of mourning was over[c]** ([c-c]*Lit. "he was comforted").* Trad. "and he was comforted" does not convey here the force of the idiom in Heb. *wa-yinnáḥem;* see Driver (p. 329), ". . . was comforted (viz. after the usual period of mourning was over). . . ." See Introduction, §c.

17. **You must leave a pledge.** Understanding Heb. *im-titten* as "Only if you give a pledge"; thus Sforno, *im titten az e'eseh ma-she-ṣiwwítha* ("if you will give, then I shall do . . ."). Trad. "Wilt thou give me a pledge . . . ?"

derives from the assumption that *im* is the equivalent of the interrogative *ha-'im*.

20. **to redeem.** Understanding Heb. *la-qáḥath* to mean not (Trad.) "to get" but "to get back." On another nuance of *laqaḥ*, see v. 23 below.

21. **cult prostitute.** Trad. "harlot" would represent *zona* (cf. v. 15); *qedesha* is a "sacred prostitute," one associated with a shrine or the like (see Jacob, pp. 717–718).

22. **the townspeople.** Trad. "the men of the place," by rendering literally, has not brought out the idiom in Heb. *anshe ha-maqom*.

23. **keep.** As noted already by Rashi, Rashbam, and Ibn Ezra (and see Driver, p. 330; Jacob, p. 718), the force of *tiqqaḥ-lah* is "keep," rather than Trad. "(Let her) take (it)."

24. **in fact.** Thus Rashbam: If you should ask, "How certain can one be that she played the harlot?" then know that she is, in fact, already pregnant (*she-hare gam harah hi kevar*).

25. **she sent this message.** Heb. *shalaḥ* often denotes not merely Trad. "send" but also "send a message." See Introduction, §c.

26. **in the right.** Heb. *ṣadaq* is a legal term (compare 18.19 above; Lev. 19.36; Deut. 1.16; 16.18, 20; etc.). Trad. "righteous" has turned it into a moral-ethical concept. See Introduction, §c.

28. **to signify.** Trad. "saying" does not do justice to the force of *lemor* here.

Chapter 39

1. **courtier . . . chief steward.** See at 37.36 above.

2. **and he stayed.** Trad. "and he was" obscures the force of *wayhi*.

his Egyptian master. Trad. "his master the Egyptian" (for Heb. *adonaw ha-miṣri*) is more Hebrew than English.

4. **he took a liking to (Joseph).** Trad. "(Joseph) found favor in his sight" is literal enough for Heb. *wa-yimṣa (yosef) ḥen be'enaw,* but it is hardly idiomatic English. See 6.8; 18.3; 32.6; etc.

6. **he paid attention to nothing.** Trad. "he knew not aught," being literal, requires clarification; thus Driver: "i.e. . . . he troubled himself about nothing. . . ."

7. **After a time.** Idiomatic, as against Trad. "And it came to pass after these things," for Heb. *wayhi aḥar ha-devarim ha-élle.* So also at 40.1 below.

9. **He wields no more authority (in this house than I . . . How then could I do) this most wicked thing . . . ?** Trad. "He is not greater . . . this great wickedness . . . ?", being a mechanical rendering, hardly does justice to the nuance of Heb. *enénnu gadol . . . mi-(ménni) . . . ha-ra'a ha-gedola ha-zoth.* Similarly in v. 10 following.

10. **And much as she coaxed (Joseph day after day).** In rendering mechanically, Trad. "And it came to pass, as she spoke to (Joseph day to day)" has not conveyed the flavor of Heb. *wayhi kedabberah el-(yosef yom yom).* See Jacob (p. 729): "als sie auf Joseph . . . einredete."

14. **to dally with us.** (Also v. 17.) Understanding Heb. *ṣaḥaq bánu* in the same sense as *meṣaḥeq eth* (26.8). Trad., "to mock us."

14–15. **but I screamed loud . . . screaming at the top of my voice.** Trad. "and I cried with a loud voice . . . I lifted up my voice and cried" is mechanical. See also v. 18 below, and Introduction, §c.

19. **he was furious.** Trad. "his wrath was kindled" is a hebraism (*wa-yíḥar appo*).

20–21. **But even while he was there in prison, the Lord was with Joseph.** The last part of v. 20 is pointless if the traditional sentence division is retained: "(And Joseph's master took him, and put him into the prison . . .) and he was there in the prison. ([21]But the Lord was with Joseph . . .)." Thus Saadia eased the siuation somewhat by adding to the first part of v. 21 "(And the Lord was with him) also" (*'aiṣan,* i.e., as noted by W. Bacher in ed. Derenbourg, *gam ba-maqom ha-ze,* "in this place also"); and similarly Malbim: *gam sham haya Ha* [*-Shem*] *immo,* "there too the Lord was with him." And cf. Radak's comment: "and he was there: he remained there; his master did not change his mind to liberate him."

22. **and he was the one to carry out everything that was done there.** Trad."and whatsoever they did there, he was the doer of it" hardly does justice to either the Hebrew or the English idiom.

Chapter 40

1. **Some time later.** See at 39.7 above.

cupbearer. Trad. "butler" is misleading. Heb. *mashqe* means literally "drink-giver."

the cupbearer and the baker of the king of Egypt. Hebrew syntax requires the order "the cupbearer of the king of Egypt and the (or his) baker"; but in reproducing this order mechanically, Trad. has not only violated English idiom but has had to add "his (baker)" where the Hebrew lacks it (*we-ha-ofeh,* "and the baker").

2. **courtiers.** See at 37.36 above.

5. **—the cupbearer and the baker . . . in the prison—.** The entire phrase is parenthetic in the Hebrew (referring to *shenehem,* "both of them"), at the end of the verse; English idiom requires that it be brought up to follow "both of them."

each his own dream and each dream with its own meaning. Trad. "each man according to the interpretation of his dream" is literal, but hardly clear enough.

8. **Surely God can interpret! (Tell me [your dreams]).**

Earlier printings read "Do not interpretations come from God? (Tell me about it)"; while more literal, this rendering ("Do not . . . ?") did not bring out the force of Heb. *ha-lo* as forcefully as "Surely . . . !" See Introduction, §c.

Tell me [your dreams]. The Heb. (*sapperu*) lacks an object. Trad. adds "(tell) it (me, I pray you)."

10. **(its clusters) ripened into (grapes).** An attempt to bring out the denominative force of the *hiphil* form *hivshilu* (see Brown-Driver-Briggs, *Hebrew Lexicon,* p. 143a, s. *bashal,* HIPH.) better than Trad. "brought forth ripe (grapes)."

16. **favorably.** Thus Sforno (*she-yiftor gam ba'ado*) *leṭov;* also Targum (*ya'uth*), Ramban, Luzzatto, and Ehrlich. Trad. "good" may denote "correct, true" (as Rashbam, *nikkarim divre emeth*) as well as "favorable."

In my dream, similarly, there were, etc. Because it was translating mechanically, Trad. "I also saw in my dream, and, behold," had to add "saw" without a Hebrew equivalent for it (*af ani baḥalomi*).

19. **impale.** (Also v. 22.) It was "impaling" rather than "hanging" that constituted a common manner of execution in the ancient Near East. In our case, the baker was apparently to lose his head before being "impaled" (hardly Trad. "hanged").

pole. Heb. *eṣ* means "pole, wood, stick," and the like, as well as (Trad.) "tree"; see Brown-Driver-Briggs, *Hebrew Lexicon,* s. *eṣ,* pp. 781–782.

Chapter 41

5. **He fell asleep.** The inchoative aspect of the Hebrew verb is unrecognized in Trad. "And he slept" (*wayishan*). See 27.34 above, and Introduction, §c.

healthy. (Also vv. 22, 24, 26.) Trad. "good" hardly does justice to Heb. *ṭovoth,* the opposite to which is *daqqoth* (vv. 6, 7, 24).

9. **offenses.** As noted by Driver (p. 341) on Trad. "faults": "His offences . . . against Pharaoh are intended."

11. **We had dreams the same night, he and I, each of us a dream with a meaning of its own.** Trad. "And we dreamed a dream in one night, I and he; we dreamed each man according to the interpretation of his dream," in being literal, is less than clear.

14. **He had his hair cut.** Trad. "And he shaved himself" overlooks two aspects of Heb. *waygallaḥ*: (a) *gillaḥ* denotes "to cut one's hair" as well as "shave"; (b) "to shave oneself" would point to the *hithpael* (cf. Lev. 13.23, 33; Num. 6.19) rather than to the *piel.*

16. **Not I!** Cf. Driver, in his comment on Trad. ("It is not in me," Heb. *biladay*): Or "Not at all!"

(will see to Pharaoh's) welfare. Trad. "(will give Pharaoh an answer of) peace" is mechanical for *shalom.*

22. **(In my) other (dream).** Hebrew idiom does not require a word such as *aḥer, od,* or *sheni* to express "other"; see at 3.2 above, and 44.19 below, and Introduction, §c.

31. **no trace of the abundance will be left in the land.** Cf. Sechel Tob (in Kasher, *Encyclopedia of Biblical Interpretation,* V, p. 147, n. 133): "I.e., the reserves will be completely consumed." Trad. "and the plenty shall not be known in the land."

32. **(As for Pharaoh) having had the same dream twice.** Trad. "(And for that) the dream was doubled (unto Pharaoh) twice" is literal, and misleading: Pharaoh's dream was not "doubled . . . twice"; it was "doubled" only once. See Ibn Ezra and Ramban.

34. **organize**[a]: ([a]*Others "take a fifth part of"; meaning of Heb uncertain*). For something like "organize" cf. Rashi (followed by Luzzatto): "*weḥimmesh* is to be understood according to the Targum (*wizarez*), 'and let him prepare (or equip, arm)'; and similarly 'and prepared (or equipped, armed)' (Exod. 13.18)." On Heb. *weḥimmesh* as involving the number "five," see Rashbam, Ibn Ezra, Radak, and Jacob (p. 748).

35. **(Let all the food . . .) be gathered, and let (the grain) be collected.** Understanding the subject of *weyiqbeṣu* and *weyiṣberu* to be indefinite; hence the use of the passive in idiomatic translation. Trad. "And let them gather (all the food) . . . and lay up (corn . . .)"—unless it is purely mechanical—construes the "overseers" (*peqidim*) in v. 34 as the subject.

under Pharaoh's authority. See Driver (p. 343). In being literal, Trad. "under the hand of Pharaoh" is not clear.

37. **The plan pleased Pharaoh.** Idiomatic, as against Trad. "And the thing was good in the eyes of Pharaoh." See Introduction, §c.

43. **(in the chariot of his) second-in-command.** Understanding Heb. (*mirkéveth*) *ha-mishneh* not as (Trad.) "the second (chariot)" but as the official next in authority to the king (so Rashbam, Ibn Ezra, Radak, Ramban, Luzzatto, Malbim, and perhaps Rashi; see also Jacob, p. 752). But the matter still requires clarification (Brown-Driver-Briggs, *Hebrew Lexicon,* s. mishneh, 1041b).

45. **emerged in charge of.** Cf. Targum, "and Joseph went out as ruler over"; so also Sforno, and see Ehrlich (*Randglossen*).

46. **when he entered the service of (Pharaoh).** Trad. "when he stood before" overlooks the inchoative aspect of the Hebrew verb; see Driver's comment (p. 345): "became his minister . . ."; also Ehrlich (*Randglossen*). See at 8.5 above.

48. **he put in each city the grain of the fields around it.** Idiomatic for the mechanical rendering of Trad. "the food of the field, which was round above every city, laid he up in the same."

49. **(until) he (ceased to measure it).** Trad. "(until) they (left off numbering)" is curious for Heb. *ḥadal* in the singular. (Is this a misprint?)

51. **meaning.** (Also v. 52.) Cf. Ibn Ezra on Heb. *ki*: "its meaning is 'for he said' " (and see the *Perush al Ibn Ezra*). Luzzatto, in declaring that "the word 'saying' (*lemor*) is lacking," has not realized that this is expressed precisely by *ki*. See Introduction, §c.

(forget) completely (my hardship and my parental home). Lit., "(forget) all (my hardship) and all (my . . .)." The idea is expressed by Ralbag (Kasher, *Encyclopedia of Biblical Interpretation,* V, p. 163, note 354): ". . . I must no longer grieve over my former sufferings."

56. **Accordingly,** etc. The Hebrew verse becomes clear if the first clause, involving the famine over the whole world, is brought down to the end of the verse, to be followed immediately in v. 57 by "So all the world came. . . ." On the numerous attempts to explain the traditional order of the clauses, see *Encyclopedia of Biblical Interpretation,* V, pp. 165–166. See also the comments by Luzzatto and Driver (p. 346).

(Joseph laid open) all that was within. On Trad. "opened all the storehouses" Driver has commented (p. 346), "This is no doubt what is intended: but the Heb. (*eth-kol-asher bahem*) is corrupt, and cannot be so rendered (it is lit. 'all that was in them')." See also Luzzatto.

rationed out grain . . . to procure rations. (Also v. 57; 42.1.) Understanding Heb. *wa-yishbor . . . lishbor* as from *shavar,* "to break (one's hunger or fast)"; see Radak, Luzzatto, Ehrlich (*Mikra,* 114f.) Hence to buy/acquire or to sell/dispense food of all kinds, e.g., grain, wine, milk (Isa. 55.1).

Chapter 42

1. **keep looking (at one another).** Trad. "look" misses the durative-continuing aspect of the *hithpael* (*tithrá'u*); thus Moffatt, "Why stand looking at each other?" See at 3.24 above.

3. **ten of Joseph's brothers.** Trad. "Joseph's ten breth-

ren" does not do justice to the Hebrew *(aḥe yosef asara),* and is misleading to boot—Joseph had eleven brothers.

4. **feared.** Trad. "said" misses the point; cf. Meyuḥas (Kasher, *Encyclopedia of Biblical Interpretation,* V. p. 181, n. 25): "thought."

10. **Truly.** The force of *waw* with initial *avadékha* is strongly adversative (= on the contrary); Trad. "but" is hardly emphatic enough.

11. **We are all of us sons of the same man.** Idiomatic (and yet also literal) for Heb. *kullánu bene ish eḥad náḥnu.* Trad., "We are all one man's sons."

have never been. (Also v. 31.) So Ramban (*me-'olam*), Sforno, Malbim (*mi-yaménu*). Trad. "are" does not do justice to Heb. *hayu.*

16. **the rest of you.** (Also v. 19.) Trad. "ye" restricts the force of Heb. (*we*)-*attem* unduly. See at 3.2 above, and 44.9 below.

19. **and take home rations for your starving households.** An attempt at reproducing the intent and idiom of Heb. *havi'u shéver ra'avon battekhem* (cf. Rashi and Luzzatto). Trad. "carry corn for the famine of your houses" is mechanical.

21. **we are being punished (on account of our brother).** Heb. *ashem* (as *ḥeṭ* and the like) means "punishment, penalty" as well as "guilt"; so Joseph Bechor Shor (Kasher, *Encyclopedia of Biblical Interpretation,* V, pp. 192–193, note 161): "These troubles are a punishment for a crime of which we were all guilty"; so also Luzzatto. Trad., "We are all verily guilty (concerning . . .)."

23. **between him and them.** So Luzzatto, Ehrlich. On Heb. *benotham* (as distinct from *benehem*) see at 26.28 above (on *benothénu* as distinct from *benénu*). Trad., "between them."

24. **He turned away (from them).** Trade. "And he turned himself about" mechanically imposes upon Heb. *wa-*

yissov (root *savav*) the idea of a complete about-turn; cf. at 2.11 and 19.4 above.

31. we have never been. See at v. 11 above.

32. sons by the same father. See at v. 11 above.

33. and take something for your starving households. See at v. 19 above. Trad. "and take care for the famine of your houses" is not very helpful.

34. free to move about. See at 34.10 above. Trad., "traffic."

36. It is always me that (you bereave) . . . (These things) always (happen) to me! An attempt to reproduce the force of initial *othi* (*shikkaltem*) . . . *alay* (*hayu kullána*). See Driver (p. 351), ". . . The emphasis is upon 'me': it is I, the father, who suffer, not you." See also Meyuḥas and Alshech (*Encyclopedia of Biblical Literature,* V, p. 199, notes 249 and 250 respectively): "These disasters befall me only, and no other person" and "But not upon you: your grief as brothers cannot compare with mine as a father." See also Luzzatto, Ehrlich (*Randglossen*).

37. (Put him) in my care. So Luzzatto, Brown-Driver-Briggs, *Hebrew Lexicon,* bottom of p. 391a. Trad. "(deliver him) into my hand" hardly reproduces the force of the preposition *al* with *yad* (*tena otho al-yadi*).

38. white head. Cf. "hoary head" in Brown-Driver-Briggs, *Hebrew Lexicon,* p. 966b. Trad., "gray hair."

Chapter 43

1. But. As noted by Jacob (p. 777), the force of the conjunction *we*(*ha-ra'av*) is here adversative; only because of this was Joseph compelled to change his mind and permit Benjamin to leave for Egypt.

4. (If) you will let (our brother go). An attempt (see Jacob, p. 778) to reproduce something of Heb. (*im*) *yeshka* (*meshalléaḥ*). Trad. "(If) thou wilt send" would represent (*im*) *teshallaḥ*.

7. **kept asking.** An attempt to capture the idiom in Heb. *sha'ol sha'al*. Trad., "asked straitly."

another brother. See at 44.19 below.

8. **in my care.** Trad. "with me" hardly brings out the force of *itti* here.

9. **I myself.** Note the emphatic use of the pronoun *anokhi*—which is not reproduced in Trad. "I." Cf. Joseph Bechor Shor and Abravanel (*Encyclopedia of Biblical Interpretation,* V, p. 212, notes 30 and 31) respectively: "I alone . . ." and "Personally . . . myself."

I shall stand guilty (before you). (Also 44.32.) Another way of expressing "I shall be guilty" (*ḥaṭáthi*). Trad. "then let me bear the blame" takes no account of following *lekha*.

10. **we could have been there and back twice.** Idiomatic for Heb. *ki-atta shávnu ze pa'amáyim*. Trad. literally, "surely we had now returned a second time"—though *pa'amáyim* means "twice," not "a second time."

11. **gum.** See at 37.25 above.

pistachio nuts. Heb. *baṭnim*; long known as a delicacy in the Near East. Trad. "nuts" would represent the generic term *egoz*—apart from the fact that immediately following "almonds" (*sheqedim*) renders nuts anomalous.

12. **with you.** (Twice. Also cf. vv. 15, 22, 26, and frequently.) As against Trad. "in your hand," see at 24.10 above.

13. **(Take) your brother too.** "Too" attempts to bring out something of the emphatic position of the object (*we-eth-aḥikhem*) before its verb (*qáḥu*); cf. Trad. "take also your brother."

16. **slaughter and prepare an animal.** Idiomatic English order for idiomatic Hebrew order: "slaughter an animal (lit., a slaughter) and prepare" (*u-ṭevóaḥ ṭévaḥ we-hakhen*). In following the Heb. order mechanically, Trad. ends up with a

less than literal "and kill the beasts, and prepare the meat."
27. **(Is he still) in good health?** (Also v. 28.) Trad. "(Is he yet) alive?" misses the idiom in Heb. *ḥay* here; So Or Ha-Ḥayyim (*Encyclopedia of Biblical Interpretation,* V. p. 225, note 145), "alive: well and in good health." See also Ehrlich: "wie geht es ihm?" and the clear case in I Ki. 20.32.
30. **hurried out.** Understanding Heb. *waymaher* ("hastened, hurried") as elliptical for "hastened to leave"; cf. Jacob (p. 788), "eilte davon." Trad., "And Joseph made haste." Others, e.g., Reggio (*Encyclopedia of Biblical Interpretation,* V, p. 227, n. 159), connect *waymaher* with *wa-yavo*: "The verse is to be understood thus: Joseph made haste to enter into his chamber, for his heart yearned," etc.

on the verge of tears. Recognizing the idiomatic force of Heb. *wayvaqqesh livkoth,* which the rendering "wanted to cry" in earlier printings failed to do. Trad. "and he sought where to weep" is incorrect, and reads into the Hebrew more than is there.
31. **Serve the meal.** Trad. "set on bread" is mechanical for *símu léḥem.*
33. **by his direction.** Cf. Rashbam: "Joseph offered to seat them thus"; so also Ehrlich (with reference to Bab. Talmud Pesaḥim 119a). See also at 10.9 and 17.18 above.
34. **several**[c] ([c]*Lit. "five"*). Similarly at 31.7; 45.22; 47.2. See Jacob (p. 791) on literally "five."

(And they) drank their fill. Earlier printings read "feasted and drank." Trad., "(And they) drank, and were merry."

Chapter 44

4. **They had just left (the city).** Trad. "and when they were gone (out of the city)" does nothing for the force of the pronoun *hem* with the verb *yaṣe'u.*

9. **the rest of us.** (Cf. also v. 10.) So the force of the pronoun *anáḥnu* (and of *we-attem* in v. 10). Trad. "we also" ("ye" in v. 10) misses the idiom. See at 42.16 above.

10. **Although,** etc. Understanding the force of the Hebrew as concessive; so Sforno: "even though . . . nevertheless" (*af-al-pi . . . mikkal maqom*). See also Ramban, Luzzatto, and Ehrlich. Trad. "Now also let it be according unto your words," etc., has created an illogical verse.

shall go free. So the force of *naqi* here; cf. Sforno: "*naqi*: from slavery or any other penalty." Trad., "shall be blameless."

14. **(they) threw themselves.** Trad. "fell" ignores the correct nuance of Heb. *nafal.* See at 14.10 above.

15. **practices divination.** See Rashi, Rashbam, Luzzatto, Malbim, Ehrlich (*Mikra*). The future tense in Trad. "will indeed divine" is hardly the intent here.

16. **uncovered.** See Ibn Ezra (and *Perush al Ibn Ezra*).

19. **or another brother.** The Hebrew does not require a word such as *aḥer* (or *od,* or the like) to express the idea of "another." Indeed, Heb. *ha'od lakhem aḥ* (Trad., "whether ye had yet a brother?"; Revised Version, "have ye *another* [italics in original] brother?") at 43.6 expresses the same idea as *hayesh lakhem . . . aḥ* in the present verse. See at 3.2 and 41.22 above, and Introduction, §c.

20. **the youngest.** Trad. "a little one" (*qaṭan*) adds little to preceding "child" (*yéled); on ha-qaṭan*="youngest," see, e.g., 42.13, 15, 20; etc. So Sechel Tob (*Encyclopedia of Biblical Interpretation,* VI, p. 8, n. 39).

his full brother. Contrast 42.38, where "his brother" —with Jacob as the speaker—suffices. Cf. Haamek Dabar (*Encyclopedia of Biblical Interpretation,* VI, p. 8, n. 40): "*His* particular brother, from the same mother."

dotes on him. So Sforno, "more than all of us." Trad. "loveth him," while ordinarily correct for Heb. *ahav,* might imply here that Jacob did not love the other sons;

see at 25.28 above on "favored" for *ahav,* and at 26.27 above on "unloved" and "hostile to" for *sane'*. See Introduction, §c.

22. **(if he were to leave) him, his father (would die).** Trad., "(for if he should leave) his father, his father (would die)"; lit., "(if he were to leave) his father, he (would die)." Some commentators identify the subject of *wa-meth* ("he will die") with Benjamin (so the Targums, Rashi, Ramban); but the majority regard Jacob as the subject (so Rashbam [at v. 30], Ibn Ezra [and *Perush al Ibn Ezra*], Joseph Bechor Shor, Sforno, Luzzatto, Ehrlich [*Randglossen*]).

31. **white head.** See at 42.38 above.

32. **stand guilty.** See at 43.9 above.

Chapter 45

1. **before all his attendants.** So Rashi, Ramban. Trad. "before all them that stood by him" is misleading for *lekhol ha-niṣṣavim,* in that it was only his Egyptian attendants who left Joseph's presence, his brothers remaining where they were.

no one else. Trad. "no man" is scarcely appropriate here; his brothers were present.

3. **well.** See at 43.27 above.

6. **no yield from tilling.** An instance of hendiadys (on which see at 1.14 above and Introduction, §c). As noted by Ehrlich, Trad. "no plowing or harvest" could be justified only by the repetition of (*en-ḥarish*) *we-en* (*qaṣir*).

10. **region (of Goshen).** So Ramban. Trad. "land" overlooks the occasional meanings "region, district, territory," and the like, for *éreṣ*; see Gen. 47.11; Brown-Driver-Briggs, *Hebrew Lexicon,* p. 76a, §2 *b–d*. See Introduction, §c.

19. **And you are bidden [to add].** So Targum Jonathan, Rashi, Sechel Tob (*Encyclopedia of Biblical Interpretation,*

VI, p. 29, n. 170), Sforno. Trad. is less than clear: "Now thou art commanded, this do ye: take your wagons. . . ."

24. **Do not be quarrelsome.** So Targum Jonathan (followed by Ehrlich, *Randglossen*); and see Luzzatto with reference to Rashi, Ibn Janaḥ, Radak, Ralbag.

26. **went numb.** So Driver (p. 364); cf. Joseph Bechor Shor and Hizkuni.

Chapter 46

4. **I Myself.** (Twice.) Trad. "I" does not bring out the force of the personal pronoun *anokhi* (*ered*) . . . *we-anokhi* (*a'alkha*).

(and Joseph's) hand shall close your eyes. Understanding Heb. *yashith yado al-enékha* as an idiom for "perform the last offices to the deceased" (Driver, p. 365); similarly many commentators, e.g., Saadia (on which see Jacob, p. 829), Ibn Ezra, Rashbam (Bab. Talmud, Baba Bathra 108a), Luzzatto. Trad., "(and Joseph) shall put his hand upon thine eyes."

7. **his daughters.** On the plural form *benothaw*—Dinah was Jacob's only daughter—see at v. 23 below.

9. **Enoch.** An old conceit transliterated Heb. *ḥanokh* sometimes by "Hanoch" (as Trad. here) and on other occasions by "Enoch" (as in Gen. 5.18–24). The name is the same. Cf. Saul/Shaul at v. 10 below.

10. **Saul.** As against Trad. "Shaul," see at 36.37 above.

15. [c]**Including Jacob.** So Ibn Ezra (at v. 23 below), Leḳaḥ Ṭov (*Encyclopedia of Biblical Interpretation,* VI, p. 53, n. 85), Rashbam (see also at v. 26 below), Luzzatto, Malbim, Jacob (pp. 832–834). Another way of reaching the total of thirty-three is by including Er and Onan and excluding Dinah (so, e.g., Driver, p. 366; thus he observes that "Dinah . . . from the awkwardness of the Heb. [. . . *we-eth*], it is in-

dependently probable, is a later insertion in the list"). The present list is the culmination of a complex process; see Jacob (pp. 832–834), G. von Rad, *Genesis* (1961), pp. 397–398.

23. **Dan's son**[d]**: (Hushim)** *([d]Heb "sons").* Already Ramban recognized that the plural form *bene* (instead of expected *ben,* "son" in the singular) is simply formulaic; this is evident from his comment at v. 7 in connection with *benothaw* "his (viz., Jacob's) daughters," when Dinah was actually the only daughter. He cites there also Num. 26.8, where *u-vene (fallu eliav),* lit., "and the sons (of Pallu: Eliab)"—Eliab being the only son—is merely formulaic, and to be understood simply as "son."

26. **All the persons belonging to Jacob who came to Egypt.** Taking *kol-ha-néfesh* with *le-ya'aqov* and *ha-ba'a* with *miṣráyma* (so Trad.; cf. v. 27). Earlier printings read "All the persons who came with Jacob to Egypt."

27. On the number 70, see Driver, p. 368; also the references to Jacob and others at v. 15 above.

29. **ordered**[g] ([g]*Lit. "hitched"*). Cf. Ibn Ezra on *wa-yesor yosef*: "by means of an order" (*al yede ṣiwwui*). See also Luzzatto at Exod. 14.6.

30. **Now I can die.** Trad. "Now let me die" can be quite misleading.

34. **the region (of Goshen).** See at 45.10 above.

Chapter 47

2. **a few**[a] *([a]Lit. "five").* See at 31.7; 43.34.

5. **As regards (your father and your brothers) who have come (to you).** Cf. Ramban, "This is an opening remark, as one might say: I have just heard that your father and brothers. . . ." Earlier printings read "Now that . . . have come. . . ." Trad. "Thy father and . . . have come to me" doesn't really say anything.

7. greeted. Trad. "blessed" has overlooked one of the nuances of *barakh;* so Rashi, Luzzatto, Driver ("saluted").

10. bade (Pharaoh) farewell. As in v. 7 preceding. Trad. "blessed" has overlooked the meaning "bid farewell, good-by" for *barakh*; see at 32.1 above and Introduction, §c.

14. as payment for. Exact and idiomatic meaning of the *bet* of exchange in *ba*(*-shéver*). See v. 16 below.

15. lest (we die). One of the generally unrecognized meanings of *lámma*; see Luzzatto and 27.45 above, and Introduction, §c. Trad., "for why (should we die . . .)?"

16. and I will sell to you against (your livestock). As in v. 14 above, the *bet* of exchange: (*we-ettena lakhem be-*(*miqnekhem*). Trad., "and I will give you [bread] for (your cattle)."

17. gave . . . in exchange for. On *bet* of exchange, see vv. 14, 16 above.

18. (with all the money and animal stocks) consigned to (my lord). Understanding *tam* (*ha-késef u-miqneh ha-behema*) *el*(*-adoni*) as a technical term meaning approximately "consigned to," with *ha-késef u-miqneh ha-behema* ("the money and animal stocks") as the compound subject of *tam*. So Sforno: for even if it were true that the money and animal stocks had come to an end and all of it had come into your possession, it is not proper that you should abandon us to die through hunger (and see Luzzatto).

19. Let us not. See at 27.45 above.

Take us . . . in exchange for. Trad. "buy us . . . for" fails to note the element of barter in *qanah*.

20. gained possession. See at v. 19 preceding on *qanah*. Trad., "bought."

22. he did not take over. Heb. *lo qanah*; see at v. 19 above. Trad., "bought he not."

allotment . . . and they lived off the allotment. Understanding *ḥoq* and *akhelu* to include both the land (cf. v. 26 below) and its yield. Trad. "portion . . . and did eat their portion" understands *ḥoq* to refer to "a fixed income in kind" (so Rashi, Luzzatto, Driver).

23. Whereas. Trad. "Behold," being mechanical, fails to recognize the *hen-* clause as the protasis of which the *he-* clause ("here is seed . . .") is the apodosis; so essentially Sforno: "This being so, you are his serfs . . . and he is obligated to provide you provisions . . ." (*we-im ken attem avadaw . . . we-hu ḥayyav latheth mezonothekhem . . .*).

25. We are grateful (to my lord). Trad. "Let us find favour in the sight (of my lord)" not only misses the idiom in *maṣa ḥen be-'ene (adoni),* but the tense ("let us find") is hardly appropriate to the people's response to Joseph's edict; so Luzzatto, Meyuḥas (*Encyclopedia of Biblical Interpretation,* VI, p. 90, n. 245): "Rather, we regard it as a great favor; we are very grateful. The expression is idiomatic"). See Introduction, §c.

26. a land law in Egypt. An attempt to indicate the intent of the Hebrew; lit., "a law . . . concerning the land (or, soil) of Egypt."

27. and were fertile and increased greatly. Cf. Trad. Earlier printings read "and increased greatly in numbers," understanding *me'od* to apply to *wa-yifru* as well as to *wa-yirbu.*

29. And when (the time approached . . .). So Ramban: *ka'asher qarevu. . . .*

as a pledge (of your steadfast loyalty). Understanding the oath proper to begin not with *we-asítha* but with *al-na.* As put by Driver on vv. 29–31 (p. 375), "Jacob exacts a solemn promise from Joseph that he will not bury him in Egypt," and he notes the parallel in 49.29 ff.

steadfast loyalty. So Luzzatto. On the hendiadys involved, see at 1.14 above and the Introduction, §c; on the combination of terms, see at 24.49 above.

Chapter 48

1. **(Joseph) was told.** Idiomatic for the indefinite subject in *wa-yomer le(yosef)*, lit. (and Trad.) "one said to (Joseph)."

2. **sat up in (bed).** Hardly Trad. "sat upon (the bed)." See Sechel Tob (*Encyclopedia of Biblical Interpretation*, VI, p. 106, note 13): ". . . to sit up, as he was already bedridden." And see Luzzatto.

6. **instead**[a] ([a]*Lit. "under* [earlier printings read *by*] *the name"*). Trad. "after the name" would indicate that they were to assume the names of their brothers. See the discussions in Rashi, Rashbam, Ibn Ezra.

7. **I [do this because].** This seems to be the general intent of the verse in its present form; see the materials in *Encyclopedia of Biblical Interpretation,* VI, p. 113, notes 57, 59 ff. On the literary criticism, see Driver, p. 376.

to my sorrow. See Driver (p. 376), and cf. Luzzatto; cf. at 33.13 above.

10. **[Joseph].** To avoid the unnecessary confusion that simple "he" (Trad.) creates here.

14. **crossing (his hands).** Understanding Heb. *sikkel* as having approximately the meaning of Arabic *shakala,* "to plait," and in line with the Septuagint translation (*enalláks,* "crosswise"); so also Rashbam, Ralbag. Trad. "guiding (his hands) wittingly" is based upon *sikkel* in the sense of "prudent" (cf. *sekhel*); in accepting this interpretation, Driver has noted (p. 377), "the philol[ogical] justification from the Arabic is questionable. LXX [Septuagint], Vulg[ate], Pesh[itta], 'changing' may be merely a paraphrase."

15. **in whose ways (my fathers . . . walked).** For this meaning of *hith-hallekh lifne* in connection with God, see at 17.1 above and Introduction, §c.

15–16. The Hebrew text of this blessing by Jacob appears to represent poetry more than it does the narrative prose employed hitherto.

19. plentiful enough for nations. Understanding *melo-ha-goyim* to mean, with Saadia, "his seed will be like a multitude of nations." See Driver (p. 378), "*shall become* THE FULLNESS OF THE *nations.* I.e. will become populousness itself: a hyperbolical expression. Comp. Dt. xxxiii. 17. . . ."

20. Thus (he put). A summing up. Trad. "And (he set)" misses this force.

Chapter 49

1. in days to come. In postbiblical times, the expression *be'aḥarith ha-yamim* (Trad., "in the end of days") acquired an eschatological-messianic connotation that it lacked within the Bible proper. In its fourteen biblical occurrences, it always (as observed by Driver, p. 381) "denotes the *closing period* of the future, so far as it falls within the range of view of the writer using it. The sense expressed by it is thus relative, not absolute, varying with the context. Thus in Nu. xxiv. 14 it is used of the period of Israel's future conquest of Moab and Edom (see vv. 17, 18). . . . Here it is evidently used of the period of Israel's occupation of Canaan,—in particular of the period of the Judges and early years of the monarchy." (On this general date see also F. M. Cross, Jr.–D. N. Freedman, "The Blessing of Moses," *Journal of Biblical Literature,* 67 [1948], 191–210.) Note also that such a similar expression as *miqqeṣ yamim* (Gen. 4.3) denotes only "in the course of time," and that *qeṣ* means "period (of time)" as well as "end."

3. honor. This meaing for *az* (Trad., "power") derives from parallel *se'eth,* "rank" (Trad., "dignity"); and note Sforno: "As our rabbis of blessed memory said, '*oz* denotes royalty' " (*en oz ella malkhuth*).

5. a pair. This is meant to bring out the force of *aḥim* here; so Targum Jonathan, "twins," and Ramban: ". . . but it is my opinion that he is saying that Simeon and Levi are completely brothers, resembling and fitting each other in their plans and acts." Trad. "brothers" is hardly meaningful here—all of them were brothers.

lawlessness. See at 6.11 above.

6. **my person.** For this meaning of *néfesh,* see at 2.7 above, and Introduction, §c.

my being. Cf. Saadia *dhāti,* "my being, self, essence." This is also in line with parallel *nafshi* "my person" (so Ibn Ezra), and cf. Rashi ("my name"). Heb. *kavod* has such sundry meanings as "glory; honor; dignity; presence."

9. **On prey . . . have you grown.** Understanding *mi-ṭéref . . . alítha* (Trad., "From the prey . . . thou art gone up") metaphorically; see Luzzatto.

the king of beasts. There is no certain evidence that Heb. *lavi* is feminine (Trad., "lioness"). Similarly at Num. 23.24, etc.

10. **tribute . . . to him.** See the detailed discussion in Driver, pp. 385–386 and Excursus II (pp. 410–415).

12. **(dark)er than (wine) . . . (whit)er than (milk).** Understanding the *mem* in *mi(-yáyin)* and *me(ḥalav)* as comparative; so Joseph Bechor Shor and Meyuḥas (*Encyclopedia of Biblical Interpretation,* VI, p. 173, note 178). Trad. "with . . . with" (so Rashi, Luzzatto, etc.) treats the *mem* as instrumental.

14. **sheepfolds.** Earlier printings had "saddlebags," on the basis of A. Saarisalo, *The Boundary between Issachar and Naphtali* (1927), p. 92—adopted, e.g., in L. Koehler, *Lexicon in Veteris Testamenti Libros* (p. 580b). However, the picture of ease and comfort represented by Trad. "sheepfolds" seems preferable; note, too, the greater probability of "sheepfolds" in Judges 5.16.

15. **how . . . how.** Understanding *ki* as an emphatic adverb ("how") rather than as a conjunction (Trad., "that"). See Introduction, §c.

burden. On the technical use of the root *sabal,* see M. Held, *Journal of the American Oriental Society,* 88 (1968), 90–96.

21. **(lovely) fawns.** Understanding Heb. *imre* as cognate to Aramaic *immar,* "lamb" (cf. Ezra 6.9 17; 7.17; so also in Akkadian, *immeru*); this accords well with parallel *ayyala,* "hind." As for Trad. "(goodly) words," Driver has commented (p. 390), that it "is supposed to refer to the eloquence . . . of the tribe . . . But . . . the two clauses do not connect well together: and the interpretation cannot be regarded as certain."

22. **(Joseph is a) wild ass /A wild ass . . ./ Wild colts on a hillside.** Understanding *porath* as a poetical feminine form of *pére,* "wild ass": (a) several of the other sons are described in the Blessing in terms of animals (v. 9, "Judah is a lion's whelp"; v. 14, "Issachar is a strong-boned ass"; v. 17, "Dan shall be a serpent by the road"; v. 21, "Naphtali is a hind let loose"; v. 27, "Benjamin is a ravenous wolf"); none, however, in terms of flora. (b) In Deut. 33.17, Joseph is likened to "a firstling bull" and "the wild-ox." It may be further noted that Trad. "a fruitful vine" is etymologically no more certain for *porath* than proposed "wild ass"; the usual explanation has it that it is the same as *poriyya* and derives from a root *parah,* "bear fruit, be fruitful" and means "Joseph is *son of a fruit-bearer,* i.e. a fruitful bough" (Brown-Driver-Briggs, *Hebrew Lexicon,* p. 826a, Qal § 2). See further Speiser, *Genesis* (pp. 367–368).

Wild colts. Ehrlich (*Randglossen*) has noted that Arabic *banāt ṣa'dat,* corresponding to Heb. *banoth ṣa'ada,* means "wild asses."

23. **bitterly assailed him.** So Driver (p. 391). Trad. "have dealt bitterly with him."

24. **the Rock.** Understanding *éven* (*yisra'el*), Trad. "the Stone (of Israel)," as the equivalent of *ṣur,* "Rock," as in Isa. 30.29, *el-ṣur yisra'el,* "to the Rock of Israel." See Luzzatto (with reference to Rashi).

28. **as he bade them farewell.** See at 47.7, 10 above.

addressing to each a parting word appropriate to him. In the comparable Blessing of Moses in Deut. 33, the tribes are all actually blessed, and the word *berakha,* "blessing," is actually employed there (v. 1); in the present chapter, on the other hand, several of the sons are hardly blessed (Rashi, e.g., has specifically noted Reuben, Simeon, and Levi in this category), and the word *berakha* is absent. Hence the inappropriateness here of Trad. "and blessed them; every one according to his blessing he blessed them."

29. **to my kin.** See above (with reference to Driver) at 17.14 and 25.8.

31. **were buried.** (Twice.) Trad. "they buried" fails to do justice to the indefinite subject in *qaveru* and creates unnecessarily the problem of identifying the "they." Cf. Luzzatto.

31–32. By construing v. 32 as the sequence of v. 30 (and treating v. 31 as a parenthetic statement, placed within dashes), v. 32 acquires syntactical meaning. In the traditional rendering, v. 32 is simply an incomplete sentence, left hanging in the air.

Chapter 50

1. **flung himself.** See at 14.10 above. Trad., "fell."

3. **It required forty days.** Idiomatic for literal (and Trad.) "And forty days were fulfilled for him."

4. **(and when) the wailing period was over.** Idiomatic for literal "his days of wailing (or weeping) had passed." Trad., "the days of weeping for him were past."

lay this appeal before Pharaoh. Idiomatic for literal (and Trad.) "speak, I pray you, in the ears of Pharaoh, saying."

5. **I made ready.** See Malbim. The point is not that he dug it (Trad., "which I have digged for me") but, as noted by Malbim, "After this grave had been made ready (*hukhan*) in his lifetime, and his eye and heart were there all the time, he wished to be buried there." Others (cf. Luzzatto) prefer "purchased" (comparing Deut. 2.6).

11. **the Canaanite inhabitants of the land.** This phrase can be expressed in biblical Hebrew only by the present text, *yoshev ha-áreṣ ha-kena'ani,* in which the adjective *ha-kena'ani* ("the Canaanite") qualifies the subject, *yoshev* ("inhabitants"). In being mechanical, Trad. "the inhabitants of the land, the Canaanites" has incorrectly construed *ha-kena'ani* as a noun in apposition to *yoshev.*

13. **the field near Mamre.** Construing *al-pene mamre* ("near Mamre") with *eth-ha-sadeh* ("the field"), as in 49.30.

15. **(What if Joseph) still bears a grudge against us (and pays us back).** See 27.41 above. Earlier printings read "seeks" (to pay us back)." Trad., "(It may be that Joseph) will hate us, (and will fully requite us)." See Introduction, §c.

17. **the offense and guilt of your brothers.** This is the only correct rendering of the Hebrew. Trad. is only mechanical: "the transgression of thy brethren, and their sin."

18. **flung themselves.** See at 14.10 above. Trad., "fell down."

Exodus

שמות

Chapter 1

5. **Joseph being (already in Egypt).** Trad. "and Joseph was" fails to bring out the circumstantial force of the Hebrew construction *we-yosef haya (bemiṣráyim)* (not *wayhi yosef*). See at Gen. 1.1–3 the construction *we-ha-áreṣ hayetha,* "the earth being" (as distinct from "and the earth was," which would represent *wa-tehi ha-áreṣ*).

9. **are much too numerous for us.** As noted at Gen. 18.18, *aṣum* means "many" no less than (Trad.) "mighty." The phrase "much too numerous" is an attempt to express idiomatically literal "are too numerous and many."

10. **(Let us,) then.** Trad. "Come, (let us)" renders *háva* as though it were a verb rather than a particle; see at Gen. 11.7 above.

(deal) shrewdly. Luzzatto has a lengthy comment on this force of *nith-ḥakkema,* as against Trad. "wisely." Driver has noted that the author of Ps. 105.25 reproduced the force of our word by *lehithnakkel,* "to deal craftily."

and rise from the ground. Reversing the position of the text and the note of earlier printings. The force of *ala min-ha-áreṣ* here is admittedly elusive; see the discussion in Luzzatto. The idea of "gain ascendancy over the country" is to be found already in the Talmud (Soṭah 11a), and is noted by Rashi and Ehrlich.

11. **(to oppress them with) forced labor.** It is now recognized that a form of corvée (forced labor) was involved; see Driver's detailed comment, and now I. Mendelsohn, "On

Corvée Labor in Ancient Canaan and Israel," *Bulletin of the American Schools of Oriental Research,* 167 (1962), 31–35; and M. Held, *Journal of the American Oriental Society,* 88 (1968), 90–96. Trad., "burdens."

garrison cities. It is clear from the other biblical passages where *are miskenoth* is used (I Ki. 9.19, parallel to II Chron. 8.6; II Chron. 8.4; 16.4; 17.12; and 32.28), that the Hebrew term points not only to provisions but also (as noted by Driver) to "materials for war, etc., perhaps also (to) trade emporia." Trad. "store cities" limits the Hebrew unduly.

12. **(so that the [Egyptians]) came to dread (the Israelites).** Reproducing the inchoative force of the verb "came to dread"—as well as the *waw* that introduces a result clause ("so that . . ."). Trad., "(and they) were adread because of (the Israelites)." On the inchoative, see Gen. 8.5 and frequently. See Introduction, §c.

16. **(When you) deliver (the Hebrew women).** Trad., "do the office of a midwife to."

17. **they let (the boys) live.** (Also vv. 18, 22.) See Luzzatto. Trad., "and have saved (the men-children) alive." See the discussion of our verb (*ḥaya*) at Gen. 6.20.

18. **summoned (the midwives).** Trad. "called . . . for" is mechanical for *qara le-*.

19. **vigorous.** So Rashbam, Luzzatto, Ehrlich. Trad., "lively."

22. **Nile.** (And elsewhere.) Heb. *ye'or* is originally an Egyptian term for "Nile"; see the article "Nile" by T. O. Lambdin in *Interpreter's Dictionary of the Bible* (*IDB*), III, 549–551. Trad., "river." The meaning of the plural form *ye'orim* (Exod. 7.19; 8.1; etc.), however, is not always certain; it may sometimes denote branches of the Nile or the "canals" associated with it.

Chapter 2

2. **how (beautiful he was).** The emphatic use of the particle *ki* (see at Gen. 49.15). Trad., "that (he was a goodly child)." See Introduction, §c.

(how) beautiful (he was). So for *ṭov* (Trad., "fair") also in Gen. 6.2. Note that there is no word for Trad. "(goodly) child" in the Hebrew.

3. **a (wicker) basket.** (Also v. 5.) Trad. "an ark (of bulrushes)" hardly conveys an appropriate picture of what the *teva* was; see the article "Basket" by E. M. Good, in *IDB*, I, 364–365.

bitumen. (Also v. 5.) Hardly Trad. "slime." See the article "Bitumen" by W. E. Staples, in *IDB*, I, 444.

reeds. (Also v. 5.) Heb. *suf* is originally an Egyptian word meaning "reed"; see below, at 10.19. Trad., "flags."

4. **stationed herself.** The inchoative force in the Hebrew verb (see at 1.12 above); cf. Driver, "took her stand," who compares 19.17. Trad., "stood."

to learn. Trad. "to know" is mechanical for *yada.*

5. **while (her maidens) walked.** Cf. Driver, "were walking." Trad. "and (her maidens) walked" is incorrect for participial *holekhoth*; it would be correct for *wa-telákhna.* See at 1.5 above.

6. **she saw that it was a child, a boy crying.** So Rashbam, Ramban—as against (literal) Trad. "and she opened it, and saw it, even the child."

This must be (a Hebrew child). So Ramban, Luzzatto—as against (literal) Trad. "This is."

11–12. **beating . . . he struck down.** While it is barely possible that *makke*—the participle!—in v. 11 denotes "killing" (so Ehrlich, *Mikra;* contrast Rashbam, Abravanel, Malbim), *wa-yakh* (. . . *wa-yiṭmenéhu*) in v. 12 certainly does. Trad.

"smiting . . . smote" is mechanical and vague. Cf. 12.29 below.

13. the next day. Idiomatic for *ba-yom ha-sheni.* Trad., "the second day."

14. (chief and) ruler. In the earlier period of its career (e.g., in the period of the *Shofeṭim*—"Chieftains" rather than Trad. "Judges"), *shofeṭ* meant "ruler" rather than (Trad.) "judge."

17. (Moses) rose to their defense. An attempt to reproduce the idiomatic force of *qum* as an auxiliary verb in *wa-yáqam* (*Moshe*) *wa-yoshi'an* ("Moses proceeded to defend/help them"); see at Gen. 23.7; 31.17. Cf. Driver, "But Moses chivalrously comes forward . . . to assist the girls." Trad. "(but Moses) stood up and helped them" takes no cognizance of this idiom. See Introduction, §c.

18. to their father Reuel. Trad. "to Reuel their father" is a hebraism (*el-re'uel avihen*).

21. consented. So Malbim; cf. Driver, "agreed" (and cites Jud. 17.11; 19.6). The root *y'l* is sometimes elusive in meaning (cf. Brown-Driver-Briggs [*BDB*], *Hebrew Lexicon,* 383 f.). Trad., "was content."

23. and their cry for help from the bondage (rose up to God). Understanding *min-ha-avoda* ("from the bondage") as going with *shawatham* ("their cry for help"). Trad. "and their cry came up to God by reason of the bondage" is mechanical, leaving open the syntax of the verse (e.g., did their cry reach God because of the bondage, rather than their cry caused by the bondage reaching God?).

Chapter 3

5. sandals. Trad. "shoes" for biblical *na'aláyim* is anachronistic; see Driver, "properly (as always) *sandals.* Cf. Jos. v. 15. . . ."

8. **to a good and spacious land.** Trad. "unto a good land and a large" ignores the Hebrew idiom in *el-éreṣ ṭova ureḥava.*

(the home of the) Canaanites, the Hittites, etc. (Also v. 17, and frequently.) Trad. "(unto the place of the) Canaanite, and the Hittite," etc., has failed to reproduce the force of the singular collective in *ha-kena'ani we-ha-ḥitti,* etc. See Introduction, §c.

9. **has reached (Me).** The idiom in *ṣa'aqath (bene-yisrael) báa elay* is approximately "I got the message" (see Ramban, Sforno; Driver cites Gen. 18.2 in this connection); and cf. "I got your payment" for *kaspekhem ba elay* in Gen. 43.23 (already noted by Ehrlich, *Mikra*).

12. **(I will be with you); and it shall be your sign,** etc. Understanding immediately preceding "that I (God) will be with you" as the sign (*oth*) that it is God Himself who has sent Moses; see Rashi (under *davar aḥer,* "Another interpretation"), Ibn Ezra (note the *Perush al Ibn Ezra),* and Malbim. This interpretation of the verse does not preclude the same sign ("that I will be with you") pointing also to a future event, namely, "And when you have freed the people from Egypt, you shall worship God at this mountain"; so Rashi (citing Isa. 37.30 as a similar use of *oth,* "sign") and Driver (who cites additionally I Sam. 2.34 and Isa. 7.11). Projected reading: ";that (shall be your sign)."

14. **Ehyeh.** So Rashbam.

15. **This shall be,** etc. The synonymous parallelism alone (*ledor dor/le'olam*) is sufficient to point to two lines of poetry in the second half of the verse.

appellation. Cf. Rashbam, Malbim. It has been insufficiently noted that *zékher* in biblical Hebrew sometimes means "name, appellation," as well as (Trad.) "memorial, remembrance." Brown-Driver-Briggs, *Hebrew Lexicon* (p. 271a, §2), in drawing attention to the parallelism with *shem,* cities our verse and Isa. 26.8; Hos. 12.6; Ps. 135.13; Prov. 10.7

(in the well-known but generally misunderstood expression, *zékher ṣaddiq livrakha*); and Eccles. 9.5.

(for all) eternity. As against Trad. "(unto all) generations"; on "age" for *dor* (vs. Trad. "generations"), see at Gen. 6.9.

16. **(I have taken note of you and) of what (is being done . . .).** Trad. has added the verb "seen" in "(I have surely remembered you, and) seen that which (is done . . .)"—which lacks a correspondent in the Hebrew—because it failed to construe *we-eth-he-asui*, no less than *ethkhem*, as the object of *paqod paqádti*.

18. **(They will) listen to you.** Idiomatic for *we-shame'u le-qolékha*, lit. (and Trad.) "hearken to your voice." See Introduction, §c.

(then) you shall go with the elders (of Israel). Idiomatic for *u-vátha atta we-ziqne (yisra'el)*, lit. (and Trad.) "(And) thou shalt come, thou and the elders (of Israel)." See Introduction, §c.

manifested Himself (to us). Cf. Malbim "revealed Himself"; and note *nir'a* ("has appeared") in v. 16 preceding. Trad., "met (with us)."

21. **And I will dispose the Egyptians favorably toward this people.** Idiomatic, for lit. (and Trad.) "And I will give this people favor in the sight of the Egyptians." On the idiom, see Introduction, §c.

22. **borrow from (her neighbor).** See 22.13 and Luzzatto; also Driver's comment on this incident. Trad. "ask of" is mechanical.

Chapter 4

3. **recoiled.** Trad. "fled" hardly does justice to the force of *wa-yánas* here. Moses could not have fled if the action in v. 4 followed immediately upon v. 3. Cf. Num. 24.11 below (on *baraḥ*).

7. **it was again.** Trad. "it was turned again" has reproduced the force of *sháva* twice ("turned" and "again"), unnecessarily.

the rest of (his body). See at Gen. 3.2. Trad., "his other flesh."

8. **pay heed to (the first sign).** See Luzzatto on the idiom, and Introduction, §c. In being literal, Trad. "hearken to the voice of (the first sign)" is absurd.

(the first sign . . .) the second. Idiomatic for (*ha-oth ha-rishon* . . .) *ha-oth ha-aḥaron* when only two are involved; see Luzzatto (who cites also Gen. 33.2). Trad. "(the first sign . . .) the latter sign" is mechanical.

11. **(Who gives man) speech?** So Ramban, Ralbag, Cassuto. Cf. (*kevad*) *pe* in v. 10 preceding, and contrast *illem,* "dumb" immediately following.

12. **(I will be) with you as you speak.** (Also v. 15.) See Sforno. Trad. "with thy mouth" is mechanical.

13. **make someone else Your agent.** Cf. Rashbam, followed by Luzzatto; see also Joseph Bechor Shor (in *Encyclopedia of Biblical Interpretation* [*EBI*], VII, p. 128, n. c.

16. **serve as your (spokesman) . . . playing the role.** On the idiom in *haya le-* —as against lit. (and Trad.) "shall be to"—see at Gen. 9.13.

with you playing the role of God to him. Earlier printings read "and you shall be an oracle[c] to him" ([c]*Lit. "god"*).

17. **(take) with you.** On this idiom for (*tiqqaḥ*) *beyadékha,* as against lit. (and Trad.) "in thy hand," see at Gen. 43.12 and Introduction, §c.

18. **went back.** (Also v. 19.) On this idiom in *wa-yélekh* (*Moshe*) *wa-yáshav* see Luzzatto at 2.1; and cf. the idiom in *wa-yáqam* at 2.17. See Introduction, §c.

how they are faring. See Cassuto; and cf. Gen. 43.27–28 (also 45.3).

20. **mounted.** Trad. "set" hardly reproduces the force of *wa-yarkivem.*

with him. Will replace "in his hand" in projected version. See Introduction, §C.

21. **stiffen.** So for root *ḥzq,* and "stubborn" for root *kvd* throughout this section. Trad. generally employed "harden" for both Hebrew terms.

22. **My first-born son.** (Also v. 25, and elsewhere.) Trad. "My son, my first-born" violates English idiom in reproducing *beni bekhori* mechanically.

31. **they bowed low in homage.** See at Gen. 24.48. Trad. "they bowed their heads and worshipped" is hardly justified.

Chapter 5

3. **has manifested Himself.** So Luzzatto, and see 3.18 above. Trad., "hath met."

4. **labors.** So Rashbam, Ramban, Malbim; and see at 1.11 above.

8. **quota.** As recognized by Rashi, Ibn Ezra, Malbim, Ehrlich, and Driver ("The Heb. here means properly *a rightly regulated amount*"), the force of *mathkóneth* is more than simply "tale (Trad.), sum, total."

shirkers. (Also v. 17.) Cf. Rashbam ("they were capable of producing more") and Malbim, and Sforno at v. 17. Trad., "idle."

9. **deceitful promises.** Cf. Ibn Ezra: "the false promises that Moses and Aaron made to them." Earlier printings read "idle chatter." Trad., "lying words."

10. **the taskmasters and foremen of the people.** Trad. "the taskmasters of the people, and their officers" does justice neither to the Hebrew nor to the English idiom (see, e.g., at 3.8 above and Gen. 40.1), and leaves the antecedent of "their (officers)" unnecessarily uncertain. See Introduction, §C.

14. **prescribed amount.** In keeping with "quota" for

mathkóneth in v. 8 above (and see Rashi); note that the term used here, *ḥoq*, is the term that the Malbim employs in v. 8 in discussing *mathkóneth.*

18. **quota.** See at v. 8 above.

19. **found themselves in trouble.** Understanding *otham* to refer to the "foremen"; so, e.g., Ibn Ezra, Ramban, Malbim, Driver. Others (e.g., Rashi, Ehrlich, Cassuto) regard *otham* as denoting the Israelites. Trad. "did see that they were set on mischief," etc., is less than clear in the matter.

trouble. So Rashi, Ibn Ezra, Malbim.

Chapter 6

6. **burdens.** (Also v. 7.) So Trad. The projected reading is "labors," as at 1.11 and 5.4; see the reference to M. Held at 1.11.

7. **I, the Lord.** See at v. 8 below, as against Trad. "I am the Lord your God."

8. **I swore.** Idiomatic for *nasáthi eth-yadi* (lit. and Trad., "I lifted up My hand"), as recognized e.g., by Rashi, Ibn Ezra, Driver ("i.e. *sware*").

I the Lord. Understanding *ani YHWH* in context as denoting a solemn promise; so Ibn Ezra, Driver ("a solemn asseverative formula, closing a Divine utterance"), Cassuto. Trad. "I am the Lord" makes the Hebrew a simple assertion that is pointless in context.

12. **appealed.** An attempt to reproduce the force of *waydabber . . . lifne* (as distinct, e.g., from *waydabber . . . el* in v. 10 preceding).

impeded (speech). (Also v. 30.) Rashi (*aṭum*), followed by Luzzatto. Trad., mechanically, "uncircumcised (lips)."

16. **lineage.** (Also v. 19.) See Gen. 5.1 ("line"). Trad., "generations."

137. (Also "133" in v. 18 and "137" in v. 20.) On the use of numerals in lists, see Introduction, §c.

28. **when.** Cf. Luzzatto on this meaning of *be-yom,* and see at Gen. 2.4b; also Introduction, §c. On construing our verse with what follows, see, e.g., Rashi, Luzzatto, Driver.

Chapter 7

1. **prophet.** So Trad. Earlier printings read "spokesman" (cf. Luzzatto, and "spokesman" for *le-fe* at 4.16).

11. **for his part . . . in turn.** Trad. "also . . . also" fails to bring out the force of *gam . . . gam.* See Ehrlich (in part) and Cassuto.

15. **station yourself.** (Also at 9.13, and elsewhere.) See at 2.4 above.

Nile. See at 1.22, as against Trad. "river."

17. **water . . . it.** (So frequently.) See at Gen. 1.2, as against Trad. "waters . . . they." Note the form *meme,* "waters, bodies of water" in v. 19.

18. **find it impossible.** Cf. Ibn Ezra "they could not" (*lo yakhelu;* based on, as explained by *Perush al Ibn Ezra, lo yakhelu* in vv. 21, 24). See also at Gen. 19.11 (the argument of Rashbam). Trad., "shall loathe."

19. **canals.** (Also at 8.1; etc.) See on "Nile" at 1.22 above.

23. **palace.** (Also v. 28.) The *báyith* of a king is "palace," that of God "Temple," that of a royal dynasty "House"; and the like. Trad., "house."

25. **When seven days had passed,** etc. Already Saadia connected v. 25 with what follows; cf. Meyuḥas (in *EBI,* VII, p. 229, n.E): after it lasted a full seven days and Pharaoh still did not submit, God told Moses to inform Pharaoh of the next plague.

27. **(your whole) country.** On "territory, country" for *gevul* (as well as "boundary, border"), see at Gen. 10.19. In

8.1, 2, 12, 13, etc., the Hebrew term is *éreṣ*. Trad., "(all thy borders." See Introduction, §c.

Chapter 8

5. (You may have this) triumph. An attempt to reproduce the precise nuance of *hithpa'er alay*; cf. Driver (followed by Cassuto), ". . . in a bad sense, *vaunt oneself,* Jud. vii. 2, Is. x. 15 . . . i.e. here, Have this glory or advantage over me, in fixing the time at which I shall ask for the plague to cease. Not so used elsewhere." Cf. Luzzatto: have your boast over Me and exhibit mastery over Me.

11. became stubborn. (Also v. 28; 8.7.) Idiomatic for lit. (and Trad.) "hardened his heart," the reading in earlier printings.

12–14. lice . . . vermin. Distinguishing between *kinnim* (vv. 12, 13, 14; also Ps. 105.31, and doubtfully in Isa. 51.6) and *hakkinnam* (only here, vv. 13, 14); Trad. "gnats . . . gnats" makes no distinction. On the identification of the insects, see Luzzatto and Driver, and the articles on "Fauna" (by F. S. Bodenheimer) and "Gnat" (by W. W. Frerichs) in *IDB*, II, respectively pp. 246–256 and 403–404.

16. Early. (Also 9.13; and frequently.) See Gen. 19.2, as against Trad. "Rise up early," for *hashkem.*

17. [a]swarms of insects[a] ([a-a]*Others "wild beasts"*). See Luzzatto, Driver.

18. region (of Goshen). See at Gen. 45.10, as against Trad. "land" for *éreṣ* here.

22. untouchable. The idea of taboo in *to'eva* here is well expressed by Luzzatto: it has the force of holy and taboo (*qódesh we-ḥérem*) . . . something set apart, not to be used.

Chapter 9

3. **will strike.** Understanding *hoya* as from the root *hwh,* "to fall upon, attack, destroy." Cf. *haya be-* in v. 11. Trad., "is upon."

7. **inquired.** The verb *shalaḥ* is sometimes used elliptically for "send messengers (or a message), send to inquire" (see Saadia; *BDB, Hebrew Lexicon,* s. *shalaḥ,* bottom of p. 1018, where I Ki. 20.17 is cited as a case in point; cf. I Ki. 5.16); cf. Ehrlich, *Randglossen.* Trad. "sent" misses the idiom. See Introduction, §c.

11. **confront.** On the idiom, see Ramban, Joseph Bechor Shor. Trad. "stand before" is mechanical.

15. **I could have (stretched forth My hand).** Cf. Rashi, Malbim. On Trad. "Surely now I had (put forth . . .)" see Driver's comment.

16. **I have spared you.** See Saadia, Abravanel, Driver (". . . i.e. *maintained thee alive* . . ."). Trad. "have I made thee stand" misses the idiom in *he'emadtíkha.*

17. **thwart.** An attempt to capture the force of elusive *mistolel;* see Driver, ". . . *'raisest thyself up as a mound* (or *obstacle*) against my people,' to oppose their release." Targum—followed by Rashi, Rashbam, Luzzatto—rendered "tread down, oppress." Saadia translated "seeking pretexts against (My people)."

19. **order.** Idiomatic for *shelaḥ;* see at v. 7 above on "inquired."

(order . . .) brought under shelter. So Luzzatto, Ehrlich. Targum, Saadia (but see n. 4 there), Rashi, and Ibn Ezra render "assemble." Trad., "hasten in."

in the open. Idiomatic for *ba-sadeh*; cf. Gen. 25.27 ("Esau . . . a man of the outdoors"). Trad., " in the field."

26. **region.** See at 8.18 above.

27. **I stand guilty.** Cf. Rashbam ("I admit that I have sinned"), Luzzatto, Ehrlich. Trad., "I have sinned."

in the right . . . in the wrong. As put by Driver in his comment on Trad. "righteous . . . wicked": "rather, *the . . . one in the right . . . those in the wrong.* The words (*ha-ṣaddiq* and *ha-resha'im*) are used not in their ethical, but in their forensic sense. . . ."

28. **(of) God's (thunder and of hail).** Trad. "these mighty (thunderings and hail)" treats the word (*qoloth*) *elohim* (*u-varad*) as denoting divine power (see Ehrlich [*Randglossen*], Cassuto). However, in view of the statement "the Lord sent thunder and hail" in v. 23 and in light of the expression *eṣba elohim hi,* "This is the finger of God!" in 8.15 (the fourth plague), it seems safest to interpret *elohim* here simply as "God"; see also Driver.

32. **emmer.** Earlier printings read "millet"; see article "Wheat" (by J. C. Trever) in *IDB*, IV, 839–840. Trad., "spelt."

Chapter 10

2. **sons and . . . sons' sons.** Trad. "son . . . son's son" has failed to reproduce the singular collective in *binkha u-ven-binkha.* See 3.8 above, and Introduction, §c.

made a mockery of. See Rashi, Luzzatto (followed by Ehrlich), Driver (in commenting favorably on Revised Version margin "Or, *how I have mocked the Egyptians*"). Trad., "wrought upon."

4. **territory.** (Also v. 19.) See at 7.27 above. Trad., "(into thy) border."

7. **is lost.** Trad. "is destroyed" hardly conveys the force of *aveda* here; it is rather "doomed to destruction, is lost" (cf. Cassuto). Rashbam, Ibn Ezra, Driver, and others, interpret "is ruined."

9. **festival.** Earlier printings read "pilgrimage" (cf. Arabic *ḥaj*) for *ḥag*; however, the site in the wilderness had yet to become a place for pilgrimage. Trad., "feast."

10. **(as I mean to let) your children go with you.** Trad. "(as I will let) you go, and your little ones" is scarcely correct; the point is (see v. 11 and 10.24) that Pharaoh was willing to let the adult men go, but not the children. So Malbim, Ehrlich (*Randglossen*), Cassuto, and apparently Rashi, Sforno, and Luzzatto.

Clearly, you are bent on mischief. Cf. Targum, Rashi, Rashbam, Ramban, Luzzatto, Driver (". . . The 'evil' is their intention of leaving Egypt altogether"). Trad. "see ye that evil is before your face," because it is literal, conveys little meaning.

13. **had brought.** So apparently Ibn Ezra (see the *Perush al Ibn Ezra*); the pluperfect force in *nasa* is not conveyed in Trad. "brought."

15. **They hid all the land from view.** Cf. Ibn Ezra: "the earth became dark because the locusts came between the sun and the earth—for the earth itself is always dark." Earlier printings read "They hid the surface of the whole land" (cf. Trad. "For they covered the face of the whole earth"), which hardly did justice to *waykhas eth-'en (kol-ha-áreṣ)* and to the picture conveyed by the phrase as a whole.

16. **I stand guilty.** See at 9.27 above, as against Trad. "I have sinned."

19. **Sea of Reeds.** See at 15.4 below.

28. **the moment.** Idiomatic for *be-yom;* see at 6.28 above and at Gen. 2.4b. Trad. "in the day" is mechanical. See Introduction, §c.

29. **rightly.** So Targum (*ya'uth*), Rashi, Ibn Ezra (citing Num. 27.7), Malbim (implying "correctly"). Trad. "well" hardly represents the force of *ken* (*dibbárta*) here.

Chapter 11

2. **objects (of silver and gold).** So Saadia (cf. Targum *manin . . . manin*). Trad. "jewels (of silver and) jewels (of gold)" limits Heb. *kele . . . kele* unnecessarily. See below at 35.22.

3. **disposed . . . favorably.** See at 3.21.

7. **snarl**[a] ([a]*Others "move (or whet) his tongue"*). An attempt to capture the idiom in *yeḥeraf leshono.* Saadia, Luzzatto, Malbim, and others interpret as "bark," to which Ibn Ezra adds "or bite" and Cassuto "and whet its tongue." Cf. Driver, "A proverbial expression, implying that not only should they suffer no actual harm, but no unfriendly sound should even be heard against them. . . ."

9. **had said.** (Also v. 10, "had done.") So Ibn Ezra ("God had already [*kevar*] said"), Cassuto. But see Driver. Trad. "said" is hardly helpful.

10. **had performed . . . had stiffened.** Rashi notes that vv. 10–11 were repeated merely to connect v. 9 with 12.1. Modern criticism, however (see Driver, at vv. 9 and 10; pp. 55 ff.), connects vv. 9–10 (along with 12.1–20) with the "marvels" (*mofethim*) that both Aaron and Moses performed before Pharaoh in 7.8–13 and 9.8–12. But the pluperfect must be used if the chapter is treated as a unit.

Chapter 12

3. **community.** So generally for *edah* (Trad., "congregation"), and "congregation" for *qahal* (Trad., "assembly"). Earlier printings read "assembly" for *edah* here; but this could be misunderstood as an elected legislative body—which it was not.

4. **then let him share one with a neighbor who dwells nearby, in proportion to the number of persons: you shall contribute for the lamb according to what each household will eat.** Understanding the phrase (*u-shekheno*) *ha-qarov el-betho* (*bemikhsath nefashoth*) to denote "(a neighbor) who dwells nearby"—in projected version will replace "(the neighbor) closest to his household (in the number

of persons)." So already Mekilta (see ed. Lauterbach, Vol. I, pp. 25–28). Present printing reads, "(the neighbor) closest to his household in the number of persons: (you shall apportion the lamb according to what each person should eat)." In reproducing the Hebrew word for word, Trad. is less than clear: "then shall he and his neighbor next unto his house take one according to the number of the souls; according to every man's eating ye shall make your count for the lamb."

5. **a yearling male.** So Septuagint, Ehrlich (*Mikra,* a long interesting discussion; with reference to Targum Onkelos *bar shatteh* and Ibn Ezra), Snaith (*Leviticus and Numbers,* in *Century Bible,* on "flock" at Lev. 1.2, p. 29); see also the Malbim's discussion. Trad., "a male of the first year" (so, e.g., Saadia, Rashi).

6. **(You shall) keep watch over (it).** See Rashi, Malbim. Trad. "(and ye shall) keep (it)" fails to convey the force of (*we-haya lakhem*) *lemishméreth.*

(and all) the assembled congregation (of the Israelites). An attempt to get at the force of the unusual combination *(kol) adath qehal (-yisrael)* (projected version; replaces "the aggregate community" from earlier printings). This pleonasm is found again only in Num. 14.5. Rashi interprets our phrase as "the *qahal* and the *edah* and *yisrael.*" Trad. renders mechanically, "and the whole assembly of the congregation of Israel."

slaughter. (Also v. 21.) Trad. "kills" does not distinguish sufficiently between *shaḥaṭ* and other, nonritual terms for "kill, slay" (e.g., *harag*).

7. **(and the lintel) of the houses.** Trad. "(and on the lintel, upon the houses wherein . . .)" may imply that the blood is to be applied to the houses as well as to the doorposts and lintel—which is hardly the case, cf. vv. 22–23 below.

8. **they shall eat it roasted,** etc. Taking the verb

yokhlúhu as governing *ṣeli-esh u-maṣṣoth*. Trad., on the other hand, ignored the *athnaḥ* under (*ba-láyla*) *ha-ze* and construed *ṣeli-esh u-maṣṣoth* with the verb preceding (*we-akhlu eth-ha-basar*). Ramban separates *u-maṣṣoth* from *ṣeli-esh*, and takes the former with (*al-merorim*) *yokhlúhu*.

9. **(Do not eat) any of it.** To bring out more clearly and idiomatically the force of *al* (*-tokhlu*) *mi-*(*ménnu*); Trad., "(Eat not) of it." Similarly in v. 7 preceding: "(They shall take) some of (the blood)" for (*we-laqeḥu*) *min* (*-ha-dam*), as against Trad. "of."

entrails. Trad. "inwards" is a hebraism, for *qirbo*.

11. **sandals.** See at 3.5 above.

it is a passover[b] **offering to the Lord.** Trad. "it is the Lord's passover" is hardly correct for *pésaḥ hu le-YHWH*. As for note *b* (*Or "protective offering"; Heb* pesaḥ), cf. the meaning "protect" for *pasóaḥ* in Isa. 31.5.

13. **(And the blood . . . shall be a sign for you): when I see.** The *we-* in *we-raíthi* is explicative. Trad. "and when I see" does not explain the purpose of the sign. See Introduction, §c.

15. **person.** See at Gen. 2.7 and Introduction, §c. as against Trad. "soul." Note Trad. "man" for *néfesh* in v. 16 following (though, again, "soul" in v. 19).

17. **the [Feast of] Unleavened Bread.** So Trad.—but without brackets around "Feast of." Understanding (*ushmartem eth-*) *ha-maṣṣoth* here as the equivalent of *ḥag ha-maṣṣoth*; cf. Rashbam: "to eat them on this very day, as a remembrance." That *ha-maṣṣoth* represents here "*Feast of* Unleavened Bread" is clear from immediately following "for on this very day (*ki be-éṣem ha-yom ha-ze*) I brought your ranks out of the land of Egypt; you shall observe this day (*ushmartem eth-ha-yom ha-ze*) throughout the ages as an institution for all time"; that is, it is the day on which the Feast of Unleavened Bread begins—and for seven days in all—that the Exodus from Egypt is to be recalled. This is

also precisely what 23.15 says, except that there the word *ḥag* is present: "You shall observe the Feast of Unleavened Bread [*eth-ḥag ha-maṣṣoth tishmor*]—eating unleavened bread for seven days as I have commanded you—at the set time in the month of Abib, for in it you went forth from Egypt. . . ." The rabbis subsequently interpreted the word *ha-maṣṣoth* to mean here literally "the unleavened bread" (cf. Mekilta, Tractate Pisḥa VIII, ed. Lauterbach, vol. I, pp. 73–74; Pesaḥim 38b; Ḥagigah 11b; Menaḥoth 53a), i.e., specially guarded unleavened bread (*maṣṣoth shemuroth*), followed, e.g., by Rashi, Ibn Ezra, Malbim. A similar case of ellipsis (*lashon qaṣar*) may be noted at 25.16, where (*we-nathata el-ha-aron eth*) *ha-eduth* is understood generally (so Ibn Ezra, Rashbam) to stand for *luḥoth ha-eduth* ("And deposit in the ark [the tablets of] the Pact"). It is not likely that the expression *ushmartem eth-ha-maṣṣoth* can really mean "and you shall keep watch over the unleavened bread"; rather would the Hebrew verb *shamar* denote "you shall preserve, maintain, protect, save, watch for," or the like. Furthermore, one would expect some details of the nature of the watching, e.g., what it was about the *maṣṣoth* that had to be watched.

21. **passover offering.** See at v. 11 above, as against Trad. "passover lamb."

Go, pick out (lambs) for your families. An attempt to reproduce the force of *mishkhu uqḥu lakhem* (*ṣon*) *le-mispeḥothekhem*. Trad. "Draw out, and take you (lambs) according to your families" is mechanical.

22. **(and apply) some of the blood.** Trad. "(and strike) with the blood" has ignored the partitive *min*(*-ha-dam*); see at v. 7 above.

27. **bowed low in homage.** See at 4.31 above, as against Trad. "bowed the head and worshipped."

29. **struck down.** See at 2.11–12, as against Trad. "smote."

33. **(The Egyptians urged the people on,) impatient to**

have them leave the country. Projected version; replaces "to make them leave in haste" (cf. Trad. "to send them out of the land in haste"), which connected *lemaher* with *min-ha-áreṣ* following, instead of with the preceding part of the verse.

35. **had done . . . and borrowed.** Trad. "did . . . and they asked" fails to indicate the correct sequence of action; see Driver, "*had done . . . and asked,*—before viz. the events just narrated (*vv.* 29–34). Cf. xi.3." So also, e.g., Cassuto.

45. **(No) bound or hired laborer (shall eat of it).** Understanding the two terms *toshav we-sakhir* as denoting two different kinds of laborers (similarly Lev. 22.10; 25.6, 40); projected version. Replaces "A resident hireling (shall not eat of it)," which treated the two words as hendiadys (i.e., a *sakhir* who is a *toshav*); however, the above-cited passages in Leviticus preclude this interpretation. Trad. "A sojourner and a hired servant" is mechanical.

48. **he shall be admitted.** So Luzzatto: "he shall be eligible" (*yihyeh kasher la'asoth pésaḥ le-aṣmo*), followed by Ehrlich (*Randglossen*). Trad. "let him come near" misses the idiom.

Chapter 13

9. **that with a mighty hand.** Understanding *ki* (*be-yad ḥazaqa*) as explicating the sign; see Ramban (followed by Luzzatto, who cites v. 16 below as further evidence), Sforno, Cassuto, and also Ibn Ezra's discussion. Trad. "for with a strong hand" treats *ki* as causal. See Introduction, §c.

13. **And you must redeem.** I.e., unlike the case with the firstling ass in the first part of the verse ("you shall redeem . . . if you do not redeem it . . ."), no alternative is given here.

14. **It was with a mighty hand.** Reproducing the force

of the emphatic (initial) position of *be-ḥózeq yad* within its clause.

16. **symbol**[c]. Approximately the meaning of obscure *ṭoṭafoth* in line with parallel *oth* ("sign"); note that in v. 9 it is *zikkaron* ("reminder") which is used in place of our *ṭoṭafoth*, again parallel with *oth*.

17. **(although it was) nearer.** Trad., "near."

18. **Sea of Reeds.** See at 15.4, as against Trad. "Red Sea."

Chapter 14

3. **astray.** Cf. Brown-Driver-Briggs, *Hebrew Lexicon*, s. *bwk* (p. 100b), "wander aimlessly." Trad. "entangled"—perhaps in line with "the wilderness has closed in on them" (*sagar alehem ha-midbar*) immediately following.

4. **(that I may)** [a-]**assert My authority against**[-a] **(Pharaoh)** ([a-a]*Or "gain glory through"*). (Also vv. 17, 18.) So Ehrlich, *Randglossen*, (who cites Lev. 10.3, and Ezek. 28:22; 39.13 as additional cases in point). Trad. "(and I) will get me honour upon (Pharaoh)" is less than clear.

5. **(Pharaoh and his courtiers) had a change of heart about (the people).** See Rashi for the idiom. Trad. "and the heart (of Pharaoh and of his servants) turned towards (the people)," in being literal, is quite meaningless.

7. **the rest of (the chariots).** See Driver—as against Trad. "all the (chariots)"—"i.e. all the *other* chariots." See also Introduction, §c.

officers[c]. See the discussion in Driver (pp. 115–116).

in (all of them). Cf. Driver: "upon (not 'over') all of them"—as against Trad. "over."

8. **defiantly.** Idiomatic for the phrase *be-yad rama*; so also Num. 33.3. Will replace "boldly" in projected version; this in light of Num. 15.30. Trad., mechanically, "with a high hand."

20. Thus there was . . . and it cast a spell[e], etc. An attempt to make intelligible an admittedly difficult passage. Trad. "and there was the cloud and the darkness here, yet gave it light by night there" has gratuitously introduced "here" and "there," and has hardly made the sentence intelligible with the phrase "and gave it light." The "here" and "there" probably represents Rashi's idea that the cloud and the darkness were meant for the Egyptians, and the light for the Israelites—which is not what the text says.

25. locked[f]. Following such ancient versions as the Septuagint, Samaritan, and Peshitta, which understood *wa-yásar* to represent *wa-ye'esor* after the manner of *azin* (for *a'azin*) in Job. 32.11. As against Trad. "took off" (Revised Version "removed"), Driver prefers Revised Version margin "*bound*" (based on Septuagint, Samaritan, Peshitta): "i.e. clogged,—presumably by their sinking in the wet sand . . . probably to be preferred. . . ."

27. normal state. So Rashi, Luzzatto, Malbim, Cassuto. Cf. Driver, as against Trad. "strength": "The [Revised Version] marg. ("wonted flow") is right: lit. to its perennial state. . . . The true meaning of the word was not recovered till in the 18th century Arabic began to be studied and compared with Hebrew. . . ."

(and the Egyptians fled) at its approach. Trad. "against it" (for *liqratho*) is neither idiomatic nor clear.

hurled. Cf. Sforno (*na'ar otham me'al ha-markavoth el qarqa ha-yam*), *Perush al Ibn Ezra* (*zaraq otham*), Luzzatto, Malbim, Driver. Trad., "overthrew." The idea is repeated in 15.1 (*rama ba-yam*).

28. (the chariots and the horsemen)—Pharaoh's entire army (that . . .). Reproducing the force of *le-khol* as a summing up of what preceded; so Rashi, who cites Exod. 27.3, 19 and Num. 4.32 as other cases in point. See Introduction, §c. Trad., mechanically, "(the chariots, and the horsemen) even all the hosts of Pharaoh."

Chapter 15

1. **He has triumphed gloriously.** So Saadia, Rashbam ("a military victory"), Ibn Ezra, Luzzatto.

2. **(my strength and) might.** In line with the meaning of the root in Arabic and in personal names (see Koehler, *Lexicon,* under II* *zimrah,* p. 260; so also Cassuto). Similarly Isa. 12.2 and Ps. 118.14. Interestingly, Rashi interpreted our word *zimrath* as from *zamar,* "to cut off" (citing Lev. 25.4 and Isa. 25.5), to denote: "The strength and vengeance of our God have become our salvation."

enshrine. Understanding *we-anwéhu* as from the same root as *naweh,* "homestead, abode." So Targum Onkelos, followed by Rashi, Ibn Ezra, Sforno.

4. **the pick (of his officers).** So Rashi ("*mivḥar* is a noun"); cf. Driver's comment on Trad. "(his) chosen (captains)": "Heb. *the choice of his. . . .*"

Sea of Reeds. The literal meaning of *yam suf*; Heb. *suf* is a loanword from Egyptian and means "reeds, rushes" (as at Exod. 2.3). Scholars have long agreed that Trad. "Red Sea" (deriving from the Septuagint, but of unknown origin) is incorrect. For a discussion of the problem and the later extension of the term *yam suf* to denote the Gulf of Aqaba (as at I Ki. 9. 26), see J. L. Mihelic, *Interpreter's Dictionary of the Bible,* IV, pp. 19–21. On *suph,* see J. C. Trever, "Reed," *IDB,* IV, 22–23.

7. **triumph.** See at v. 1 above, as against Trad. "excellency"—on which see Driver.

8. **wall.** Cf. Targum Onkelos, Rashi, Ibn Ezra, Luzzatto (see his discussion). Trad., "heap."

9. **desire.** On this and other meanings of *néfesh,* as against Trad. "soul," see at Gen. 2.7, and Introduction, §c.

11. **celestials.** A more poetic term than "divine beings, gods" for *elim.*

15. **clans.** See at Gen. 36.15, as against Trad. "chiefs."
tribes. Parallel to "clans," as against Trad. "mighty men."

16. **ransomed.** Cf. Driver, ". . . The word [*qanítha*] . . . is commonly used in the sense of to *get by purchase*, or *buy* . . . and this no doubt is its meaning here, the idea being that Jehovah has 'redeemed' Israel (*v.* 13, vi.6), like a slave, from servitude. . . ." So Ibn Ezra, Luzzatto, Ehrlich, Cassuto. See Isa. 11.11. Trad., "gotten."

21. **He has triumphed gloriously.** See at v. 1 above.

25. **a piece of wood.** Trad. "a tree" for *eṣ* is mechanical; see at Gen. 40.19 above.

a fixed rule. Treating *ḥoq u-mishpaṭ* as hendiadys, see Introduction, §c. Trad., "a statute and an ordinance."

Chapter 16

4. **instructions.** So Driver: "properly, my direction. . . ." See Introduction, §c, as against Trad. "law" for *tora*.

5. **apportion.** For this force of *hekhin,* cf. Deut. 19.3; Jos. 3.17. Will replace "prepare" in projected version.

7. **Presence.** Cf. Ehrlich (*Randglossen*). An attempt at reproducing the nuance of the *qavod* of God, as against Trad. "glory." The same nuance is apparent, e.g., in Exod. 24.17; 40.35; Ezek. 1.28; chaps. 9 and 10. Thus Luzzatto has noted (against Ibn Ezra) that the *qavod* here is not the same as the *qavod* in the cloud in v. 10, and that (following Rashi, Rashbam, Ramban, and Abravanel; cf. Driver) the *qavod* here will manifest itself by the miraculous gift of manna.

12. **I the Lord am your God.** Cf. Luzzatto (*ki ani YHWH mashgiaḥ alekhem*). Trad. "I am the Lord your God" is mechanical, and really says nothing. See at 6.8 above.

13. **a fall of dew.** (Also v. 14.) Understanding *shikhvath-ha-ṭal* (the expression occurs only here in the Bible) as from *shakav,* "to pour out"; see Orlinsky, "The Hebrew Root *shakab,*" *Journal of Biblical Literature,* 63 (1944); pp. 36–39 on *shikhvath-*. Trad. "layer" derives, erroneously, from root *shakab,* "to lie."

20. maggots. (Also v. 24.) Trad. "worms," on which see W. S. McCullough, *Interpreter's Dictionary of the Bible,* IV, 878.

22. food. As recognized long ago (see Saadia), *léḥem* has the meaning "food" as well as (Trad.) "bread." See 18.12 below.

23. a day of rest. Cf. Driver—as against Trad. "a solemn rest"—"a *cessation* or *resting;* Heb. *shabbathon* . . . there is nothing in the word to suggest the idea of 'solemn.' . . ." See also 31.15 below.

29. Mark. See Luzzatto, as against Trad. "See" for interjectional (not imperative) *re'u.*

34. Pact. Understanding *eduth* as synonymous with *berith,* "covenant," and as representing "P's standing expression for the Decalogue" (Driver); thus *ushne luḥoth ha-eduth be-yado* in Exod. 32.15 is the equivalent of *ushne luḥoth ha-berith al shte yaday* in Deut. 9.15.

Chapter 17

2. (The people) quarreled (with Moses). See Introduction, §c. Trad., "strove."

14. document. Trad. "book" is anachronistic; *séfer* may denote simply a "letter" (I Ki. 21.8). As for the definite article in *ba-séfer,* it has frequently been noted, e.g., by Driver that —as against Trad. "the (book)"—"the Hebrew always writes in *the* book . . . an object being conceived as definite in Heb. not only because it is already known or has been mentioned before, but also because it is taken for a particular purpose, and so made definite in the speaker's or writer's mind. See numerous examples in. . . ." Or see Luzzatto.

:(I will utterly blot out). The particle *ki* is not causal—Trad. "for"—but serves merely to introduce the statement that follows; it is thus the equivalent of our "i.e." or "namely"—here indicated by the colon. See Introduction, §c.

Chapter 18

2. **(after she had been) sent home.** The technical term (*aḥar*) *shilluḥéha* does not mean here "send away" (Trad.) but "send (to her father's) home." See Luzzatto at Exod. 4.23 (end).

4. **meaning.** On this force of *ki*—as against Trad. "for" —see at 17.14 above.

5. **Jethro . . . brought Moses' sons and wife to him.** To avoid the ambiguity inherent in Trad. "Jethro . . . came with his sons and his wife unto Moses" (Jethro's sons and wife?).

6. **sent word (. . . I . . . am coming).** So Mekilta (namely, by letter or by messenger), followed by Rashi, Rashbam, Ibn Ezra, Luzzatto, Malbim, Driver, etc. Trad. "said" creates—unnecessarily—an incongruity with "Moses went out to meet his father-in-law" in v. 7 immediately following.

12. **(to partake of the) meal.** As noted at 16.22 above, *léḥem* means "food, meal" as well as "bread" (in Arabic it means "meat"). Here it is the sacred meal that is associated with Jethro's offerings to God; see Luzzatto (on "before God"), Driver. In reproducing the Hebrew mechanically, Trad. "(to eat) bread" has inadvertently suppressed this religious custom.

14. **act**[d] ([d]*Lit. "sit" as magistrate; cf. v.* 13). See Ibn Ezra ("for the judge sits"), Luzzatto.

16. **dispute.** (So also v. 22.) See Sforno (*riv*), Luzzatto. Trad. "matter" misses the legal force of *davar*.

the laws and teachings of God. On the Hebrew

syntax and English idiom, as against Trad. "the statutes of God, and His laws," see Introduction, §c.

18. **(you cannot do it) alone.** In rendering *levaddékha* literally, "(thou art not able to perform it) thyself alone," Trad. has overlooked the fact that the suffix here is a purely Hebraic phenomenon—the unsuffixed form *levad* is not used ordinarily in this context—and is not required in English idiom: either "yourself" or "alone" suffices.

22. **judge.** (Also v. 26.) Earlier printings read "exercise authority over."

23. **unwearied.** An attempt to get at the nuance of *be-shalom* here. Earlier printings read "content." Trad. "in peace" is mechanical.

27. **bade . . . farewell.** As at Gen. 26.31. Trad. "let . . . depart" misses the idiom.

Chapter 19

1. **On the (third) new moon.** This interpretation of *ba-ḥódesh* (*ha-shelishi*) follows the Mekilta, Shabbat 86b, Rashi, Ibn Ezra (who refers to Moses Ha-Cohen), and such modern scholars as Luzzatto and Cassuto; on *ḥódesh* with the meaning "new moon" elsewhere in the Bible, see Brown-Driver-Briggs, *Hebrew Lexicon,* p. 294b, §1 (where such passages as I Sam. 20.4, 18; and Isa. 1.14 are cited). It may be noted that when Driver, e.g., comments on *ba-yom ha-ze* ("on that very day") that "The day of the month must in some way have fallen out in the early part of the verse," the day of the month is actually provided by *ba-ḥódesh.*

5. **My treasured possession.** See Luzzatto. For a recent discussion of *segulla,* see M. Greenberg, *Journal of the American Oriental Society,* 71 (1951), 172–4.

9. **ever after.** "Thereafter" in earlier printings did not bring out sufficiently the "forever" element in *le-olam.*

10. **and warn them to stay pure.** (Also v. 14.) Cf. Rashi (followed by Ehrlich, *Randglossen*): "*we-qiddashtam* means 'and prepare them' . . . that they make themselves ready today and tomorrow"; or Driver—as against Trad. "sanctify them" —"viz. by enjoining ablutions and abstention from anything that would render 'unclean.' . . ."

19. **in thunder.** Understanding *qol* here exactly as in v. 16 (Trad. "thunders"); cf. Driver. Trad., "by a voice."

Chapter 20

2. **I the Lord am your God who,** etc. So Luzzatto (following Weisel and followed by Ehrlich), construing *anokhi YHWH* as the subject and *elohékha,* etc. as the predicate.

5. **impassioned (God).** Understanding *qanna* in its primary sense of "be zealous, emotionally involved, impassioned"; cf. Luzzatto's discussion. Trad., "jealous."

reject. On this nuance of *sane'*—as against Trad. "hate"—see at Gen. 26.27; 29.31; and Introduction, §c.

7. **(You shall not)** [b-]**swear falsely by**[-b] **(the name of the Lord)** ([b-b]*Others "take in vain")*. Jewish tradition has tended to interpret *tissa . . . la-shaw . . . yissa . . . la-shaw* as denoting perjury ("swear falsely") rather than impropriety or profanity (Trad., "utter in vain"), though at times the latter merged into the former, e.g., when the Mekilta distinguishes between the use of the name of God when swearing that something known to be made of wood is made of wood and when swearing that something known to be made of stone is made of gold; so apparently also the Targum, and see the discussions in Rashi, Ibn Ezra, Sforno, and Luzzatto. In support of "swear falsely," it has been noted that *shaw* and *shéqer* are interchanged in the commandment dealing with the false witness (*ed shéqer* in Exod. 20.13, *ed shaw* in Deut. 5.17) and that in Ps. 24.4 *nasa la-shaw* is associated with *nishba le-mirma* ("swear deceitfully"). On the other hand, "swear falsely" is close enough to "bear false witness" (v. 13) to make one wonder why the former should be included separately as one of the Ten Commandments. Further, if "swear falsely" were intended, surely clear terms such as *nishba* and *shéqer*—rather than *nasa* and *shaw*, whose association with "swear; oath" is less than certain—would have been employed; in this connection, *nasa la-shaw* in Ps. 24.4 may be merely parallel to, rather than synonymous with, *nishba le-mirma.* The biblical expression for "swear falsely" is usually *nishba la-shéqer* (Lev. 19.12; Jer. 5.2; 7.9; Zech. 5.4; Mal. 3.5); on the other hand, *nasa* or *dabber la-shaw* usually denotes insincerity rather than perjury (Lev. 23.1; Ps. 12.2; 16.4; 41.7). Ehrlich's analysis of our phrase is instructive: whereas in his *Mikra* he argued (citing, e.g., the Mekilta at 13.19 and Berakoth, bottom of 33a) that it indicated that one should not utter the name of God unnecessarily, in his *Randglossen* he began his long discussion with the confession, "What is forbidden here is not altogether clear." Perhaps the problem should be left here with that.

10. **settlements.** *Shá'ar,* lit. (and Trad.) "gate," frequently denotes the town itself; see Driver, and Introduction, §c.

15. **witnessed.** This term goes well with both "thunder" and "flashes of fire," as against Trad. "perceived." Cf. "paid heed to" (for *shama,* Trad. "heard") your suffering" in Gen. 16.11.

flashes of light. Will replace "lightning" in projected version, to distinguish *lappidim* from *beraqim* in 19.16. Trad. "lightnings" for both terms.

they fell back (and stood at a distance). Understanding *núa* to mean here "wander," as in Num. 32.13 and Amos 8.12. Trad. "they trembled (and stood afar off)" indicates that the people, fearful of what they were witnessing, remained at a distance from the beginning (so, e.g., Luzzatto); this does not seem to jibe with 19.17, 21, 23–24.

19. **from the very heavens.** The use of "very" is to reflect something of the emphatic position of *ki min-hashamáyim* (see Driver, ". . . these are the emphatic words in the sentence"): it is from the heavens that I spoke to you.

21. **sacrifices of well-being.** Although *shelamim* is an ancient term—it is found, e.g., in Canaanite (Ugaritic) texts of the 15th century B.C.E.—its meaning is uncertain. As noted, e.g., by Driver, the Septuagint rendered our term mostly by "a welfare (or safety) sacrifice," and Snaith (*Leviticus and Numbers,* 1967, pp. 37–38, at Lev. 3.1) has followed this with ". . . good health, prosperity, and well-being, and this is not far from the true meaning. . . ." Moreover, the term "sacrifice of well-being" accords well with the nature of this sacrifice as it is known from the Bible itself. Trad. "peace-offering" derives from the Septuagint rendering of our word (*shalom,* "peace") in the books of Samuel and Kings, by way of the Vulgate rendering, *pacificorum.*

22. **And.** Earlier printings read "But"; however, it was subsequently felt that no real contrast was intended here.

Chapter 21

1. **rules.** Earlier printings read "norms" for *mishpaṭim*; this was subsequently given up because it is not a legal term. Trad. "ordinances," like "regulations, judgments," and the like, hardly conveys the sense of *mishpaṭim,* namely, legal precedents, judicial decisions (see Driver); and such terms as "statutes" and "laws" were preempted for *ḥuqqim* and *tora.*

2. **acquire.** Trad. "buy" for *qana* does not reflect adequately the manner of acquiring or paying for slaves, property, goods, etc., in the economy of ancient Israel before coinage came to be introduced (beginning about 500 B.C.E.); see the long article on "Money" by H. Hamburger in *Interpreter's Dictionary of the Bible,* III, pp. 423–435.

go free. (Also vv. 5, 11.) Earlier printings read "be

freed." However, not only does "go free" reflect the active force of *yeṣe* but "be freed" could lead the reader to believe that the owner had to take the initiative in the liberation of the Hebrew slave; so far as the Hebrew text is concerned, the Hebrew slave simply walked out a free man at the end of six years of service. (Later on, Driver has noted, "The philanthropic legislator of Deuteronomy [xv. 13f.] enjoins the master to bestow a handsome present upon his slave when he thus leaves him.") Trad. "go out free" overtranslates; Heb. *yaṣa* is used here as a technical term in the sense of "go free (from slavery)."

3. **single.** In contrast to *bá'al ishsha* ("married"). Trad. "by himself" does not necessarily indicate bachelorhood.

7. **be freed.** Projected version will read "go free"; see end of v. 2 above.

8. **designated (her for himself).** (Also v. 9.) Cf. Driver, ". . . *ya'ad* does not mean to 'espouse': to 'designate' a woman *for* any one may indeed be equivalent to 'to espouse,' but that does not justify 'designate,' used absolutely, being rendered 'espouse.' "

10. **from this one.** I.e., the "daughter" of vv. 7–9 (see Rashi). Trad. "her (food)" can readily be misunderstood to denote the other wife ("another") mentioned immediately preceding in our verse.

14. **and kills him.** I.e., if the planned murder actually succeeds; see Mekilta, Rashi, Ibn Ezra, Driver ("the protection of the altar is not to be extended to the wilful murderer . . ."). Trad. "to slay him" could indicate, erroneously, that the death penalty is imposed even if the planned murder fails.

16. **still holding him.** On this idiomatic use of *be-yad*, see Introduction, §c.

17. **insults.** Earlier readings read "repudiates," on the ground that, in Mesopotamia, repudiation of a parent by a son was punishable by death; however, it is not certain that the text here (*meqallel*) denotes repudiation—or that biblical

law must conform to Mesopotamian law. On "insult," and the like, for *qallel*—as against Trad. "curse"—see Ehrlich, Cassuto.

19. **(he must pay for . . .) his cure.** So Targum, followed by Rashi and Luzzatto. Trad. "and shall cause him to be thoroughly healed" hardly represents the force of (*werappo*) *yerappe*; on "thoroughly" for the infinitive absolute in this construction (*rappo*), see Introduction, §c.

22. **and a miscarriage results.** Trad. "so that her fruit depart" is mechanical.

(but no) other damage (ensues). (Also v. 23.) See Driver, "but no (other) mischief happen"; for "other," see at Gen. 3.2, and Introduction, §c. Trad., "and yet no harm follow."

(the payment to be based) on reckoning. An attempt to get at the meaning of elusive *biflilim*. In rejecting Trad. "as the judges determine," Ehrlich (*Mikra*) has noted that the Hebrew would have had to read the definite article (*ba-pelilim*). Driver has observed that *pelilim* in the sense of "judges, arbitrators" is "rare and poetical." See also Gen. 48.11; Deut. 32.31.

23. **the penalty shall be.** Trad. "thou shalt give" fails to bring out the force of *we-nathata* here as "impose, exact," or the like; cf. Trad. "and he shall pay" for *we-nathan* in v. 22 preceding.

26. **on account of (his eye).** Trad. "for (his eye's) sake" hardly does justice to the force of *taḥath ('eno)*.

27. **(If he) knocks out.** On Trad. "smites out" see Introduction, §c.

28. **(gores . . .) to death.** In being literal rather than idiomatic, Trad. has had to translate *wa-meth*—lit., "so that he dies"—ungrammatically: "And if an ox gore a man or a woman, that they die."

31. **a minor, male or female.** Cf. Mekilta (*élu ha-qeṭanim*, "these are the minors"), followed by Luzzatto. Trad.

"a son, or . . . a daughter"—who may be adults!—does not bring out the force of *ben . . . bath* as a technical term for "a minor."

Chapter 22

1. **the (thief).** Trad. "a (thief)" leaves indefinite what is clearly definite: *ha-gannav* refers back to *ki-yignov ish* in v. 37 preceding (and that is why the paragraph begins with 21.37 rather than with 22.1; see Introduction, §c), exactly as *ha-mavir* refers back to *ki yaver-ish* (22.4–5) and as *ha-shor* to *ki yiggaḥ shor* (21.28–29). Note also that if our paragraph were to begin with v. 1, the Hebrew would read not *ha-gannav* (for to what *gannav* would the definite article apply, if not to the one in v. 37 preceding?) but *we-khi yignov ish*; cf. *ish* in 22.4, 6, 9, 13, 15 (as well as in 21.7, 14, 20, 26, 32); *anashim* in 21.18, 22; and *shor* in 21.28, 35.

tunneling[a] ([a]*I.e. under a wall for housebreaking*). So Luzzatto, Driver, ("*digging through* . . . Still the usual method of housebreaking in Syria . . ."). Trad. "breaking in" is too vague.

there is no bloodguilt in his case. Scholars are divided between the housebreaker and the killer as the antecedent of (*en*) *lo* (*damim*); see the discussion in Luzzatto. Trad., "there shall be no bloodguiltiness for him."

4. **impairment**[c]. See the discussion by Luzzatto (who cites the Mekilta; Baba Kama, 6b center; and Rashbam), followed by Ehrlich.

5. **or growing grain.** Understanding all three terms, *gadish . . . ha-qama . . . ha-sade,* to denote grain in various stages. Ehrlich would distinguish between the first term (without the definite article) and the last two (that have the definite article).

7. **depose.** Trad. "come near" fails to bring out the

legal connotation of *we-niqrav* (*el-ha-elohim*) *im-lo;* cf. Mekilta ("for an oath"), followed by Rashi, Ibn Ezra, Ramban, Malbim (keeping in mind *shevuath . . . im-lo shalaḥ yado* in v. 10), Cassuto. Luzzatto (followed by Ehrlich), however, rejects the element of "swear, oath" because in such contexts *im-lo* would indicate "that he *did* lay hand on . . ."; "that he did *not* . . ." would be expressed by *im* alone. Yet as the Malbim has observed, the phrase *im-lo shalaḥ yado* is not the one employed by the "defendant"; and v. 10 is not readily disposed of.

the other's (property). Projected version; replaces (Trad.) "his neighbor's," which is mechanical.

8. **declares guilty.** Trad. "condemn" does not convey the technical, legal aspect of *yarshi'un*; see Introduction, §c.

10. **and no restitution shall be made.** By retaining the active voice of *we-lo yeshallem,* Trad. "(and the owner thereof shall accept it,) and he shall not make restitution" has made it possible for the reader to believe that the antecedent of "he" is "the owner."

13. **borrows [an animal].** So already, in effect, Mekilta and Baba Meṣia 95a, followed, e.g., by Rashi, Rashbam, Malbim (at v. 14), Driver. Trad. "(And if a man) borrow aught" is unnecessarily vague.

14. **(but if) it was hired.** Trad. "(if) it be a hireling" presupposes a person rather than an animal, running counter to vv. 11–14a; see Driver's comment.

he is entitled to the hire. (Earlier printings read "he is still entitled to the hiring fee.") Understanding *ba biskharo* in accord with Mekilta (see ed. Lauterbach, III, pp. 128–9 and n. 10), Rashi, Malbim, Ehrlich, among others. Another common interpretation is that of Trad. "he loseth his hire"; see the discussion in Luzzatto.

15. **for whom the bride price has not been paid.** Earlier printings read "who has not been spoken for." Trad. "that is not betrothed" for *orása* is misleading, in that it is

not betrothal (or engagement) that was involved; this custom is not known in ancient Israel. The prospective bridegroom and the girl's father agreed upon a price (namely, the *móhar*, "bride price"), and when this was paid, the girl became legally the groom's wife. The English language has no adequate term for this biblical institution (which is dealt with in Deut. 20.7; 22.23, 25, 27; 28.30).

bride price. As against Trad. "dowry" for *móhar*, see preceding note, Driver's comment ("marriage-price"), and at Gen. 34.1.

17. tolerate[g]. See Luzzatto (followed by Ehrlich) as against Trad. "suffer . . . to live."

19. proscribed. *Ḥérem* is a technical term denoting "set apart for God, devoted exclusively to sacred use"; thus the object or person that is *ḥérem*, being wholly God's, may not be spared or (as in the case of certain vessels, see Josh. 6.17–25) be enjoyed by anyone other than God or His priests. An exact English term for *ḥérem* and its sundry forms is lacking. Trad. "utterly destroyed" (cf. "accursed thing" in Deut. 7.26) is inadequate; see Driver's comment in favor of "devoted, devoted thing."

24. among you. Projected version; replaces "in your power," on the assumption that *immakh* in this context denoted "to be, remain with you" (namely, with the creditor), i.e., to be, remain under the creditor's authority (see at Lev. 25.35).

27. revile. So Trad., on which see Driver. Earlier printings read "offend."

28. [i-]**. . . the skimming of the first yield of your vats**[-i]**.** Understanding *mele'athkha we-dim'akha* as hendiadys (see Introduction, §c). Several scholars (e.g., Rashi, Ehrlich [*Mikra*]) admit that the meaning of the Hebrew phrase eludes them; cf. our note: *Meaning of Heb uncertain.* On Trad. "of the fulness of thy harvest, and of the outflow of thy presses" see Luzzatto and Driver.

Chapter 23

2. **mighty.** Understanding *rabbim* here as the opposite of *dal,* "a poor man," in v. 3. On Trad. "multitude," in the sense of majority, see Rashi, Luzzatto.

5. **raising . . . raise.** Understanding *azov ta'azov immo* in accordance with the parallel in Deut. 22.4 *haqem taqim immo* ("you must help him raise it"), cited in Mekilta; and cf. Deut. 32.36 (*aṣur we-azuv*) and Neh. 3.8, 34, cited by Rashi.

7. **acquit the wrongdoer.** Trad. "justify the wicked" has failed to reproduce the legal idiom in *aṣdiq rasha.* See Introduction, §c.

7–8. **him who is innocent and in the right . . . those who are in the right.** Projected version; to bring out the technical, legal force of *ṣaddiq(im),* which "the innocent and the righteous . . . the just" fails to do.

11. **the wild beasts.** (Also v. 29.) Trad. "beast of the field" is mechanical. See Gen. 3.14 and Introduction, §c.

12. **cease from labor.** Cf. Driver ("desist from work"), and see Gen. 2.2. Trad., "rest."

your bondman. Understanding the use of *ben* in *ben-amathekha* as merely denoting the species or category; Driver, ". . . intended, it must be supposed, to represent slaves in general. . . ." Trad. (cf. Mekilta, Rashi, Luzzatto) literally: "the son of thy handmaid."

16. **the results of your work.** Trad. "your labours" overlooks the fact that such words as our *ma'asékha* mean both "your work" and "the results, gain from your work" (cf. Driver, ". . . here of the product of the year's work in agriculture"); similarly, *yagía,* "toil" and "product"; *amal,* "toil" and "gain"; and *pó'al,* "work" and "wages of work."

17. **the Sovereign, the Lord.** Trad. "the LORD GOD" for *ha-adon YHWH* is misleading, in that "GOD" hardly

represents *YHWH. Ha-adon,* as noted by Driver and others, represents the Master, the "Sovereign of the land." See Introduction, §c.

18. **(with) anything leavened.** Trad. "leavened bread" restricts the meaning of *ḥameṣ* here unnecessarily; even Mekilta and the commentators, who connect our verse with v. 15 (*ḥag ha-maṣṣoth,* Feast of Unleavened Bread), think in terms of everything unleavened, not merely bread, that must be removed from the premises before the passover sacrifice may be offered. In rejecting any connection with v. 15, Ehrlich (*Mikra,* but not in *Randglossen*) notes that nowhere does *zébaḥ* by itself denote the passover offering.

20. **to guard you on the way.** Trad. "to keep you by the way" is hardly clear, and is even misleading.

23. **When (My angel goes before you . . .), and I annihilate them, [24]you shall not (bow down . . .).** Trad. "For . . . ; and I will cut them off. [24]Thou shalt not . . ." does not do justice to the construction and intent of vv. 23 and 24. On the literary history of vv. 23–25a, see Driver.

Amorites . . . Hittites, etc. As against Trad. "Amorite . . . Hittite," etc., see at 3.8 and 10.2 above, and Introduction, §c.

Chapter 24

1. **You and Aaron, Nadab and Abihu.** (Also v. 9.) Trad. "thou, and Aaron, Nadab, and Abihu" has failed to note that the Hebrew construction is one of two pairs: *atta we-aharon nadav* (not *we-nadav*!) *wa-avihu.* See Driver at v. 9; also Num. 3.2.

2. **(and the people) shall not even come up (with him).** The use of "even" (as against earlier printings which read "shall not come up with him at all") is to bring out more clearly the emphatic position and force of *we-ha-am* (*lo* *ya'ale immo*), namely, whereas Aaron, his two sons, and the elders were to accompany Moses and "come up (*ale*) to the Lord" (v. 1), then remain at a distance while Moses alone approached God (v. 2), the people at large were not even to come up with Moses in the first place. (See Driver, comments on "they" and "neither.") Trad. "neither shall the people go up with him" fails to bring out this sequence.

4. **Early (in the morning).** As against Trad. "rose up early" for *wa-yashkem,* see at Gen. 19.2.

5. **designated.** Earlier printings read "delegated." Cf. Saadia. Trad. "sent" has little meaning here; they went nowhere.

offerings of well-being. See at 20.21 above.

6. **one part (. . . the other part).** See Ibn Ezra at 26.12, followed by Ehrlich. Trad. "half (. . . half)" restricts the meaning of *ḥaṣi* unnecessarily; see Jud. 9.43, where Abimelech divided his troops—*wa-yeḥeṣem*—into three columns.

7. **record (of the covenant).** As against Trad. "book," see at 17.14 above.

14. **he had said.** Only the pluperfect tense fits the context, as against Trad. "he said." See Rashi, Sforno, Ehrlich (*Randglossen*), Driver ("before going up into the mount").

16. **Presence.** See at 16.7 above.

Chapter 25

2. **the Israelite people.** So when God is the speaker; otherwise, "the Israelites."

accept. (Also v. 3.) So Cassuto. Trad., "take."

gifts . . . gifts. (Also v. 3.) Cf. Driver's comment in favor of "contributions," as against Trad. "offering." On the failure of Trad. to recognize the singular collective in *teruma,* see Introduction, §c.

(gifts) for Me. Trad. "My (offering)" fails to bring

out the objective genitive in *(eth-teruma)thi,* "for Me," as distinct from the subjective ("My").

3. **copper.** As against Trad. "brass," see at Gen. 4.22.

4. **crimson (yarns).** Trad., "scarlet." There is some uncertainty about the exact color denoted by *toláʿath shani,* whether it is a brilliant red (scarlet) or a deep red of various hues (crimson); see C. L. Wickwire's articles in *IDB*: "Crimson" in vol. I, p. 744; "Scarlet" in IV, pp. 233–234.

yarns. As noted, e.g., by Driver, we are dealing here with "yarn of stuff so coloured by means of a dye. . . ." Colored yarns were twisted together.

5. **tanned.** In all probability, "the skins were reddened as a result of the tanning process employed" (S. A. Cartledge, article "Tanner, Tanning," *IDB*, IV, p. 516), whence Septuagint (and Trad.) "dyed red"; cf. also "Leather" (by W. S. McCullough), *IDB*, III, p. 104.

dolphin skins. A reasonable guess, based on Arabic *tuḥas,* the cognate of Heb. *táḥash,* "which makes it probable" —as put by Driver—"that the DUGONG . . . is meant, an animal in general appearance not unlike a dolphin, though with a larger and blunter nose . . . species of which are common in the Red Sea . . ."; followed, e.g., by Cassuto. Trad., "sealskins." On "goatskin" for *táḥash,* see W. S. McCullough, *IDB*, II, 407.

7. **and other stones for setting,** etc. Understanding the phrase *avne shóham we-avne millu'im* to indicate that the *shóham* stones were to be used for setting along with other stones; cf. 28.9 ff. (the two *shóham* stones for the ephod) and 28.17 ff. (the twelve stones, including the *shóham* in v. 20, for the breastpiece), and see the discussion in Ramban (in disagreement with Rashi) and Cassuto. Trad. "onyx stones, and stones to be set" is literal and unclear.

9. **Exactly (as I show you).** Idiomatic for *kekhol,* literally (and Trad.) "According to all."

furnishings. As noted by Driver, *kelim* includes

"here all articles, vessels, utensils, &c., belonging to the sanctuary." Trad., "furniture."

12. **(to be attached) to (its four feet).** (Also v. 26.) Trad. "(and put them) in (the four feet thereof)" is incorrect for (*we-nathata*) *al*; cf. Driver, "fasten them *on to*."

16. **[the tablets of] the Pact.** Cf. Rashbam (the tablets that were the *eduth* and the *berith* between God and Israel . . .) and Ibn Ezra (who cites, *inter alia,* I Ki. 8.9). Trad., "the testimony."

21. **after depositing.** See Rashi, Ibn Ezra, Ramban. Trad., "and . . . thou shalt put."

27. **as holders (for poles).** Trad. "for places (for the staves)" is not clear.

29. **bowls, ladles, jars, and jugs.** Trad., "dishes . . . pans . . . jars . . . bowls." The exact meaning of many biblical terms for pottery or metal vessels is not yet known; see J. L. Kelso, *The Ceramic Vocabulary of the Old Testament* (*Supplementary Studies,* Nos. 5–6, *Bulletin of the American Schools of Oriental Research,* [1948]); also his articles on "Pottery" and "Vessels" in *IDB,* respectively in vols. III (pp. 846–853) and IV (p. 783).

with which to offer libations. See Rashbam, Driver ("for making the libations with"), Cassuto. Trad. "wherewith to pour out" is literal and unclear.

31. **lampstand.** Trad. "candlestick"—candles were not used in biblical times—hardly gives a true picture of this *menorah*; see L. E. Toombs, "Lampstand," *IDB,* III, 64–66.

its base and its shaft, its cups, (calyxes, and petals shall be of one piece). Trad. "(. . . be made), even its base, and its shaft; its cups," etc., has construed the sentence incorrectly, putting the semicolon after "shaft" instead of after "be made"; the *entire* lampstand is to be made of hammered work and of one piece. See Rashi, Rashbam.

37. **on its front side.** So Rashbam, Luzzatto, Driver.

Trad. "(to give light) over against it" leaves the reader in the dark as to the meaning of (*we-he'ir*) *al-éver panéha.*

38. fire pans. See the article on "Firepan" by J. L. Mihelic in *IDB,* II, 270; also "Snuffers"—cf. Trad. "snuff-dishes"—in IV, 394. Driver comments: "*snuffdishes* . . . The same word (*maḥtothéha*; lit., [*fire-*] *catcher*) is also used for what we should denote by the separate terms *fire-pan* . . . and *censer*. . . ." But the exact identification of these vessels is not easy (cf. at v. 29 above).

Chapter 26

1. As for the tabernacle. Trad. "Moreover (thou shalt make) the tabernacle" hardly brings out the emphatic position of *we-eth-ha-mishkan* at the beginning of the verse. As to note *a,* see Rashbam, Driver.

strips of cloth. In the verses following, "cloth" alone. Trad. "curtains" hardly indicates any longer this meaning of *yerioth.*

with a design (of cherubim worked into them). (Also v. 31; 28.6) Understanding (*keruvim*) *ma'aseh ḥoshev* (*ta'aseh otham*) to mean that the various yarns should be woven together so that the figure of cherubim emerges; so essentially Rashi, Driver, Cassuto. Similarly *ma'aseh roqem* in 27.16 and 28.39, and *ma'aseh oreg* in 28.32; 39.22, 27. See Driver's comment on these terms (pp. 280–281). Trad., "(with cherubim) the work of the skilful workman."

12–13. An attempt to reproduce the layout of the clothes; cf. Rashbam, Cassuto, and see Driver's comment.

14. tanned (ram skins) . . . dolphin skins. See at 25.5 above.

17. parallel to each other. Understanding *meshullavoth* as connected with *shelav,* "ladder rung." So Septuagint, Targum, Baraita di-Meleket ha-Mishkan, Saadia, Rashi,

Rashbam, Cassuto. Driver, on the other hand, likewise beginning with "post-Biblical *sheliba,* the 'rung' of a ladder," reaches the meaning *"joined by a cross-piece . . . ,"* and see his references to Skinner and especially Kennedy. Earlier printings read "braced together." The note: *"Meaning of Heb* meshullaboth *uncertain,"* is much in order. Trad. "joined one to another."

18. **on the south[c] side** ([c]*Heb uses two terms for "south"*). So Targum, Luzzatto, Cassuto. Trad. "for the south side southward" is hardly clear.

24. **They shall match.** Cf. Luzzatto, Driver ("And they shall be twinned"; see his discussion), Cassuto. Trad., "And they shall be doubled."

25. **under each of the other planks.** Trad. "under another board" leaves the Hebrew idiom unnecessarily vague.

31. **design,** etc. See at v. 1 above.

Chapter 27

3. **pails . . . scrapers, basins,** etc. On the difficulty of exact identification, see at 25.29 above.

—make all its utensils. On *le-khol* as a summing up, see at 14.28 above, and Introduction, §c.

7. **so that (the poles) remain.** Trad. "and the . . . shall be" is more literal than meaningful.

8. **Make it hollow, of boards.** Trad. "Hollow with planks shalt thou make it" is hardly clear.

9. **a hundred cubits of hangings . . . for the length (of the enclosure) on that side.** In rendering literally, Trad. "there shall be hangings . . . a hundred cubits long for one side" obscures unnecessarily the intent and idiom of the Hebrew.

14. **on the one flank.** In Trad. "for the one side [of the gate]," the added phrase is less than helpful; it is hardly

the side of the gate that is involved here. See Rashbam, Rashi (on v. 13).

16. **done in embroidery.** See at 26.1 above.

17. **All the posts round the enclosure.** In reproducing the Hebrew order of (*kol-ammude he-ḥaṣer*) *saviv* mechanically, Trad. "(All the pillars of the court) round about" has obscured the passage.

(All the posts . . .) shall be banded with silver and their hooks shall be of silver; their sockets shall be of copper. Trad. has disregarded the Hebrew accents (. . . *wawehem kásef we-adnehem neḥósheth*) and created an un-English sentence: "(All the pillars of the court round about) shall be filleted with silver; their hooks of silver, and their sockets of brass."

18. **[with hangings] of fine twisted linen.** Cf. Rashi, Cassuto.

19. **of the Tabernacle**[b] ([b]*I.e. of the Tabernacle enclosure* . . .). Cf. Rashi. On *le-khol* as a summing up, see at v. 3.

20. **clear oil of beaten olives for lighting.** Trad. "pure olive oil beaten for light" for *shémen záyith zakh kathith la-ma'or* is hardly clear; it is the olives, not the olive oil, that are beaten.

for kindling lamps regularly. See Ibn Ezra, Ramban, Luzzatto, Cassuto. Earlier printings read "to maintain lights regularly." Trad. "to cause a lamp to burn continually," indicating something of a Ner Tamid (a perpetual lamp), is hardly correct; note "from evening to morning" in v. 21 following, and cf. Driver's comment on "not *continuously* . . . but *regularly*, as a standing practice. . . ." See also Lev. 24.2.

21. **[the Ark of] the Pact.** See at 25.16 above; projected reading.

[to burn]. Trad. "to burn" fails to inform the reader that there is no word for this phrase in Hebrew.

Chapter 28

1. **(to serve Me) as priests.** (Also v. 21.) Cf. Driver, "*be* (or *act as*) *priest.*" Trad. "(that they may minister unto Me) in the priest's office" can be misleading.

3. **skillful.** Trad. "wise-hearted," while literal, hardly reproduces the force of *ḥakhme-lev.* Cf. Driver, "*wise* . . . *wisdom* of artistic cleverness or skill."

for consecrating him. Trad. "to sanctify him" would mean something else nowadays; thus Driver explains "sanctify" here to the effect that "the investiture is a part of the consecration, xxix. 5ff." Cf. 29.27 below.

4. **a fringed (tunic).** See at v. 39 below.

5. **they, therefore, (shall receive).** Trad. "And they (shall take)" has failed to reproduce the significance of the initial (emphatic) position of *we-hem.* On "receive," as against "take," see at 25.2 above.

6. **worked into designs.** (Also v. 15.) As against Trad. "the work of the skilful workman," see at 26.1 above.

7. **they shall be attached at its two ends.** Cf. Rashbam, Cassuto, Trad. "(It shall have two shoulderpieces joined to the two ends thereof); that it may be joined together" is literal, but unclear.

8. **decorated band.** (Also v. 27.) Trad. "skillfully woven band (with which to gird it on)" is too much for *ḥéshev* and hardly does justice to it. The point is that the band (*afuda*) had a design woven into it (*ḥéshev*) rather than that it was skillfully woven; cf. Driver ("the band . . . perhaps of a different pattern . . .").

26. **at its inner edge, which faces the ephod.** Cf. Driver, ". . . on the *inner* side, towards the ephod . . ."). Trad. "upon the edge thereof, which is toward the side of the ephod inward," being literal, is unclear.

28. **(so that the breastpiece) rests.** Cf. Ehrlich (*Rand-*

glossen), Cassuto. Trad. "(that it may) be" is hardly adequate. Similarly Trad. "be" in v. 37 below.
35. Aaron shall wear it while officiating. Trad. "And it shall be upon Aaron to minister" is literal and unclear.
37. remain. On Trad. "be" see at v. 28 above.

Chapter 29

1. **(a young) bull of the herd.** Trad. "(one young) bullock," denoting as it now does "a castrated bull," is no longer correct.
2. **choice . . . flour.** (Also v. 40.) As against Trad. "fine flour," see at Gen. 18.6.
3. **(and) present (them).** Trad. "bring" is inadequate for *we-hiqravta;* cf. Driver at 28.1 on "bring near" in "the special, sacred sense of *present,* or, of a sacrifice, *offer.* . . ."
9. **and wind turbans upon them.** Brought forward in the verse so as to apply to Aaron's sons alone; Aaron did not wear a turban (cf. Driver, ". . . 'Aaron' had no 'cap' "). In reproducing the Hebrew order, Trad. has placed a *migba'a* ("turban") upon Aaron's *miṣnéfeth* ("*headdress*"). It may further be noted that the *avneṭ* ("sash") is not mentioned previously (e.g., in vv. 5–6) in connection with Aaron. Since the phrase "Aaron and his sons" is lacking in the Septuagint and makes for awkward Hebrew to boot, its deletion as a gloss solves all difficulties. See Driver's comment.
13. **the protuberance on (the liver).** (Also v. 22.) Cf. Driver (following G. F. Moore; and cf. N. H. Snaith, *Leviticus and Numbers,* at Lev. 3.4, p. 38), "*the* APPENDIX . . . *upon the liver* . . . what is called technically the *lobus caudatus,* or tail-shaped lobe, a small finger-shaped appendix—in the Mishnah, *Tamid* iv. 3, it is actually called 'the *finger* of the liver'—projecting from the liver close to the right kidney. . . ."

Trad. "the lobe above (the liver)" is misleading, in that this can denote the lobe that is above (and not part of) the liver.

and turn them into smoke. Cf. Driver, "*turn into sweet smoke*" (and see also his *Genesis,* at 19.28, p. 202). Trad. "and make them smoke" (cf. "And thou shalt make the whole ram smoke" in v. 18 below; and so regularly) is hardly clear.

16. **(and dash it) against all sides of the altar.** Cf. Driver, ". . . the blood was thrown against its four sides (*Zebāḥim* v. 4 ff.; Rashi on Lev. i.5). . . ." See also v. 20 below.

17. **(Cut up the ram into) sections.** Trad. "(And thou shalt cut the ram into) its pieces" has turned what is idiomatic in Hebrew (the suffix "its" in *linthaḥaw*) into unidiomatic English. Cf. Driver, "i.e. divide it by its joints."

22. **broad tail.** Cf. Driver, "What is meant is the large tail of certain species of sheep, still bred in Palestine, and elsewhere, which was esteemed a delicacy. The tail is often so heavy [according to Snaith (*Leviticus and Numbers,* at Lev. 3.9, p. 39), 'as many as ten pounds of fat'] as to need the support of a little cart. . . ."

23. **. Add.** Used for *we(-khikkar)* for clarity, since vv. 22–23 really constitute a single long sentence in the Hebrew. Trad., "; and."

(one) flat loaf (of bread). Trad. "loaf" gives the wrong impression of the shape; cf. Driver, "A circular flat 'cake' is meant, not what we should call a 'loaf.' "

24. **and offer them (as a wave offering).** (Also v. 26, and elsewhere.) Trad. "and thou shalt wave them" reproduces literally the cognate construction *wehenafta . . . tenufa,* which is idiomatic in Hebrew but not in English. Similarly, Trad. "the judges judged" in Ruth 1.1 for *shefoṭ ha-shofṭim* (idiomatically, "the chieftains ruled"); or see Num. 11.4.

25. **with (the burnt offering).** So Ehrlich (*Mikra,* at Lev. 3.5), who notes—against Rashi's (and Trad.) "upon"—

that there was only one "regular offering" (*olath tamid,* Exod. 29.42) but any number (hundreds or thousands) of *shelamim* offerings; were the latter to be offered only upon the regular morning offering and only when it was still burning upon the wood that was on the fire?

27. consecrate (the breast that was offered as a wave offering). Trad. "sanctify" is hardly appropriate here. See at 28.3 above.

28. —(and) those parts. Earlier printings read "These." Trad. "it" is ambiguous.

a gift. Understanding *teruma* in the sense of "contribution" (so, e.g., Driver), since Trad. "a heave-offering" would designate the "wave offering" (*tenufa*) of v. 27 along with the *teruma* as a "heave offering!" Cf. 25.2; and 35.24, "make gifts" (Trad. "set apart an offering") for *merim teruma.*

(their) sacrifices of well-being. As against Trad. "the sacrifices of (their) peace-offerings," see at 20.21 above.

29. shall pass on to (his sons). Trad. "shall be for" fails to reproduce the idiom in *yihyu le-,* "become the possession of, belong to."

33. These things shall be eaten only by those for whom expiation was made with them when they were ordained and consecrated. Earlier printings read—more literally but less clearly: "Only they for whose expiation those things were used, to ordain and consecrate them, shall eat them." Trad., "And they shall eat those things wherewith atonement was made, to consecrate and to sanctify them." See Driver on Old English *"atonement*] i.e. *at-one-ment, setting at one, reconciliation. . . .*"

36. a (bull as a sin offering) for expiation. So Rashi, Ehrlich (*Mikra*), Driver. Trad. "the (bullock of sin-offering), beside the other offerings of atonement" follows Ibn Ezra and Ramban.

37. shall become (most holy). Trad. "shall be" overlooks the inchoative force of the verb; cf. Driver, and see Introduction, §c.

38. **(two) yearling (lambs).** As against Trad. "(two lambs) of the first year," see at 12.5 above.

42. **For there I will meet with you,** etc. Having completed the instructions for Aaron and his sons and descendants with the words "at the entrance of the Tent of Meeting before the Lord," God breaks off to advise Moses that it is at the Tent of Meeting that He will meet with him ("For there . . ."); see Driver, Cassuto.

Chapter 30

4. **(on its two side walls) on opposite sides.** So Ehrlich (*Randglossen*), Cassuto; and this is what Ibn Ezra may have intended to convey.

8. **a regular (incense offering).** Trad. "a perpetual (incense)" does not convey the true force of *tamid*; cf. Driver, and see at 27.20 above.

13. **who is entered in the records.** (Also v. 14, and elsewhere.) Trad. "that passeth among them that are numbered" is literal and unclear.

19. **[in water drawn] from it.** Trad. "thereat" hardly conveys the meaning of *mi-mennu*.

23. **Next.** An attempt to bring out the emphatic force of *we-atta*; see Driver.

choice (spices). Trad. "chief" is a mechanical rendering of *rosh*; cf. Driver, "i.e. finest, best." Cf. "choice (first fruits . . .)" for *reshith* (*bikkure admathek*) in 23.19 above.

solidified (myrrh). Cf. Cassuto (but contrast Driver and J. Lewy [see reference on *deror* at Lev. 25.10]); see the article on "Myrrh" by J. C. Trever, *IDB*, III, 478–479. Trad. "flowing" would represent *mor over* (Cant. 5.13).

aromatic cane. Trad. "sweet calamus" is inadequate. See Driver; "Flora" by M. Zohary, *IDB,* II, §A7e, pp. 290 f.; "Sweet Cane" by J. C. Trever, *IDB,* IV, 468 f.

33. **kin.** (Also v. 38.) As against Trad. "people" for the plural form *ammaw* (as distinct from singular *ammo*), see Driver's pertinent comment here and at Gen. 25.8.

35. **refined.** So Targum, Rashi, Luzzatto, Cassuto; and cf. Driver (". . . Salt, from its purifying and antiseptic properties . . ."). Trad. (following, e.g., Ibn Ezra, Ramban), "seasoned with salt"—on which Driver comments ". . . a doubtful paraphrase; for the incense was not a food. . . ."

Chapter 31

2. **I have singled out (by name).** See Targum, Luzzatto, Ehrlich (*Randglossen*), Cassuto; cf. Driver, "specially chosen." Trad. "I have called (by name)" misses the idiom in *qaráthi* (*beshem*).

4. **to make designs.** See at 26.1 above.

10. **the service (vestments).** Following the Septuagint, Targum, and Syriac versions, and Rashi. Trad. "plaited"—against which see Ehrlich. But note Driver, ". . . the Heb. a peculiar expression, of most uncertain meaning. . . ."

13. **Nevertheless, you must (keep).** So Rashi (Even though I have charged you to command them concerning the work involved in the Tabernacle, do not think for a moment of setting aside the laws of Sabbath because of that), Rashbam, Ibn Ezra, Ramban, Sforno, Malbim (following Mekilta), Ehrlich (*Randglossen*), Cassuto. Trad. "Verily ye shall (keep)" has missed the force of *akh.*

15. **(a sabbath of) complete rest.** So Rashi (cf. Sforno), Driver ("*entire rest*"); see at 16.23 above.

17. **was refreshed.** Trad. "rested"—though correctly "refreshed" in 23.12 above. As noted by Driver, the Hebrew (*wa-yinnafash*) is "a strong anthropomorphism: elsewhere used only of men, xxiii. 12. . . ."

Chapter 32

1. **(gathered) against (Aaron).** See Brown-Driver-Briggs, *Hebrew Lexicon* (pp. 874–875), Ehrlich (*Randglossen*), Cassuto, with reference to *hiqhil al* in Num. 16.3; 17.7; 20.2. Trad., "unto."

for that man Moses, (who brought us . . .). (Also v. 23.) In rendering "for as for this Moses, the man (that brought us up . . .)," Trad. has—unnecessarily—run counter to the accents.

2. **Take off.** Cf. Rashi. Trad. "Break off" is too vigorous a rendering for *parequ*.

6. **sacrifices of well-being.** As against Trad. "peace-offerings" for *shelamim*, see at 20.21 above.

to dance. Cf. Luzzatto (with reference to II Sam. 6.21; Jer. 31.4), Driver ("to amuse themselves, e.g. by singing and dancing, *vv.* 18, 19 . . ."). See also Jud. 16.25. Earlier printings read (with Trad.) "to make merry"—a somewhat vague rendering.

11. **Let not.** (Also v. 12.) As against Trad. "why" for *lama*, see Introduction, §c.

12. **renounce.** (Also v. 14.) Trad. "repent" reproduces *niḥam* mechanically. Cf. Rashi: Devise another plan, to deal well with them, instead of the evil one which You planned for them. See further Introduction, §c.

32. **[well and good].** See Rashi, followed by Ramban, Ehrlich, Cassuto.

Chapter 33

6. remained stripped (. . . from Mount Horeb on). Hardly Trad. "stripped themselves" in context.

12. singled you out (by name). (Also v. 17.) Cf. Cassuto (with reference to Jer. 1.1; Amos 2.3); and see 31.2 above.

13. (that I may . . .) continue in Your favor. Trad. "find grace in Thy sight" overlooks the "ongoing" aspect of the verb and adds nothing to "if I have found grace in the sight" at the beginning of the verse.

14. [a]I will go in the lead and will[a] (lighten your burden) ([a-a]*Lit. "My face will go and I will"*). (Also "You" in v. 15.) It is not any avoidance of anthropomorphism but the idiomatic force of *panay* (*yelékhu*), lit. "My face," in context that justifies the rendering "I (will go in the lead)." This was understood long ago by, among others, Targum Onkelos, Rashi ("*panay* is to be understood here in accordance with the Targum [Onkelos: "My Divine Presence (*Shekhina*) will go"], namely, I will not send again an angel, I Myself will go" [*ani be-aṣmi elekh*]), Rashbam (see his comments on vv. 12 and 13 as well as on 14: *ani be-aṣmi*), Ibn Ezra (*ani be-aṣmi,* rejecting Saadia's rendering—which is cited as *ḥamathi* in the Rabbinic Bible, as against *nuri,* "My light," in ed. Derenbourg), and Sforno; the last named goes beyond his predecessors by interpreting our phrase not merely "I Myself will go" but "I Myself will go before you, in the lead" (. . . *yelékhu panay lifnekhem lo be-thokhekhem*). Both Rashi and Ibn Ezra correctly cited the phrase *u-fanekha holekhim ba-qerav* in II Sam. 17.11 ("you yourself going in the lead into the battle") in this connection, and they should have included reference also to Deut. 4.37 (as S. R. Driver did, in his *Samuel,* bottom of p. 322; and see Ibn Ezra on the Deuteronomy passage), where *wa-yoṣi'akha be-fanaw* (*be-khoḥo ha-gadol mi-miṣráyim*) is correctly rendered, "He Himself,[b](in His great might, led you out of Egypt)," with note *b* reading: *Lit. "With His face (or, Presence)"; cf. note at Ex. 33.14.* Trad. "My presence (shall go with thee"—though note the absence of a Hebrew term for "with thee") has recognized this use of *panay,* following the Targum, etc.

Chapter 34

6. **The Lord passed before him,** etc. See S. Zeitlin, *Jewish Quarterly Review,* 52 (Oct. 1961), 130.

12. **against which (you are advancing).** Trad. "whither (thou goest)" hardly does justice to the force of *asher* (*atta ba*) *aléha.*

13. **sacred posts.** Cf. Driver (with reference to such passages as Deut. 16.21; Judg. 6.25–30. Note verbs such as *karath* and *gada,* "to cut down"), followed by Cassuto; see "Asherah" by W. L. Reed, *IDB,* I, 250–252.

14. **Impassioned.** As against Trad. "jealous" for *qanna,* see at 20.5 above.

19. **that drop a male.** So Rashi, taking *tizzakhar* as third person feminine singular. Trad. "thou shalt sanctify the males," taking the Hebrew form as second person masculine singular.

21. **cease from labor.** As against Trad. "rest," see at Gen. 2.2 above.

even (at plowing time). Reproducing the force of the emphatic (initial) position of *be-ḥarish u-va-qaṣir*; cf. Luzzatto (*afílu*), Driver ("i.e. even at times when the need of working continuously might seem most urgent"), Cassuto.

23. **Sovereign.** See at 23.17 above.

29. **So Moses came down.** Actually, the Hebrew construction would require "When Moses came down," etc. (so Trad.) to go with v. 30, with most of v. 29 (from *beridti* on)

construed parenthetically (see Ehrlich, *Randglossen*). The present translation, however, has avoided what would be awkward in English, namely, Trad. "And when Moses came down . . . when he came down . . .[30]And when Aaron . . . saw Moses. . . ."

was radiant. (Also vv. 30, 35.) Cf. Driver ("was rayed"), Cassuto (with reference to the concept in Mesopotamia). Trad., "sent forth beams."

Chapter 35

22. **brooches.** See "Brooch" by J. M. Myers, *IDB,* II, 467. Trad., "nose-rings."

(gold) objects of all kinds. Trad. "all jewels (of gold)" limits (*kol-*)*kele* (*zahav*) unnecessarily. See above at 11.2.

25. **skilled (women).** As against Trad. "(women) that were wise-hearted," see at 28.3 above.

27. **(and) other stones (for setting).** See at 25.7.

32. **to make designs.** As against "skilful workmanship," see at 26.1 above.

Chapter 36

2. **to undertake (the task).** On the verb *qarav "to* DRAW NEAR, viz. for a sacred purpose, as often in P . . . ," see Driver. See at 12.48 above.

4. **artisans.** Trad. "wise men" misses the force of *ḥakhamim* here, which is that of *ḥakhme lev* (cf. vv. 1,2).

Chapter 37

16. **with which to offer libations.** See at 25.29 above.

Chapter 38

7. **hollow, of boards.** See at 27.8 above.

Chapter 40

31. **would wash.** See Driver, "The tenses are frequentative, USED TO WASH. . . ." Hardly Trad. "that (Moses . . .) might wash."

38. **in it**[a] (*[a]I.e. in the cloud*). See Luzzatto, Driver—with reference to Num. 9.15, 16, 21.

Leviticus

ויקרא

Chapter 1

2. **an offering of cattle (. . . offering from the herd . . .).** So Ibn Ezra, Sforno, Snaith (*Leviticus and Numbers*). Trad. attempts this construction—hardly successfully—by adding "(your offering of the cattle,) even (of the herd . . .)."

3. **for acceptance in his behalf.** (Also v. 4 and frequently.) Understanding *lirṣono* to denote acceptance of the sacrifice in behalf of the worshipper; so Targum, Rashbam, Luzzatto, Ehrlich (*Mikra*). Trad. "that he may be accepted" is hardly clear.

9. **turn . . . into smoke.** See at Exod. 29.13 (with further reference there to Driver, at Gen. 19.28).

14. **pigeons.** Understanding *bene* (*yona*) to indicate merely the species (similarly *ben-adam* as denoting the species man [Num. 23.19, "mortal"], not a young person); see Snaith, and Introduction, §c. Trad., "young pigeons." Cf. Gen. 15.9.

16. **contents.** So Targum, Sifra, Rashi. Trad., "feathers."

Chapter 2

1. **choice flour.** As against Trad. "fine flour," see at Gen. 18.6.

2. **token portion.** Understanding thus the technical term *azkara,* in light of all its seven occurrences in the Bible (six of them in Leviticus, one in Numbers), and as distinct

from *zikkaron,* "reminder, remembrance" (Trad., "memorial"); see G. R. Driver, "Three Technical Terms in the Pentateuch," *Journal of Semitic Studies,* 1 (1956), 99 f.; followed by Snaith. Trad. "memorial-part" scarcely distinguishes between the two Hebrew terms.

4. **[it shall be].** Trad. "it shall be" does not indicate the lack of a verb in the Hebrew (contrast *tihye* in v. 5; *te'ase* in v. 5; *taqriv* in v. 14).

(choice flour): The word *sóleth,* as indicated by the colon in the translation, applies to both the cakes and the wafers. Trad. "it shall be of unleavened cakes of fine flour mingled with oil, or unleavened wafers spread with oil" does not indicate this; it would even seem to exclude wafers.

5. **on a griddle.** Trad. "baked on a griddle" does not indicate that (unlike *ma'afe* in v. 4) there is no Hebrew equivalent for "baked."

8. **in any of these ways.** So Rashi (following Sifra), and see Malbim. Trad. "of these things" is unsatisfactory, since it is the different ways in which the meal is offered that is meant here by *me-élle.*

12. **choice products**[a] ([a]*Exact meaning of Heb* [*reshith*] *uncertain*). Hardly Trad. "first-fruits," which is the regular term for *bikkurim* (e.g., v. 14). See Snaith at vv. 12 and 14.

14. **new ears . . . fresh grain.** Projected version; replaces "grain in season . . . the fresh ear." Trad., "corn in the ear . . . even groats of the fresh ear."

Chapter 3

1. **(a sacrifice of) well-being.** (And frequently.) As against Trad. "peace-offering" (here incorrectly in the plural: "peace-offerings"), see at Exod. 20.21.

4. **protuberance (on the liver).** As against Trad. "lobe above," see at Exod. 29.13.

5. **with (the burnt offering).** As against Trad. "upon," see at Exod. 29.25. Cf. Rashi: *al* here means *levad* ("beside, apart from").

9. **broad tail.** As against Trad. "fat tail," see at Exod. 29.22.

Chapter 4

12. **(all the) rest of (the bull).** Trad. "(even the) whole (bullock)" is misleading, in that the blood and the fat (vv. 5–10), for example, were not removed outside the camp; see Snaith (p. 44, at v. 11).

in a wood fire. In accord with 1.7–8. Will replace "with wood" in projected version. Trad. "(and burn it) on wood with fire" is mechanical.

13. **(the matter) escapes the notice of (the congregation).** Trad. "being hid from" is misleading, in that it might indicate deliberate concealment.

they realize their guilt. (Also vv. 22, 27; 5.2, 3, 4.) See Rashbam, Luzzatto, and see at 5.17 below. Will replace "thus incur blame" (or "draw blame" or "find themselves culpable") in projected version.

14. **becomes known.** Trad. "is known" is mechanical, and does not do justice to the inchoative force of the Hebrew verb. See Introduction, §c.

20. **the [priest's] bull of sin offering.** So Rashi; cf. Ehrlich (also at v. 21 following).

27. **the populace[b]:** ([b]*Lit. "people of the country"*). Trad., "(the) common people." The (somewhat elusive) expression *am ha-áreṣ* denotes here the general population, the laymen who are neither priests (vv. 2 ff.) nor chieftains (*nasi,* vv. 22 ff.).

Chapter 5

1. The paragraphing of vv. 1–5 will help the reader to see at a glance that the phrase "If a person incurs guilt" in v. 1 is completed by "when he realizes his guilt . . ." in v. 5, with the intervening section consisting of four different kinds of circumstances. Also, it is thus seen clearly that vv. 7 ff. ("But if his means do not suffice for a sheep . . .") follow immediately upon 4.35, and round out the sin offering "of any person from among the populace . . ." of 4.27 ff. On the whole problem, see Snaith, pp. 47 f.

a public imprecation. Trad. "the voice (of adjuration)," by rendering mechanically, has obscured the force of *qol* in context. Cf. Exod. 36.6 (*wa-ya'aviru-*) *qol* "(had this) proclamation (made)"; (Trad., "And they caused it to be proclaimed").

so that he is subject to punishment. As noted, e.g., by Snaith (p. 48)—as against Trad. "he shall bear his iniquity"—the phrase *nasa awon* often means " 'bear the responsibility' of sin or guilt" or "pay the penalty."

3. **and, though he has known it, the fact has escaped him.** (Also v. 4.) Cf. Rashi (followed by Luzzatto): he had known it (*yada*; see Luzzatto on this reading) and had forgotten (his) uncleanness.

4. **to bad or good purpose.** I.e., to any purpose, involving anyone, even himself; see Rashi (in part; following Bab. Talmud, Shebuoth 27a), Luzzatto. On merismus, see Introduction, §c.

12. **token portion.** As against Trad. "memorial-part," see at 2.2.

with (the Lord's offerings by fire). As against Trad. "upon," see at 3.5.

15. **convertible into payment in silver.** As recognized; e.g., by Rashi (see at 27.3), Luzzatto, and Ehrlich, the final *kaf* in *erkekha* is not to be understood as the pronominal suffix ("your"; cf. Trad. "according to thy valuation in silver by shekels"). A recent study (E. A. Speiser, in *Yehezkel Kaufmann Jubilee Volume,* Jerusalem, 1960, pp. 30–33) explains final *kaf* as "a pronominal suffix that became fossilized and thus absorbed in the nominal stem," i.e., " 'your valuation' . . . became through common usage simply 'valuation' (by an outside party), with the pronoun inactivated and absorbed"; furthermore, usage among the Hurrians at Nuzi (east of the Tigris River, about the middle of the second millennium B.C.E.) is adduced to indicate that the term *erkekha* denotes the "specified monetary equivalent in terms of animals," which may, however, "be commuted to currency."

17. **and then realizes his guilt.** (Also vv. 23, 24.) Cf. Ibn Ezra: "At first he did not know, but afterwards he became aware of it." See at 4.13 above. Trad. "(though he know it now,) yet is he guilty" is less than adequate.

21. **by defrauding.** See Ehrlich (*Randglossen*). Trad. "having oppressed" hardly goes well with "dealing deceitfully (or: falsely)" in the matter of "deposit," "pledge," and "robbery."

23. **and, realizing his guilt.** Cf. Rashi.

24. **or anything else.** This indicates that swearing falsely was the sin in every instance in vv. 21–23 preceding. Earlier printings read "or anything."

(he shall repay) the principal amount. Cf. Rashi on *rosho*: "This is the principal." Trad. "(and he shall even restore it) in full" is less than clear.

when. On this idiomatic meaning of *be-yom,* as against Trad. "in the day," see at Gen. 2.4 and Introduction, §c.

he realizes his guilt. See v. 17 above. Trad. "(in the day) of his being guilty," is mechanical and meaningless.

26. **to draw blame thereby.** As noted by Snaith (p. 52;

6.7 in the English versions)—who prefers "and thereby incur liability" to RSV "and thereby becomes guilty" and Trad. "so as to be guilty thereby"—"the distinguishing feature of the guilt-offering is that the offender is liable to pay full restitution plus 20 percent. He is guilty over a sin-offering offence, but he must pay up for a guilt-offering offence."

Chapter 6

2. **ritual.** (And elsewhere.) One of several meanings of *tora*; cf. Snaith (p. 52), "The Ritual of the Whole-Offering." Trad., mechanically, "law." See Introduction, §c.

The burnt offering itself shall remain where it is burned (upon the altar). Understanding *hi ha-ola* in its usual sense of "burnt offering" (as in the word immediately preceding and throughout our section, culminating in 7.37), and *moqedah* in the sense of "place of burning" (cf. *moshav, morad, maqom*). Trad. "it is that which goeth up on its fire-wood," while a common interpretation of *ola* as the *qal* feminine participle scarcely fits the pattern throughout this section (chaps. 6–7), where none of the terms for the sacrifices is explained (cf. *ha-minḥa* v. 7; *ha-ḥaṭṭath* v. 18; *ha-asham* 7.1; *zébaḥ ha-shelamim* 7.11); moreover, it is in chap. 1, if anywhere, that an explanation of the term *ola* would have been expected.

14. **baked slices**[b] ([b]*Meaning of Heb* tuphine *uncertain).* Interpreting *tufine* as from the root *afa*, "bake" (see Rashi, Rashbam). Trad., "broken pieces."

19. **(who offers it) as a sin offering.** Trad. "for sin" is hardly clear; see Snaith's comment (at 9.15): "the rendering is unfortunate, since it suggests that the sin-offering was offered to God. This is not the case. . . . Translate 'performed the de-sinning rite.' "

Chapter 7

10. **But every other (meal offering).** Trad. "And every" hardly conveys the nuance of *we-khol(-minḥa)*. See Introduction, §c.
19. **As for other flesh.** Trad. "And as for flesh," being literal, has no meaning here. See Introduction, §c.
21. **creature.** Cf. Luzzatto: *shéqes* refers to "swarming things" (*shéreṣ*) or fish or fowl which may not be eaten.
35. **perquisites**[d] *([d]Lit. "anointment," i.e. accruing from anointment).* See Ehrlich. Trad. "consecrated (portion)" has no correspondent in Hebrew *mishḥa*—unless "consecrated" derives from "anointing."
37. **(the offering of) ordination.** On RSV (and Trad.) "consecration (-offering)" Snaith has commented (p. 62): ". . . The use of such terms as 'consecration' is unfortunate, since it imports later ecclesiastical ideas into the original."

Chapter 8

15. **for making expiation upon it.** Projected version; replaces "and purged it." Trad., "to make atonement for it."
17. **The rest of the (bull).** Trad. "But the (bullock)" has overlooked the clear nuance of *we-eth-ha(-par)*. See Introduction, §c.
20–21 (. . . **into smoke):** [21]**Moses washed the entrails and the legs with water, and (turned all of the ram . . .).** Projected version; replaces "(. . . into smoke)— [21]the entrails and the legs having been washed with water. Moses (turned all of the ram . . .)."
27. **palms.** Heb. *kaf.* Trad. "hands" is less accurate.
31. **as I commanded**[c] *([c]Or, vocalizing* ṣuwwethi, *"I have been commanded . . .").* See the discussion by Ehrlich, who

refers to the Septuagint, Targum Onkelos (in some manuscripts and printed editions—on which see S. B. Schefftel, *Biure Onkelos,* ed. J. Perles [1888], p. 135), and Syriac. It may be further noted that it is overwhelmingly the Lord, and only very rarely Moses, who does the commanding; see *ṣiwwa* and related forms in Mandelkern's *Concordance,* pp. 988–990.

34. **[seven days].** Cf. Rashi: all seven days.

Chapter 9

3. **yearlings.** As against Trad. "of the first year," see at Exod. 12.5.

15. **sin offering.** As against Trad. "for sin," see at 6.19 above.

19. **the covering [fat].** So Rashi: the fat that covers the entrails.

Chapter 10

2. **at the instance of.** So Ehrlich *(Randglossen),* who would render similarly *mi-lifne* (*YHWH*) in the first part of our verse ("auf JHVHS Anordnung"). See at Gen. 10.9.

6. **(Do not) [c]bare your heads[c]** *([c-c]Or "dishevel your hair").* Earlier printings read "Do not dishevel your hair,[c]" with the note reading: *Lit. "heads."* Trad., "(Let not) the hair of your heads go loose." The root of *tifrá'u* is of uncertain meaning; any of the meanings offered here is possible.

9. **other intoxicant.** Earlier printings read "ale." Trad. "strong drink." In his article on "Strong Drink," *IDB,* I, 448, J. F. Ross has noted, "While it seems to have meant 'barley beer' at one time, it later came to denote any intoxi-

cating beverage prepared from either grain or fruit . . ."; or cf. Snaith (p. 78), ". . . the word *šēkār* occurs so often in conjunction with *yáyin* (wine) that the former would seem to refer to intoxicants made from other ingredients."

14. **But.** Trad. "And" is mechanical, and fails to do justice to the emphatic (initial) position of *we-eth ḥaze.*

17. **to remove the guilt.** Cf. Snaith (p. 80), ". . . The purpose . . . was to take away sin and get rid of it. . . ." Hardly Trad. "to bear the iniquity."

Chapter 11

3. **any animal that has true hoofs.** Idiomatic for *kol mafréseth parsa . . . ba-behema.* Trad., "Whatsoever parteth the hoof . . . among the beasts."

25. **(and whoever carries) the carcasses of any of them.** (Also v. 37.) Understanding (*we-khol-ha-nose*) *mi-nivlatham* in accordance with (*we-ha-nose*) *eth-nivlatham* ("And anyone who carries their carcasses") in v. 28. Trad., "(And whosoever beareth) aught of the carcass of them."

29. **of every variety.** As against Trad. "after its kinds" for *le-minéhu,* see Gen. 1.11.

Chapter 13

2. **scaly (affection).** Based on Greek *lepra* (a disease which makes the skin rough, scaly), the word used in the Septuagint for *ṣaráʿath;* and see note *b* in v. 3. See the article "Leprosy" by R. K. Harrison in *IDB,* III, 111–113.

it shall be reported. (Also v. 9.) So Luzzatto, Ehrlich; and see below, 14.1–3, where the priest has to go out to the leper, outside the camp.

4–5. **isolate . . . examine.** Trad. "shut up . . . look upon" translates mechanically terms (*hisgir, ra'a*) that are probably intended here technically.

Chapter 15

2. **member.** Trad. "flesh" has failed to reproduce the idiomatic force of *basar* here.
8. **the latter.** Trad. "he" leaves the antecedent open.
9. **Any means for riding.** Cf. Snaith (p. 107). Trad. "saddle" (deriving ultimately from Septuagint "ass's pack-saddle") unnecessarily limits the meaning of *merkav.*
13. **(he shall) count off.** (Also v. 28.) Trad. "number to himself" hardly does justice to the idiom in (*we-safar*) *lo.*
16. **(his whole) body.** Trad. "(all his flesh)" is literal rather than idiomatic for (*eth-kol-*) *besaro.*
26. **Any bedding.** Trad. "Every bed" is hardly the force of *kol-ha-mishkav* here.

Chapter 16

3. **Thus only (shall Aaron enter).** Bringing out the force of emphatic (initial) *be-zoth* (*yavo aharon*). Trad., "herewith."

6–11. Aaron is to offer his own (bull of sin offering) . . .[11]Aaron shall then offer his (bull of sin offering). This rendering, and the paragraphing of vv. 11 ff., make it clear that vv. 7–10 describe the procedure that Aaron was to follow in preparing his sin offering. The mechanical rendering of Trad. ("And Aaron shall present the bullock of the sin-offering. . . .[11] And Aaron shall present the bullock of the sin-offering . . ."), with no paragraphing at all, makes vv. 11 ff. a meaningless repetition of vv. 1 ff.

8. **(he shall) place (lots upon the two goats).** Trad. "cast" is misleading here; see Ehrlich (*Randglossen*), Snaith (p. 112).

13. **[the Ark of] the Pact.** See Exod. 16.34; 25.16; 27.21; and Snaith (113 f.).

16. **(Thus he shall) purge (the Shrine) of (the uncleanness) and (transgression of the Israelites).** Trad., mechanically, "(And he shall) make atonement for (the holy place) because of (uncleannesses of the children of Israel,) and because of their (transgressions)." So also v. 33.

19. **cleanse it of the uncleanness . . . and consecrate it.** The phrase *mi-ṭumoth* (*bene yisrael*) belongs with *we-ṭiharu* rather than with *we-qiddesho* (cf. the use of *ṭaher* in such passages as Jer. 33.8; Ezek. 36.25, 33; Ps. 51.4; Neh. 13.30)—overlooked in the mechanical rendering of Trad. "cleanse it, and hallow it from the uncleannesses. . . ."

21. **whatever (their sins).** On *le-khol* as a summing up, see Exod. 14.28; 27.3, 19. See Introduction, §c.

29. **(you shall) practice self-denial.** (Also v. 31.) As noted by Snaith (p. 117), already the Jerusalem Targum interpreted *te'annu eth-nafshothekhem* as abstention "from food, drink, bathing, perfuming, sandals, and intercourse." Trad. "afflict your souls" is mechanical.

31. **(a sabbath of) complete rest.** As against Trad. "solemn rest," see at Exod. 31.15.

Chapter 17

7. **goat-demons.** See Snaith (119 f.), as against Trad. "satyrs." See T. H. Gaster, "Demon(ology)," *IDB*, I, 817 ff.

11. **assigned it to you for making expiation . . . upon the altar.** Trad. "and I have given it to you upon the altar . . ." is literal, and misleading.

it is the blood, as life, that effects expiation. Cf.

Rashi. Trad. "for it is the blood that maketh atonement by reason of the life" is hardly intelligible.

Chapter 18

3. **You shall not copy the practices of (the land of Egypt).** Trad. "After the doings (of the land of Egypt . . .) shall ye not do" is beyond the call even of mechanical translation duty.

4. **My rules alone.** Bringing out the force of emphatic (initial) *eth-mishpaṭay*. Trad. "Mine ordinances" is mechanical.

7. **that is.** See Luzzatto, Ehrlich (*Mikra*), Snaith (122f.: " 'one nakedness,' so to speak"); and cf. 20.11. Trad., mechanically, "and."

17. **a woman and her daughter.** Cf. 20.14. Earlier printings read "your wife's[b] daughter *([b]Lit. 'a wife and her . . .')*."

Chapter 19

5. **(so that) it may be accepted on your behalf.** See at 1.3. Trad. "(that) ye may be accepted" is misleading.

13. **defraud.** Earlier printings read "coerce" (cf. Trad. "oppress"). See at 5.21 above.

fellow. (Also vv. 16, 18.) Projected version; replaces mechanical (and Trad.) "neighbor." See Introduction, §c.

15. **(You shall not) render an unfair decision.** Trad. "(Ye shall do no) unrighteousness in judgment" has failed to reproduce the legal idiom in the Hebrew, and is hardly acceptable English to boot.

16. [a]**deal basely with**[a] *([a-a]Others "go about as a tale-bearer among"; meaning of Heb uncertain).* The expression *holekh rakhil* is elusive. In such passages as Jer. 6.28 and Ezek. 22.9 the wickedness of the people is surely more grievous than that of talebearing.

[b]**profit by**[b] **(the blood of your neighbor** [projected version: **fellow**]) *([b-b]Lit. "stand upon"; precise meaning of Heb phrase uncertain).* See Ehrlich, who cites *amad al* in Ezek. 33.26 (comparing *ḥaya al* in Gen. 27.40).

20. **an indemnity.** Connecting *biqqóreth* with Akkadian *baqrum* (Nuzi-Hurrian *pirqu*) in the sense of obligation to make good a valid claim, or the like; see E. A. Speiser, in *Yehezkel Kaufmann Jubilee Volume* (1960), pp. 33–36. Trad., "inquisition."

35. **(You shall not falsify) measures (of length, weight, or capacity).** Understanding *mishpaṭ* in the sense of "custom, standard" rather than as a legal term. Trad., "(Ye shall do no unrighteousness) in judgment, (in meteyard, in weight, or in measure)."

Chapter 20

9. **insults.** Earlier printings read "repudiates"—on which see at Exod. 21.17. Trad., "curses."

Chapter 21

14. **(of his own) kin.** Trad. "people" is meaningless here; as noted by Ehrlich, *ammaw* must denote here priestly descent, for even the ordinary Israelite may marry only a fellow Israelite. On *am,* see Introduction, §c.

17. **qualified.** (Also vv. 18, 21.) See Exod. 12.48. Trad.

"approach" misses the idiom in *yiqrav*. See Exod. 12.48; 22.7; 22.3 below, and Introduction, §c.

Chapter 22

2. **to be scrupulous about (the sacred donations).** See Snaith (p. 146), citing Septuagint "give heed to, hold fast to." Trad. "that they separate themselves from" is misleading.

3. **partakes.** Cf. Rashi: the term *yiqrav* denotes here "eating."

10. **(No) bound (or hired) laborer.** See Rashi, Ehrlich, (*Randglossen*), and Exod. 12.45. Trad., "a tenant (of a priest)."

15. **But [the priests] must not allow,** etc. So Rashi (by giving them as food to laymen); Luzzatto.

16. **incur guilt requiring a penalty payment.** Cf. Snaith (pp. 147 f.), "guilt and repayment."

24. **You shall have no such practices.** Cf. Rashi (following Sifra), Malbim. Trad. "neither shall ye do thus" leaves open, unnecessarily, the antecedent of "thus" (is it "ye shall not offer unto the Lord"?).

25. **such [animals] from a foreigner,** etc. Trad. "neither from the hand of a foreigner shall ye offer the bread of your God of any of these," by reproducing the Hebrew mechanically, has made it unclear.

Chapter 23

7. **(you shall not work at your) occupations.** (Also vv. 8, 25, 35, 36.) So Ehrlich (*Randglossen*), who notes the distinction between our *kol-melékheth avoda* (so also in v. 8) and *kol-melakha* in v. 3; and see Exod. 12.16; 20.10). Trad.

"(Ye shall do no manner of) servile work" is unclear, even misleading.

16. **an offering of new grain.** Cf. Rashi. Trad. "a new meal-offering" is hardly clear.

24. **loud blasts.** See at Num. 10.3, 5; E. Werner, "Musical Instruments," *IDB*, III, p. 474a. Trad., "the blast of horns."

27. **practice self-denial.** See at 16.29 above.

Chapter 24

2. **kindle lamps regularly.** As against Trad. "to cause a lamp to burn continually," see at Exod. 27.20; Snaith (p. 159). Projected version, replacing "maintain lights."

3. **(Aaron shall set them up . . .) [to burn] . . . regularly.** (Also v. 4.) So Rashi (after Menaḥoth 89a, bottom), followed by Ehrlich (*Mikra*). Trad. ". . . shall (Aaron order it) . . . continually" is misleading.

11. **pronounced the Name in blasphemy.** Cf. Snaith (p. 160), ". . . uttered a curse containing the Name of God." Trad. "blasphemed the Name, and cursed" is mechanical and misleading, making two actions out of a single one. On *wayiqqov* as "pronounced" (also v. 16), see Targum, Rashi, Ehrlich (*Randglossen*).

Chapter 25

6. **But you may eat whatever the land during its sabbath will produce—you, your male and female slaves, the hired and bound laborers . . .[7] and your cattle and the beasts in your land,** etc. Earlier printings read, "The

land at rest shall yield your food: for you, for your male and female slaves, for your hired and bound laborers . . . [7]and for your cattle and for the beasts in your land," etc. Trad., "And the sabbath-produce of the land shall be for food for you: for thee, and for thy servant and for thy maid. . . ."

(the hired and) bound laborers. (Also v. 40.) See at 22.10 above. In context, *toshav* must belong in some way to the category of male slave, female slave, and hired laborer. Trad. "(for thy hired servant and for) the settler by thy side" hardly reproduces *toshavekha*.

10. release. Cf. "redemption" (*ge'ulla*) of holdings of land in the summing up in v. 24, and the expression *we-shav la-aḥuzzatho* in vv. 27 and 28. The Hebrew term and concept of *deror* has been discussed recently in its Mesopotamian setting by J. Lewy ("The Biblical Institution of *Dᵉrôr* in the Light of Akkadian Documents," *Eretz-Israel,* 5 [1958], pp. 21–31) and F. R. Kraus ("Ein Edikt des Königs Samsu—iluna von Babylon," in *Studies in Honor of B. Landsberger* [*Assyriological Studies,* No. 16; Chicago, 1965], 225–231.

30. (the house . . .) shall pass (to the purchaser). See Rashi and Gen. 23.17. Trad. "shall be made sure (. . . to him that bought it)" is mechanical, showing no regard for either Hebrew or English idiom.

(it shall not) be released. (Also v. 31.) Trad. "(it shall not) go out" has failed to do justice to the technical force of *yeṣe*; thus our word means "go free (from slavery)" in Exod. 21.2, 5, 11.

35. comes under your authority, and you hold him as though a resident alien. Understanding *u-maṭa yado immakh we-heḥezáqta bo* in the light of Mesopotamian (Old Babylonian and Hurrian) parallels; see E. A. Speiser, *Yehezkel Kaufmann Jubilee Volume* (1960), 36–39—following some leads by Ehrlich. Trad., "and his means fail with thee; then thou shalt uphold him: as a stranger and a settler. . . ."

let him live by your side: [36]do not, etc. Earlier

printings read "so that he remains under you, [36]do not," etc. (after Ehrlich), on the assumption that *ḥay* meant "reside" (rather than "subsist") and that *immakh* reflected the Old Babylonian (Alalakh) usage of "remain in the household of (the creditor)," i.e., remain under his authority (see preceding note). Trad., "shall he live with thee."

36. advance or accrued interest. (Also v. 37.) This brings out the two kinds of interest involved. Trad. "interest . . . or increase" is not very helpful.

39. give himself over. (Also vv. 42, 47.) I.e., to work off his indebtedness. Trad. "sell himself" ("be sold" in v. 42) misses the point.

40. by your side. See v. 35 above. Projected version, replacing earlier "with you."

Chapter 26

6. vicious beasts. Trad. "evil" hardly represents the force of (*ḥayya*) *ra'a* here.

12. I will be ever present. So Ehrlich (*Randglossen*), and cf. Sforno. Trad., "And I will walk." On the durative aspect of the *hithpael*, see at Gen. 3.24.

16. I in turn. (Also v. 40.) Trad. "I also" hardly reproduces the force of *af ani*.

30. cult places. Trad. "high places" is misleading. Heb. *bama* is simply a place where God was worshipped, a shrine, a sanctuary. In time, the ever-increasing importance of the royal shrine in Jerusalem led to the downgrading of the legitimate *bamoth* throughout the country and their eventual disappearance; see, e.g., "High Place, Sanctuary," by G. Henton Davies, *IDB*, II, 602–604.

incense stands. The *ḥamman* is now known archaeologically; see "Incense Altars" by K. Galling, *IDB*, II, 699–700. Trad. (erroneously), "sun-pillars."

36. put (them) to flight. Trad. "chase (them)" is mechanical—"the sound of a driven leaf" will not chase them; it will panic them into headlong flight.

40–41. and they shall confess . . .[41] When I, in turn, etc. The rendering of these two verses removes the difficulty in the Trad. translation, according to which God inflicted further punishment following a confession.

Chapter 27

2. the equivalent. (So throughout the chapter.) As against Trad. "thy valuation," see at 5.15 above.

12. (and the priest shall assess it.) Whether, etc. On the construction of the verse, see E. A. Speiser, in *Yehezkel Kaufmann Jubilee Volume* (1960), 39–41.

Numbers

במדבר

Chapter 1

2. **Take a census.** Trad. "Take ye the sum" does not reflect *se'u eth-rosh* as a technical term.
16. **contingents.** Trad. "thousands" hardly does justice to *alfe* as a technical military term. Cf. *alpi,* "my clan," in Jud. 6.15; and see Gen. 36.15.
20. **They totaled as follows:.** Initial *wa-yihyu* is to be understood also for the succeeding groups in the list beginning with *livne* (*shimon, gad,* etc.).
40. **Of (the descendants).** Thus many Hebrew manuscripts, Septuagint, Samaritan; note *li(vne),* "Of (the descendants)," throughout the list (vv. 22–40).
53. **(the Levites shall) stand guard around (the Tabernacle).** See Ibn Ezra. Earlier printings read "perform the duties of." Trad., "keep the charge of."

Chapter 2

3. **division.** Trad. "camp" hardly brings out the nuance here of the military term *maḥane.*
9. **shall march.** (Also vv. 17, 24, 31.) Earlier printings read "marched." Trad., "shall set forth."

Chapter 3

1. **line.** As against Trad. "generations," see at Gen. 5.1.
at the time. For this idiom in *be-yom,* as against

Trad. "in the day," see at Gen. 2.4b ("When"), and Introduction, §c.

2. **Nadab . . . and Abihu, Eleazar and Ithamar.** As so often (see v. 19 in this chapter; Exod. 24.1), names are listed in pairs: *nadab wa-avihu elazar we-ithamar*. Trad. "Nadab . . . , and Abihu, Eleazar, and Ithamar" fails to take note of this.

4. [a]**by the will**[a] **of** ([a-a]*Others "before"*). See at Gen. 10.9 and Introduction, §c.

in the lifetime of. As against Trad. "in the presence of," see at Gen. 11.28.

31. **screen**[d] ([d]*I.e. the screening curtain; cf. 4.5*). So Rashi, referring to Exod. 35.12.

Chapter 4

6. **dolphin skin.** See at Exod. 25.5.

10. **(on a) carrying frame.** (Also v. 12.) See Luzzatto, Snaith (p. 195). Trad., "bar."

13. **[copper] altar.** Cf. Rashi.

18. **Do not let (the group of Kohathite clans) be cut off.** See Rashi, Ibn Ezra (at v. 17), Sforno, followed by Ehrlich (*Randglossen*). Trad. "cut ye not off" misses the nuance.

20. [b]**witness the dismantling of the sanctuary**[b]. See Ibn Ezra (first explanation), Ehrlich.

Chapter 5

6. **realizes his guilt.** As against Trad. "be guilty," see at Lev. 5.17.

9. **gift.** As against Trad. "heave-offering," see Exod. 25.2; 29.28. Cf. Rashbam.

12. **has gone astray.** Trad. "go aside" hardly does justice to *tisṭe.*

13. **and she keeps secret the fact that she has defiled herself.** Trad. "she being defiled secretly" reproduces the *niphal* form *niṭmáʼa* mechanically as passive, and in the process treats *we-nistera* adverbially. However, the reflexive is a common function of the *niphal,* and both *we-nistera* and *niṭmáʼa* are to be so understood here; see Ibn Ezra ("she did not reveal the matter"), Luzzatto, Ehrlich (*Randglossen*).

without being forced. So Sifre, Rashi (citing Deut. 22.28), Rashbam, Sforno, Ehrlich, Malbim. Trad., "neither she be taken in the act."

15. **(a meal offering of) remembrance (which recalls wrongdoing).** On "remembrance," as against Trad. "memorial, (bringing iniquity to remembrance)," see at Lev. 2.2; also Snaith's comment here (pp. 201–202).

20. **But if you have gone astray while married to your husband.** (Also v. 29). On the force of *táḥath* here, see Ehrlich (*Randglossen*). Trad. "but if thou hast gone aside, being under your husband" is less than clear.

23. **rub it off (into the water).** Trad. "and he shall blot them out" is hardly clear enough.

26. **a token part.** As against Trad. "memorial-part," see at Lev. 2.2.

Chapter 6

3. **any other intoxicant.** See at Lev. 10.9.

13. **he shall be brought.** Understanding the subject of *yavi otho* as indefinite; cf. Sifre ("others shall bring him"). The same sense is achieved by Sifre (quoting Rabbi Ishmael) —followed by Rashi, Ibn Ezra, Sforno, Malbim—when the object *otho* is construed as referring back to the subject of *yavi,* namely, "he shall bring himself." Trad. "he shall[a] bring

it (unto the door . . .)," with note *a* reading: "That is, bring his consecrated head (come with his consecrated hair unshaven)"; so, e.g., Luzzatto, followed by Ehrlich.

25. **deal kindly.** Understanding thus the idiomatic force of *ya'er (YHWH) panaw*; so Ibn Ezra, and cf. Snaith (p. 207). ". . . The phrase indicates outgoing activity in goodwill."

26. **bestow His favor.** Understanding thus the idiomatic force of *yissa (YHWH) panaw (elêkha)*. See Gen. 19.21, with which the Sifre connects our verse.

peace[g] ([g]*Or "friendship"*). Cf. Snaith (p. 207), "all translate literally (peace), but *šālôm* has a much wider meaning and involves prosperity, good health, wholeness, and completeness in every way. . . ."

Chapter 7

1–2. **(On the day that Moses) finished (setting up the Tabernacle,) he anointed and consecrated (it and all its furnishings, as well as the altar and its utensils.) When he had anointed and consecrated them, [2]the chieftains,** etc. By reproducing mechanically the sentence division, Trad. has made the Hebrew less than meaningful: "(And it came to pass on the day that Moses) had made an end (of setting up the tabernacle) and had anointed and sanctified (it, and all the furniture thereof, and the altar and all the vessels thereof,) and had anointed them and sanctified them; [2]that the princes," etc.

3. **draught carts.** So the Akkadian cognate of the Hebrew. Trad., "covered wagons," following Sifre, Targum, Rashi. Symmachus, "wagons for military service" (apparently interpreting *ṣav* as from *ṣava'*).

8. **under the direction.** Trad. "under the hand" for *be-yad* is neither literal nor idiomatic.

9. **[most] sacred objects.** So Rashi, Sforno. Trad. "holy

things" is hardly clear: all "holy things" were handled by the Levites.
89. **(Ark of the) Pact.** See at Exod. 16.34.

Chapter 8

2. **(When you) kindle (the lamps, let the seven lamps) give light at (the front . . .).** Projected version; replaces "mount . . . throw their light forward toward (the front . . .)." Similarly in v. 3: kindled (the lamps) at (the front), as against earlier "mounted . . . to face (the front)."
11. **designate**[b] ([b]*Lit. "wave"*). See Ehrlich, Snaith (p. 216).
12. **(one) shall be offered.** Employing the passive, to avoid rendering the awkward imperative *wa-ase* ("and you offer"; Trad., "and offer thou").
15. **be qualified.** (Also v. 22.) Understanding *bo* here as something of a technical term; cf. the root *qarav,* Exod. 12.48; 22.7; Lev. 21.17. See Introduction, §c.
26. **by standing guard.** See at 1.53 above.

Chapter 9

1. **on the first new moon.** See at Exod. 19.1; and cf. 28.14 and 29.6 below. Trad., "in the first month."
10. **would offer.** As in v. 14 (Trad., "And if . . . will keep"), where *we-'asa* is followed, in both instances (vv. 11 and 14), by *ya'asu/ya'ase,* "they/he shall offer." Trad., "yet he shall keep (the passover)."
15. **it rested . . . in the likeness of fire.** I.e., the subject of *yihye* is "the cloud." Trad. "there was . . . as it were the appearance of fire" has erroneously made *kemare-esh* the subject of *yihyeh.*

Chapter 10

3, 5. long blasts, short blasts. Suggested by the discussion in Sifre. But nothing certain has been achieved in the interpretation of *ṭaqa* and *teru'a* (Trad. respectively "blow" and "blow/sound an alarm"); see Ehrlich (*Mikra*) and the reference to E. Werner at Lev. 23.24.

30. to my native land. On the hendiadys, as against Trad. "to mine own land, and to my kindred," see at Gen. 12.1, and Introduction, §c.

36. You who are, etc. Understanding *rivevoth* (*alfe yisrael*) as in the vocative, in apposition to (*shuva*) *YHWH*; so Ehrlich. Sforno interprets "O Lord of the myriads," etc., comparing "Lord of the hosts of Israel," etc.

Chapter 11

1. (a fire of the Lord) broke out. See Exod. 22.5; 35.3. Trad. "burnt" does not indicate the initiation of the action.

4. and then the Israelites too wept. Projected version, replacing earlier "and the Israelites, moreover, wept."

15. I beg You. Idiomatic in context for *im-maṣáthi ḥen be-enékha* (Trad., mechanically, "if I have found favour in Thy sight")—on which see Introduction, §c.

25. spoke in ecstasy. (Also v. 26.) The *hithpael* form of *nb'* (*wa-yithnabbe'u*) is usually employed for ecstatic utterances; see Luzzatto, Snaith (p. 231, "This is the frenzy. . .").

29. wrought up. As against Trad. "jealous," see at Exod. 20.5.

31. (and some two cubits) deep on (the ground). See Ehrlich. Trad. "above the face of" is unclear.

32. set to gathering. The auxiliary use of *wa-yáqam*; cf. at Gen. 33.7, and see Introduction, §c.

35. When they were, etc. Joining with 12.1. See Ehrlich (*Randglossen*), and Introduction, §c.

Chapter 12

1. **"He married,"** etc. Understanding the clause introduced by *ki* as constituting Miriam's accusation. See Introduction, §c.
2. **through (Moses) . . . through (us).** Trad. "with . . . with" hardly reproduces the force of *be(moshe dibber YHWH . . .) bá(nu).*
5. **"Aaron and Miriam!"** See Ehrlich.
6. **When a prophet of the Lord arises among you.** See Ehrlich. Earlier printings read "When the Lord speaks through one of you"; but as the footnote reads: *Heb. clause obscure.*
8. **riddles.** So already Septuagint; and see Rashi (referring to Ezek. 17.2). Trad., "dark speech."

Chapter 13

2. **scout.** See Luzzatto, who cites Rashi and Radak at Isa. 44.13. Note that in Deut. 1.22 the term employed is *we-yaḥperu,* "reconnoiter."
18. **(and see) what kind of country it is.** Trad. "the land, what it is" is mechanical.
20. **take pains.** See Ehrlich. Trad., mechanically, "and be ye of good courage."
21. **at Lebo-hamath.** Understanding *levo* (*ḥamath*) as part of the name (modern Lebweh, on the Orontes River); so most modern scholars. Trad., "at the entrance to Hamath," on which see H. G. May, "Hamath, Entrance of," *IDB,* II, 516–7.
23. **they cut down . . . and some pomegranates and figs.** Construing *umin-ha-rimmonim umin-ha-ṭe'enim,* as well as *zemora,* as the object of *wa-yikhrethu* ("they cut down"). Trad., in limiting the object of "they cut down" to *zemora* ("a branch"), gratuitously added a verb ("and they

took") lacking in the Hebrew: "and cut down figs (from thence a branch . . .); they took also of the pomegranates, and of the."

26. **They went straight (to Moses).** An attempt to get at the idiom in lit. (and Trad.) "And they went and came (to Moses)."

Chapter 14

1. **broke into loud cries.** On the idiom *nasa qol,* as against Trad. "lifted up their voice, and cried," see Gen. 29.11 and Introduction, §c.

4. **head back.** See Ehrlich, citing Neh. 9.17.

17. **my (Lord's forbearance).** Understanding (*ado*)*nay* as the pronominal suffix; see Gen. 18.27.

25. **Sea of Reeds.** As against Trad. "Red Sea," see at Exod. 15.4.

29. **(you who) have muttered.** Projected version; replaces "mutter," which fails to distinguish between the perfect tense here (*halinothem*) and the participle (*mallinim*) in v. 26 preceding.

34. **what it means to thwart Me.** See Luzzatto, and R. Loewe, pp. 137–158 in the C. D. Winton-Thomas Jubilee Volume (1968). Trad., "My displeasure."

37. **by the will (of the Lord).** On the idiom in *lifne* (Trad., "before"), see at Gen. 10.9, and Introduction, §c.

40. **Early (next morning).** As against Trad. "And they rose up early (in the morning)," see at Gen. 19.2.

45. **at (Hormah).** For this meaning of *ad,* see at Gen. 13.12.

Chapter 15

20. **baking[c].** Trad., "dough."

Chapter 16

1. **[a-]betook himself[-a]** (*[a-a]Lit. "took"; Heb obscure*). Trad. "took men"—but without advising the reader that the Hebrew has no word for "men" or that *wa-yiqqaḥ* is not used thus idiomatically.
9–10. **and given (you access . . .) [10]Thus . . ; yet you seek . . . ;** projected version: **[10]Now that . . . , do you seek,** etc. Earlier printings read "by giving (you access . . .)."
34. **"The earth might swallow us!"** On the idiomatic rendering of *pen,* see Introduction, §c. Trad. "[for they said,] 'Lest the earth,' " etc.

Chapter 17

3. **[a][Remove]** (*[a]Parts of v. 3 are obscure*). Trad. "even" —for which, however, there is no term in the Hebrew.
20. **incessant murmurings (of the Israelites).** Idiomatic for lit. (and Trad.) "the murmurings (of the children of Israel,) which they murmur."
25. **rebels.** On *bene(-meri)* as indicating the species, see Introduction, §c. Trad., "rebellious children."
may be stopped. Projected version, to bring out the *piel* force of *u-thekhal,* which "may cease" fails to do.
28. **Alas.** So Targum.
we are doomed to perish. Cf. Rashi: "Have we then been consigned to death?"

Chapter 18

1. **and your ancestral house.** Projected version; replaces "and the ancestral house under your charge," assuming a meaning for *ittakh* that could not be proved. Similarly in

vv. 2 and 7 (*your sons,* as against earlier "your sons under your charge").

shall bear any guilt connected with the sanctuary . . . shall bear any guilt connected with your priesthood. See Ehrlich (*Mikra,* at v.7). Trad. "shall bear the iniquity of the sanctuary . . . the iniquity of your priesthood" reproduces *awon* mechanically and is unclear.

9. **(. . . as) most holy sacrifices . . . (shall belong to you and your sons).** In retaining the Hebrew word order and rendering literally, Trad. "shall be most holy (for thee and for thy sons)" has made the Hebrew unclear; note Trad. "the most holy things" for *qódesh ha-qadashim* in the first part of the verse.

guilt (offering). In accordance with Lev. 5.19; 7.1. Projected version, replacing earlier "penalty."

10. **(You shall partake of them) as most sacred donations.** Understanding the preposition *be(qódesh)* in the sense of "as, in the capacity" (*bet essentiae*; as in *be[el shadday]* "as [El Shaddai]" in Exod. 6.3); see Ramban, Ehrlich. Trad., "in a most holy place."

16. **the money equivalent.** On this meaning of *erkekha,* see at Lev. 5.15.

20. **(you shall,) however,** etc. Bringing out the emphatic force of initial *be-arṣam* (*lo tinḥal*).

Chapter 19

3. **in his presence.** Trad. "before his face" is neither literal ("to his face") nor idiomatic ("before him"="in his presence").

9. **water of lustration**[a] ([a]*Lit. "water for impurity"*). I.e., water for de-impurification, exactly as immediately following *ḥaṭṭath* means "cleansing" (i.e., de-sinning), Trad., "purification from sin." Trad. "water of sprinkling" goes

back to Septuagint and Rashi—against which see Ehrlich *(Mikra)*.

18. or on him. As against Trad. "and on him" to distinguish between two different acts, one inside the tent (first part of verse) and the other outside the tent (*we-ha-nogé'a*).

Chapter 20

1. on the first new moon. See at Exod. 19.1.

3. at the instance of. See at Gen. 10.9, and Introduction, §c.

5. (There is not) even water. Bringing out the emphatic force of initial *u-máyim* (*áyin lishtoth*).

18. else. For the idiomatic rendering of *pen,* as against Trad. "lest," see Introduction, §c.

19. it is but a small matter. Both more idiomatic and literal for *en-davar* than Trad. "there is no hurt."

24. : (he is not to enter). Understanding *ki* (*lo yavo*) as explicative. Trad., "for (he shall not enter)."

Chapter 21

5. miserable (food). Cf. Snaith, ". . . almost any derogatory word will do." Trad. "light (bread)" is hardly meaningful today.

6. (sent) . . . against. In accordance with Deut. 7.20; 28.20 (for *shillaḥ be-*). Projected version; replaces "among."

18. started. So sometimes for *kara,* "begin to dig," as distinct from *ḥafar,* "dig"; see Gen. 26.25; Exod. 21.33.

24. as far as [Az] of the Ammonites. Something like "Az" is to be understood here, for Israel did not capture at this time any territory beyond the Jabbok.

27. it is built firm; /(Sihon's city) is well founded.

Taking *tibbane* as the last word in line 1, parallel to *we-thikkonen* in line 2, thus producing a 3:3 meter. Trad. "Let the city of Sihon be built and established!" makes the meter unnecessarily 2:4.

Chapter 22

6. **numerous.** As against Trad. "mighty" for *aṣum,* see at Gen. 18.18; Exod. 1.9.
7. **versed in divination.** Ehrlich (*Randglossen*), comparing the use of *bidakh* in Ezra 7.25. Trad., "with the rewards of divination in their hand."
9. **What do these people want of you?** See Ehrlich. Trad., "What men are these with thee?"
10. **sent me this message.** An idiomatic use of *shalaḥ* for "send a message/messenger"; see Brown-Driver-Briggs, *Hebrew Lexicon,* p. 1018a, bottom of §c ("very often without object . . ."), and Introduction, §c. In vv. 5 and 15, and in 24.12, an object (*malakhim; sarim*) is given; but not so in v. 37 in this chapter. Trad. "hath sent to me [saying]," in adding "[saying]," has missed the idiom.
17. **I will reward you richly.** (And cf. v. 37.) See Rashi, Ibn Ezra. Trad., "for I will promote thee unto very great honour."
24. **in a lane.** Cf. Targum, Rashi, Ibn Ezra. Trad. "in a hollow way" is less than clear.

Chapter 23

3. **alone.** See Targum (*yeḥidi*), Rashi, Ehrlich. Trad., "to a bare height"—though "to" has no Hebrew correspondent.
10. **dust-cloud.** See W. F. Albright, *Journal of Biblical*

Literature, 63 (1944), 213, n. 28 (comparing Assyrian *turbú-tu,* "dust"). Trad., "stock."

14. Sedeh-zophim[f] ([f]*Or "Lookout Point"*). Trad., "the field of Zophim."

19. to be capricious. I.e., is not reliable; cf. the root *kazav* in Isa. 58.11; Jer. 15.18; Hab. 2.3; Job 41.1. So Ehrlich. Trad., "that He should lie."

mortal. Understanding *ben(-adam)* to indicate merely the species; see *bene ha-yonah* at Lev. 1.14 above, and Introduction, §c.

21. harm . . . woe. See Ehrlich (*Mikra*). Trad. "iniquity . . . perverseness" is mechanical and without meaning in context.

23. Jacob is told at once, /Yea Israel, etc. Trad. "Now it is said of Jacob and of Israel" has failed to heed the 3:3 meter of the verse.

24. lion. Trad. "lioness" is not justified for *lavi* (contrast *leviyya* in Ezek. 19.2). See at Gen. 49.9.

Chapter 24

3. (whose eye is) true. Understanding *shethum (ha-áyin)* as *sh-thm* (Old Hebrew-Canaanite employed the relative *she- or sha-*); see W. F. Albright (after J. Wellhausen, Von Gall), *Journal of Biblical Literature,* 63 (1944), 216, n. 56, with reference to extrabiblical data.

6. palm-groves. See Brown-Driver-Briggs, *Hebrew Lexicon,* p. 636b, § II *naḥal*; the root in Arabic means "palms." Trad. "valleys" seems out of place in a verse where all three correspondents involve trees (cf. Snaith, p. 297).

9. king of beasts. As against Trad. "lioness," see 23.24 above, and at Gen. 49.9.

11. Back with you at once. Trad. "Therefore now flee thou," in rendering mechanically, has hardly done justice to the idiom, and scorn, evident in *beraḥ-lekha;* see Sforno, followed by Ehrlich. One thinks, of course, of Amos 7.12. Cf. Exod. 4.3 (on *wa-yánas*).

reward you richly. See at 22.17 above.

14. **in days to come.** As against Trad. "in the end of days," see at Gen. 49.1.

15. **true.** See at v. 3 above.

16. **Who obtains knowledge from the Most High.** Trad. "And knoweth the knowledge of the Most High," in rendering mechanically, is unclear, even misleading.

17. **What I see for them (is not yet).** So Rashbam, Sforno; cf. Rashi. Trad. "I see him" is misleading.

scepter. So Trad. Projected version; replaces "meteor[f]" ([f]*Heb* shebet; *cf. Berakoth 58b*")— on which see Ehrlich (*Randglossen*) and Snaith (p. 300). But S. Gewirtz has made the rendering "meteor" questionable (*Journal of Biblical Literature,* 87 [1968], 267 ff.).

Chapter 25

1. **profaned themselves by whoring.** See Ehrlich (*Randglossen*), who cites especially Lev. 21.9 (*teḥel liznoth*).

4. **impaled.** As against Trad. "hang." see at Gen. 40.19.

publicly. Cf. Rashi: "in the sight of everyone."

11. **passion.** (Also v. 12.) As against Trad. "jealous(y)" (cf. 11.29 above), see at Exod. 20.5.

12. **friendship.** As against Trad. "peace," see at 6.26 above.

Chapter 26

8. **Born to.** (Also v. 19.) The fact that only one son is listed indicates that *u-vene* is not to be rendered mechanically "The sons of" (Trad.). See at Gen. 46.23.

54. **with larger groups increase the share,** etc. Trad. "to the more thou shalt give the more inheritance," etc., is hardly acceptable English.

Chapter 27

3. **for (his own sin).** Trad. "in" is mechanical, and without meaning, for *be(ḥeto meth*).
4. **Let not.** As against Trad. "Why" for *lámma,* see Introduction, §c.
7. **The plea . . . is just.** Trad. "speak right" fails to recognize the technical (legal) idiom in *ken . . . doveroth*; cf. 36.5.
16. **Source of the breath.** See 16.22.
20. **authority.** See Sforno, I. S. Reggio (cited by Luzzatto). Trad. "honour" is mechanical.
21. **By such instruction,** etc. I.e., "the decision of the Urim," (*be-mishpaṭ ha-urim*). Trad. "at his word" refers *al-piw* back to the priest.

Chapter 28

7. **fermented drink**[c] ([c]*I.e. wine*). See Snaith's comment (p. 314).
18. **occupations.** (Also v. 26.) As against Trad. "servile work," see at Lev. 23.7.

Chapter 29

1. **occupations.** (Also vv. 12, 35.) See at 28.18 above.
7. **practice self-denial.** As against Trad. "afflict your souls," see at Lev. 16.29 and 23.27.

Chapter 30

4. **or (assumes).** The making of a vow (*néder*) is not the same as assuming an obligation (*issar*; cf. vv. 3, 5, 6, 11, 13—as against v. 12, where both are included). Projected version; replaces (Trad.) "and."

10. **—The vow . . . upon her—.** Understanding this verse as parenthetic, so that v. 11 resumes v. 9; against this view, see Snaith (p. 322, § 6–8).

14. **self-denial.** See at Lev. 16.29 and 23.27.

Chapter 31

3. **(Let men) be picked out.** The root *ḥalaṣ* is often used in the sense of "withdraw," and in Arabic its meaning is "select" (cf. Ehrlich, *Randglossen*); this meaning is indicated also by *wa-yimmaseru* in v. 5 (Targum, "were picked"). Trad. "Arm ye (men)" hardly reflects the *niphal* form *heḥaleṣu*. See also 32.17, 20.

15. **You have spared every female!** As noted by Ehrlich (*Randglossen*), the interrogative—cf. Trad. "Have ye saved all the women alive?"—makes no sense after *wa-yiqṣof moshe* in v. 14.

23. **lustration.** As against Trad. "sprinkling," see at 19.9 above.

27. **combatants.** Trad. "skilled in war" mistranslates *tofese ha-milḥama*; see Orlinsky, *Jewish Quarterly Review*, 34 (1943–44), 281–295. Ehrlich (*Randglossen*) suggests *ha-yoṣe'im laṣṣava* (v. 36) as being synonymous with our phrase; note that in v. 28 immediately following (also in 49) *tofese* is replaced by *anshe*.

Chapter 32

1. **a region suitable (for cattle).** Trad., mechanically, "the place was a place."
5. **It would be a favor to us.** As against mechanical Trad. "If we have found favor in thy sight," see at Gen. 6.8, and Introduction, §c. Cf. 11.15 above.
17. **shock-troops.** (Also vv. 20, 21, 29, 30, 32.) Understanding *ḥalaṣ* (as in 31.3 above) to denote "picked troops." Trad. "armed" is unlikely, since these two and a half tribes were no more armed than the rest of the tribes. See Ehrlich (*Mikra*).
20. **at the instance (of the Lord).** (Also vv. 21, 22, 29, 32.) As against Trad. "before," see at Gen. 10.9; 17.18; Introduction, §c.

Chapter 33

52. **cult places.** As against Trad. "high places," see at Lev. 26.30.

Chapter 34

4. **its limits.** (Cf. v. 5, "terminate.") Trad. "the goings out thereof" renders *toṣe'othaw* virtually the same as *moṣa'im,* "the goings forth" (e.g., 33.2; really "starting points"), and is unclear.

Chapter 35

2. **pasture land.** See v. 3 for the purpose of the *migrash.* Trad. "open land" is without meaning here.

20. **on purpose.** See Luzzatto; Brown-Driver-Briggs, *Hebrew Lexicon,* p. 841a: "lying-in-wait . . . i.e. with malicious intent." Trad., "lying in wait." Cf. *be-lo ṣediya,* "unintentionally" in v. 22.
31. **(guilty of a) capital crime.** Trad. "(guilty of) death" is not altogether clear.

Chapter 36

5. **plea . . . is just.** See 27.7 above.

Deuteronomy

דברים

Chapter 1

14. **What you propose to do is good.** Trad., in rendering literally, has had to add "for us": "The thing which thou hast spoken is good for us to do."
16. **(decide) justly.** Trad. "(judge) righteously" fails to recognize the legal aspect of the term *ṣédeq*. See Introduction, §c.
17. **Fear (no man).** Trad. "(Ye shall not) be afraid of the face (of any man)" has erroneously rendered as a noun (as though *eth-pene*) what is simply a preposition (*mi-pene*).
25. **(took . . .) with them.** Trad. "in their hands" fails to reproduce the idiom in *be-yadam*; see Gen. 24.10, Introduction, §c.
It is a good land that, etc. Trad. "Good is the land which" is mechanical and stilted.
32. **Yet for all that.** Cf. Luzzatto (note**). Trad., mechanically, "Yet in this thing."
37. **Because of you the Lord was incensed with me too.** Trad. "Also the Lord was angry with me for your sakes" hardly reproduces the force of initial *gam-bi* and is unclear to boot ("for your sakes").
44. **at (Hormah in Seir).** On this meaning of *ad,* see at Gen. 38.1. Trad. "(in Seir,) even unto (Hormah)."

Chapter 2

1,3. **skirted the hill country of Seir.** Cf. Rashi: its entire south, as far as the land of Moab. Trad. "compassed mount Seir" is erroneous.

hill country. As against mechanical Trad. "mount" for *har,* see Gen. 10.30.

4–5. **Though they will be afraid of you, be very careful [5]not to start a fight with them.** See Rashi, Ehrlich. Trad. "and they will be afraid of you; take ye good heed unto yourselves therefore; [5]contend not with them" is mechanical and without much meaning.

28. **just let me pass through.** Cf. Luzzatto: the Hebrew is just a way of saying, "I do not ask you for any assistance whatever." And see Num. 20.19.

36. **mighty.** So Targum. Trad., "high."

Chapter 3

18. **shock-troops.** See at Num. 32.17.

24. **You who let Your servant see the first works of (Your greatness . . .).** Trad., mechanically, "Thou has begun to show thy servant (thy greatness . . .)."

You whose powerful deeds no god . . . can equal! Idiomatic for rhetorical "What god is there . . . who can do according to Your deeds and according to Your might/mighty acts?"

powerful deeds. On the hendiadys (lit. "Your deeds and Your might/mighty acts"), see Gen. 12.1, and Introduction, §c.

Chapter 4

1. **(so that you may) live to enter and (occupy the land).** Earlier printings read "thrive and be able to."

3. **in the matter of Baal-peor.** See Ehrlich (*Randglossen*) for this force of the preposition *be*. Trad., "in."

24. **impassioned.** As against Trad. "jealous," see at Exod. 20.5.

31. **(nor will) He let you perish.** Trad. "(neither) destroy thee" unnecessarily restricts the full range of the *hiphil.* Cf. v. 36 below, "let you see . . . let you hear."
37. **(He) Himself.** See the discussion at Exod. 33.14 above.
38. **populous.** As against Trad. "mighty" for *aṣum,* see at Gen. 18.18; Exod. 1.9; Num. 22.6; 32.1.

Chapter 5

21. **His majestic Presence.** On the hendiadys (lit. "His Presence and His majesty"), see Introduction, §c.
Presence. As against Trad. "glory," see at Exod. 16.7.
22. **Let (us) not (die).** As against Trad. "why" for *lámma,* see Introduction, §c.
24. **we will willingly do it.** On the hendiadys (lit. "we will hear and we will do"), see Introduction, §c.

Chapter 6

4. **The Lord is (our God, the Lord) alone.** So Rashbam and Ibn Ezra, followed, e.g., by Luzzatto and Ehrlich. Similarly, in Zech. 14.9, "in that day the Lord shall be *eḥad,*" the word *eḥad* means "the only one, alone." Trad. "The Lord (our God), (the Lord) is one" is mechanical and unclear (one what?).
5. **(You) shall (love).** Earlier printings read "must."
13. **(Revere) only the Lord your God.** Trad. "(Thou shalt fear)" has failed to bring out the emphatic force of initial *eth-YHWH elohékha* (*tira*).
18. **enter (to occupy).** (Also 8.1) Projected version; replaces "be able." (See 9.4, 5.
25. **(to our) merit.** As against Trad. "righteousness

(unto us)" for *ṣedaqa,* see at Gen. 15.6; and cf. "virtues" at 9.4 below. See Introduction, §c.

Chapter 7

1. **much larger.** On *aṣumim,* see at 4.38 and Introduction, §c.
10. **instantly.** Cf. Ehrlich, noting immediately following *lo ye'aḥer.* Trad. "to their face" has missed the idiom in *el-panaw* here.

Chapter 8

2–3. **(that He might) test you by hardships . . . [3]He subjected you to the hardship of hunger.** Cf. Luzzatto. Trad. "afflict thee, to prove . . . thee . . . [3]And He afflicted thee, and suffered thee hunger" has overlooked the hendiadys involved; see Introduction, §c.
8. **olive trees.** So Trad. Earlier printings read "olive oil."

Chapter 9

1. **about to (cross).** Idiomatic force of (*atta over*) *ha-yom.* Trad., "this day."
3. **none other than the Lord your God.** Reproducing the emphatic force of initial *ki YHWH elohékha.* Trad. "the Lord thy God is He who," etc.
4. **virtues.** (Also vv. 5,6.) Cf. "merit" for *ṣedaqa* in 6.25 above, and Gen. 15.6. Trad., "righteousness."
4–5. **has enabled me . . . be able.** Understanding *bo* in

the sense of "be in a position, be able, proceed"; cf. Ehrlich, and see at Gen. 23.2. See Introduction, §c.

Chapter 10

16. **(Cut away, therefore,) the thickening about (your hearts).** See Rashi. Trad., "(Circumcise therefore) the foreskin," etc.

19. **befriend.** For this nuance of *ahav* (Trad., "love), see Introduction, §c.

Chapter 11

2–7. As noted, e.g., by Rashi (cf. Rashbam) and Ibn Ezra, followed by Ehrlich (*Randglossen*), *ki* (*enekhem ha-ro'oth*) in v. 7 resumes v. 2a, with the section vv. 2b–6 being in apposition to, and explicating, *eth-musar YHWH elohekhem* in 2a.

24. **territory.** As against Trad. (mechanically) "border" for *gevul*, see at Introduction, §c.

28. **experienced.** See Ehrlich, and Gen. 4.1, note *a*.

30. **Both are.** Idiomatic for rhetorical *halo-hémmah*. Trad., mechanically, "are they not?"

Chapter 12

4. **Do not worship . . . in like manner.** So Rashi, Ibn Ezra. Trad., "Ye shall not do so."

9,12. **allotted haven** and **territorial allotment.** On the hendiadys construction, as against Trad. "to the rest and to the inheritance" and "no portion nor inheritance," see Introduction, §c.

12. **settlements.** (Also vv. 18, 21.) Cf. Ehrlich (*Randglossen:* as distinct from the capital city). Trad., "gates."
13. **(any place) you like.** For the idiom, cf. Rashi, Luzzatto. Trad., mechanically, "that thou seest."
27. **other (sacrifices).** See Introduction, §c.

Chapter 13

6. **urged disloyalty (to the Lord).** Trad. "hath spoken perversion (against the Lord)" is unclear. Earlier printings read "uttered falsehood (about)."

Chapter 14

1. **shave (the front of your heads).** Cf. Lev. 21.5. Trad., "make any baldness (between your eyes)."
25. **(Wrap up the money) and take it with you (to the place).** On this idiom involving *be-yadekha,* as against Trad. "(then shalt thou bind up the money) in thy hand, and shalt go," see 1.25 and Introduction, §c.

Chapter 15

1. **remission of debts.** As the context, vv. 2 ff., makes clear. Trad., "a release."

Chapter 16

4. **be found.** Understanding *yera'e* in the light of Exod. 12.15, 19. Trad., "be seen."

6. **there alone.** Reproducing the emphatic force of *sham* at the beginning of its clause.
18. **officials.** Earlier printings read "clerks." Trad., "officers."
19. **the just.** I.e., those in the right. Trad. "the righteous" fails to comprehend *ṣaddiqim* as a legal term.

Chapter 17

6. **(two or) more.** Trad. "three," by rendering *shelosha* here literally rather than idiomatically, is misleading: would the testimony of four or more witnesses negate the penalty?
8. **be it a controversy over homicide, civil law, or assault.** Trad. "between blood and blood, between plea and plea, and between stroke and stroke" is literal, and meaningless.

courts. Understanding *she'arékha* as the place where such disputes were regularly dealt with. Trad., mechanically, "gates."
9. **the levitical priests.** Trad. renders the Hebrew mechanically, "the priests the Levites." Modern scholarship has not been able to agree on what the Hebrew phrase was meant to convey.

Chapter 18

6. **If (a Levite) would go . . . he may do so.** Understanding *u-va* as introducing the apodosis to which the clause beginning with *we-khi yavo* is the protasis. Trad. begins the apodosis with *we-shereth* in v. 7: "And if (a Levite) come . . . and come . . . then he shall minister. . . ." Others (e.g., Driver, Ehrlich, *Randglossen*) would begin the apodosis with v. 8.

Chapter 19

3. **survey.** As against Trad. "prepare" for *takhin,* see at Exod. 16.5.
6. **Otherwise.** As against Trad. "lest" for *pen,* see Introduction, §c.
12. **shall have him brought back.** Trad. "shall send and fetch him" is mechanical, overlooking the idiomatic use of *shalaḥ*; see at Num. 22.10 above and Introduction, §c.
15. **(may not) validate.** Trad. "(shall not) rise up" is mechanical for *yaqum,* overlooking its technical use here as a legal term; cf. Driver (p. 235), "be treated as valid."

Chapter 20

1. **—forces (larger than yours—).** Trad. " and a people (more than thou)" has overlooked a frequent use of *am* in the sense of "troops" (cf. vv. 2 and 5 in this chapter); and in misconstruing the syntax of *am rav mimekha,* it has had to introduce an "and" where the Hebrew does not have it.
4. **to bring (you) victory.** Trad. "to save (you)" for *lehoshi'a (ethkhem)* is mechanical, overlooking the common use of the word for "military victory, triumph"; cf., e.g., *moshi'a* "military leader, champion" in the book of Judges.
7. **paid the bride-price.** Earlier printings read "spoken for a woman[a] ([a]*I.e. has paid the bride-price*"). See at Exod. 22.15.
11. **shall serve you at forced labor.** Trad. "shall become tributary unto thee and shall serve thee"—in addition to missing the hendiadys here (see Introduction, §c)—has failed to note the significance of the term *mas*; thus Driver (p. 235), in preferring "forced labour": " 'tributary' . . . expresses the general sense, but not the special ideas associated

with the Heb. *mas. . . .*" And see I. Mendelsohn's article referred to at Exod. 1.11.

19. **(Are trees of the field human) to withdraw before you into the besieged city?** Understanding *eṣ* as the subject of *lavo,* and *maṣor* (cf. *maqom, malon,* and the like) as "besieged place." See Ehrlich (*Randglossen*). Earlier printings read "under siege," with "into the besieged city" as an alternate reading. Trad., "(for is the tree of the field man) that it should be besieged of thee?"

Chapter 21

4. **a rugged[a] wadi** ([a]*Or watered*"; projected version: *Or "a wadi with a perennial stream"*). Earlier printings read "a watered wadi," with the same alternative rendering. Trad., "a rough valley"—on which see Luzzatto.

5. **and every lawsuit and case of assault[b] is subject to their ruling.** Earlier printings read "and every disputed case of assault," etc., on the assumption that *kol-riv wekhol-néga* constituted hendiadys. Trad., mechanically, "and according to their word shall every controversy and every stroke be."

15. **unloved.** As against mechanical Trad. "hated" for *sane',* see Gen. 29.31; and Introduction, §c.

Chapter 22

1. **If you see . . . do not ignore it.** (Also v. 4.) On the construction, see Ehrlich (*Mikra*), with reference to Num. 23.19. Trad., "Thou shalt not see . . . and hide thyself."

gone astray. Cf. Exod. 23.4 ("wandering"; Trad., "going astray"); Ehrlich (*Mikra*). Trad., "driven away."

ignore (it). (Also v. 4.) Cf. Rashi: "as though you do

not see it." Trad. "hide thyself" gives a false picture; cf. Ehrlich (*Randglossen*). In v. 3 below, (*lo thukhal*) *lehithallem* was rendered "(you must not) remain indifferent" because—unlike vv. 1 and 4, where *mehem* is used—the Hebrew lacks a complementary object.

2. **or (you do not know who he is).** On this force of *we-*(*lo yedato*), after *we-im-lo*—as against mechanical Trad. "and"—see Ehrlich (*Mikra*).

claims. *Trad.* "require" has little meaning here for *darash.*

13. **takes an aversion to (her).** (Also v. 16.) Cf. Driver (p. 254), "i.e. turn against her." Against mechanical Trad. "hate" for *sane'*, see at 21.15 above.

18. **flog.** Cf. Rashi (following Ketubot 46a), Driver. Trad. "chastise" is too vague.

23,25,27. **engaged.** See at 20.7 above, and at Exod. 22.15.

24. **another man's (wife).** Projected version; replaces Trad., and mechanical, "his neighbor's (wife)."

Chapter 23

1. **so as** [a]**-to remove his father's garment**-[a] ([a-a]*I.e. lay claim to what his father had possessed. See Ezek. 16.8* [to be deleted in projected version]; *Ruth 3.9*). Earlier printings read: "so as [a]-to displace his father's skirt-[a] ([a-a]*I.e. to uncover what his father had kept covered. See Ezek. 16.8; Ruth 3.9*)." Trad., "and shall not uncover his father's skirt."

18. **cult prostitute.** Trad. "harlot" would represent *zona* rather than *qedesha.*

20. **deduct interest.** As against Trad. "lend money on interest," see at Lev. 25.37.

25–26. **you may eat as many grapes as you want, until you are full . . . [26]When you enter another man's field of standing grain,** etc. Projected version; replaces "you may, if you desire, eat your fill of the grapes . . . [26]When you find yourself amid your neighbor's standing grain," etc.

Chapter 24

3. **rejects.** As against Trad. "hateth" for *sane'*, see reference at 21.15.
20. **beat down.** See Driver (p. 278). Earlier printings read "shake." Trad., "beatest."

Chapter 25

1. **declaring the one in the right and the other in the wrong.** Trad. "by justifying the righteous and condemning the wicked"—on which Driver had to comment (p. 279): "*Righteous* and *wicked* are here used in their forensic sense . . . *i.e.* they are equivalent to *innocent* and *guilty* respectively. . . ."
5. **outside the family.** Trad. "abroad" hardly brings out the correct force of *haḥúṣa;* cf. Jud. 12.9.

Chapter 26

5. **a fugitive (Aramean).** See Ehrlich. Trad., "a wandering."

Chapter 28

30. **pay the bride-price.** See the reference at 20.7 above.
34. **(you are driven mad) by what your eyes behold.** Trad. "(thou shalt be mad) for the sight of thine eyes which thou shalt see" is less than clear.

Chapter 29

5. **other (liquor** [projected version: **intoxicant]).** See Introduction, §c.

17. **stock.** For this meaning of *shóresh* see Isa. 11.1 and Amos 2.9. Trad., "root."

18. **to the utter ruin of moist and dry alike**[b] ([b]*I.e. everything*). The Hebrew expression is one of many—as indicated in the note—to denote totality. See the article on "*Merismus* in Biblical Hebrew" by A. M. Honeyman, in *Journal of Biblical Literature,* 71 (1952), 11–18; Introduction §c. Trad., "that the watered be swept away with the dry."

Chapter 30

5. **(and He will make you) more prosperous and more numerous (than your fathers).** Trad. "(and He will do thee) good, and multiply thee above (thy fathers)" has failed to recognize that the comparative *me-(avothékha)* applies to *both* verbs preceding (*we-heṭivekha we-hirbekha*).

8. **You, however, will again heed.** Trad. "And thou shalt return and hearken" overlooks the emphatic force of initial *we-attah,* as well as the idiomatic use of *shuv* in *tashuv we-shamata.*

Chapter 31

1. The Septuagint—cf. note *a-a*—derives from, and a Dead Sea Scroll fragment of Deuteronomy reads: *waykhal moshe ledabber* (cf. 32.45), as against received *wa-yélekh moshe waydabber;* see Bibliography, under Dead Sea Scroll.

Chapter 32

17. On note *e-e,* see Driver (bottom of p. 363) with reference to the Septuagint.
19. **saw and was vexed / And spurned (His sons . . .).** See Luzzatto, Ehrlich (*Randglossen*). Trad., "saw, and spurned, / Because of the provoking of (His sons . . .)."
36. **take revenge for.** Cf. Luzzatto, Ehrlich.

Chapter 33

28. **abode.** Understanding *'en* (Trad. "fountain") here as from the same root from which *ma'on,* "dwelling, habitation," derives; cf. *wa-yishkon* ("dwells") in the parallel clause, and *me'ona* in v. 27 preceding.

Bibliography

Bibliography

The *Jewish Encyclopedia* (12 volumes, 1904; reissued recently by KTAV Publishing House) is still the best convenient reference work for information on the Jewish texts and commentators listed below or referred to in the *Notes* generally. The rabbinic texts (Sifra, Sifre, etc.) are readily identified in M. L. Margolis's English version of H. L. Strack's *Introduction to the Talmud and Midrash* (JPS, Philadelphia, 1931). Translations of the Bible up to half a century ago are conveniently dealt with in M. L. Margolis's *The Story of Bible Translations* (JPS, Philadelphia, 1917) and more recently in H. G. May's account of *Our English Bible in the Making,* 2nd edition (Philadelphia, 1965). A useful survey of Bible translations, commentaries, lexicons, dictionaries, and the like may be found in H. M. Orlinsky's chapter on "Old Testament Studies," pp. 51–109 (and see the Index there) in *Religion,* ed. P. Ramsey (Prentice-Hall, 1965, in the series *Humanistic Scholarship in America: The Princeton Studies*). Those who read Yiddish will find very useful M. Kosover's *Lexicon of Sources and Exegetes in Yehoash's Notes on the Bible* (6+62 pp.), published with Yehoash's own *Notes* (*He'aros tsum Tanakh fun Yehoash*), ed. B. and E. Dworkin (New York, 1949/5710; iv+317 pp.). In 1917 the Jewish Publication Society reproduced, "For Private Circulation Only," *Notes on the New [1917] Translation of the Holy Scriptures* compiled in typewritten form by M. L. Margolis; these notes are rather on the technical-factual side.

Abravanel, Isaac (1437–1508): commentary (*Perush*) on the Pentateuch. See B. Nethanyahu's biography, *Don Isaac Abravanel,* 2nd edition (JPS, Philadelphia, 1968); on the name, see pp. 261–63.

Albright, W. F.: "Historical and Mythical Elements in the Story of Joseph," *JBL,* 37 (1918), 111–143.

———: "The Names *Shaddai* and *Abram*," *JBL,* 54 (1935), 173–204.

———: "The End of 'Calneh in Shinar,'" *JNES,* 3 (1944), 254–55.

———: "Abram the Hebrew: A New Archaeological Interpretation," *BASOR,* 163 (Oct. 1961), 36–54; see also 164 (Dec. 1961), 28.

Alshech, Moses (16th century): *Torath Mosheh,* a commentary on the Torah, based on his Sabbath lectures on the sidra of the week.

An American Translation (University of Chicago, 1927); revised edition by T. J. Meek (1939; reprinted frequently).

Barrois, G. A.: "Oven," *IDB,* III, 612–13.

Baumgartner, W.: see L. Koehler.

Berlin (Netsiv), Naphtali Zevi Yehudah (1817–1893): *Ha'ameq Davar,* a commentary on the Torah.

La Bible de Jérusalem: see *La Sainte Bible.*

Bodenheimer, F. S.: "Fauna," *IDB,* II, 246–56.

Brin, G.: "On the Expression *ben-ham-mélekh*," *Leshonenu,* 31 (1966–7/5727), 5–20, 85–96.

Brown, F.; Driver, S. R.; Briggs, C. A. (*BDB*): *A Hebrew and English Lexicon of the Old Testament* (Oxford, 1906; often reprinted, and a new, revised edition in process).

Cartledge, S. A.: "Tanner, Tanning," *IDB,* IV, 516.

Caspi, Joseph (ibn) (1297–1340): commentator on the Bible, on Ibn Janaḥ's grammatical work, Ibn Ezra's commentary on the Bible, etc.

Cassuto, M. D. (U.): *From Adam to Noah* (Hebrew; Jerusalem, 1944/5704).

———: *From Noah to Abraham* (Hebrew; Jerusalem, 1949/5709).

———: *A Commentary on the Book of Exodus* (Hebrew; Jerusalem, 1953/5714).

All three works now available in English translation (by I. Abrahams).

———: "*'Alluf*," *Encyclopediah Miqra'ith,* I (1950), 332.

Cooke, G. B.: "Mist," *IDB,* III, 406.

Cross, F. M., Jr.; Freedman, D. N.: "The Blessing of Moses," *JBL,* 67 (1948), 191–210.

Davies, G. H.: "High Place, Sanctuary," *IDB,* II, 602–04.

Dead Sea Scroll: For the reading *waykhal moshe ledabber* at Deut. 31.1, see *Discoveries in the Judaean Desert,* I: *Qumran Cave I,* ed. D. Barthélemy–J. T. Milik (Oxford, 1955), § 13 on pp. 59 f. (and plate X).

Driver, G. R.: "Three Technical Terms in the Pentateuch," *Journal of Semitic Studies,* 1 (1956), 97–105.

Driver, S. R.: *The Book of Genesis,* 3rd edition (in *Westminster Commentary* series; 1904; often reprinted).

———: *The Book of Exodus* (*Cambridge Bible* series; 1911).

———: *A Critical and Exegetical Commentary on Deuteronomy* (*International Critical Commentary* [ICC] series; 1896).

———: *Notes on the Hebrew Text . . . of the Books of Samuel,* 2nd edition (Oxford, 1913).

———: *An Introduction to the Literature of the Old Testament,* rev. edition (New York, 1914).

(See also Brown-Driver-Briggs (*BDB*)

Ehrlich, A. B.: *Mikrâ Ki-Pheschutô,* 3 volumes (Hebrew; Berlin, 1899–1901/5659–5661; KTAV reissue, 1969).

———: *Randglossen zur hebräischen Bibel,* 7 volumes (Leipzig, 1908–14).

Encyclopedia of Biblical Interpretation (*EBI*), edited and translated by H. Freedman, 7 volumes to date (New York, 1953—), an abbreviated and select version of *Torah Shelemah.*

Epstein, Baruch Halevi: see *Torah Temimah.*

Epstein, J. N.: see *Mechilta.*

Evans, G.: " 'Coming' and 'Going' at the 'City Gate'—a Discussion of Professor Speiser's Paper," *BASOR,* 150 (April 1958), 28–33.

———: "Ancient Mesopotamian Assemblies," *JAOS,* 78 (1958), 1–11, 114.

Evans, O. E.: "Kingdom of God of Heaven," *IDB,* III, 17–26.

Finkelstein, J. J.: "An Old Babylonian Herding Contract and Genesis 31:38 f.," *JAOS,* 88 (1968) 30–36.

Freedman, D. N.: see under F. M. Cross, Jr.

Freedman, H.: see under *Encyclopedia of Biblical Interpretation.*

Frerichs, W. W.: "Gnat," *IDB,* II, 403–04.

Galling, K.: "Incense Altars," *IDB,* II, 699–700.

Gaster, T. H.: articles in *Interpreter's Dictionary of the Bible* (*IDB*): "Demon(ology)" (I, 817 ff.); "Firmament" (II, 270); and "Heaven" (II, 351–52).

Gersonides: see Ralbag.

Gesenius, W.; Kautzsch, E.; Cowley, A. E.: *Hebrew Grammar,* 2nd English edition (Oxford, 1910).

Gewirtz, S.: "A New Look at an Old Crux: Amos 5_{26}," *JBL,* 87 (1968), 267–76.

Ginsberg, H. L.: *The Ugarit Texts* (Hebrew; Jerusalem, 1936).

———: "A Preposition of Interest to Historical Geographers," *BASOR,* 122 (April 1951), 12–14.

———; with B. Maisler (Mazar): "Semitised Hurrians in Syria and Palestine," *Journal of the Palestine Oriental Society,* 14 (1934), 243–267.

Ginsburg, C. D.: *Introduction to the Massoretico-Critical Edition of the Hebrew Bible* (1897; KTAV reissue, 1966).

Goldbaum, F. J.: "Two Hebrew Quasi-Adverbs: *lakhen* and *'akhen,*" *JNES,* 23 (1964), 132–35.

Good, E. M.: "Basket," *IDB,* I, 364–65.

Gordon, C. H.: "Abraham and the Merchants of Ura," *JNES,* 17 (1958), 28–31.

———: "Calneh," *IDB,* I, 490.

———: *Ugaritic Textbook* (=*Analecta Orientalia;* Rome, 1965).

Greenberg, M.: "*Hebrew* sᵉg̱ullå: *Akkadian* sikiltu," *JAOS,* 71 (1951), 172–74.

———: "Another Look at Rachel's Theft of the Teraphim," *JBL,* 81 (1962), 239–48.

Greenfield, J. C.: "Caphtor," *IDB,* I, 534.

———: "Philistines," *IDB,* III, 791–95.

Ha'ameq Davar: see Berlin (Netsiv).

Hamburger, H.: "Money," *IDB,* III, 423–35.

Harrison, R. K.: "Leprosy," *IDB,* III, 111–113.

Ḥayyim ben Attar: see *Or Ha-Ḥayyim.*

Heidel, A.: *The Babylonian Genesis: The Story of Creation,* 2nd edition (Chicago, 1951).

Held, M.: "The Root *ZBL/SBL* in Akkadian, Ugaritic and Biblical Hebrew," *JAOS,* 88 (1968), 90–96.

Hershberg, J.: *Pardes Ha-Lashon* (Hebrew; New York, 1950/5710).

Hertz, J. H. (1872–1946): *The Pentateuch and Haftarahs with Commentary* (1936; frequently reprinted).

Hezekiah ben Manoah: see *Hizkuni.*

Hizkuni (more correctly, *Ḥazzequni*): a cabalistic commentary on the Torah by Hezekiah ben Manoah (13th century), based on a score of other commentaries and studies.

Honeyman, A. M.: "*Merismus* in Biblical Hebrew," *JBL,* 71 (1952), 11–18.

Ibn Ezra, Abraham (1089–1164): his noted commentary on the Bible may be found in most editions of the rabbinic Bible (*Miqra'oth Gedoloth*).

Ibn Janah, Jonah Abu'l Walid (11th century): *Perush le-Kithve Ha-Qodesh* (collected biblical comments from his several works), ed. A. D. Rabinowitz, 2nd edition (Tel Aviv, 1935/36–5696).

Interpreter's Dictionary of the Bible (*IDB*): 4 volumes (Abingdon Press, 1962).

Iwry, S.: "A Striking Variant Reading in 1QIs[a]," *Textus,* 5 (1966), 34–43.

Jacob, B.: *Das erste Buch der Tora: Genesis* (Berlin, 1934).

Jacobsen, T.: "Shinar," *IDB,* IV, 332.

The Jerusalem Bible: an English version (1966) of *La Bible de Jérusalem–La Sainte Bible* (1956).

Joseph ben Isaac Bechor Shor (12th century): rationalist commentator on the Bible, acquainted with the Vulgate and Christian exegesis.

Kelso, J. L.: *The Ceramic Vocabulary of the Old Testament* (*BASOR, Supplementary Studies* 5–6, 1948).

———: articles in *IDB* on "Pottery" (III, 846–53) and "Vessels" (IV, 783).

Koehler, L.: *Lexicon in Veteris Testamenti Libros* (Leiden, 1948–53) with *Supplementum* (1958). A second, much-revised edition, ed. W. Baumgartner (who was responsible for *Daniel* in the first edition), is now in process (part I, *'aleph-ṭévaḥ,* appeared in 1967).

Kramer, S. N.: "Sumer," *IDB,* IV, 454–63.

Kraus, F. R.: "Ein Edikt des Königs Samsu-iluna von Babylon," in *Studies in Honor of B. Landsberger* (*Assyriological Studies,* No. 16; Chicago, 1965).

Lambdin, T. O.: "Egyptian Loanwords in the Old Testament," *JAOS,* 73 (1953), 145–55.

Lauterbach, J. Z.: see *Mekilta.*

Leḳaḥ Ṭov: a midrashic commentary on the Torah and Megilloth by Tobiah ben Eliezer (11th–12th centuries).

Lewy, J.: "The Biblical Institution of *D*[e]*rôr* in the Light of Akkadian Documents," *Eretz-Israel,* 5 (1958), 21–31.

Loewe, R.: "Divine Frustration Exegetically Frustrated—Num. 14:34 *T*[e]*nu'athi,*" in *Words and Meanings: Essays Presented to D. W. Thomas,* ed. P. R. Ackroyd; B. Lindars (Cambridge, 1968), 137–58.

Luzzatto, Samuel David (Shadal; 1800–65): *Commentary to the Pentateuch* (Hebrew), ed. P. Schlesinger (Dvir, Tel Aviv, 1965–5726).

McCullough, W. S.: articles in *IDB* on "Goatskin" (II, 407), "Leather" (III, 104), and "Worms" (IV, 878).

Maimonides: see Rambam.

Maisler (Mazar), B.: see under H. L. Ginsberg.

Malbim (Meir Leibush ben Yehiel Michael; 1809–79): *Ha-Torah we-ha-Miṣwah,* a notable commentary on the Torah (and Sifra).

Mandelkern, S.: *Concordanṣiah le-Tanakh,* revised edition by M. Goshen-Gottstein (Schocken, 1962/5722).

Margolis, M. L.: *The Story of Bible Translations* (JPS, 1917).

———: (unsigned article) "The New English Translation of the Bible," *American Jewish Year Book,* 19 (1917–18), 164–93 (reprinted by JPS, 1917; 33 pp.).

See also introductory statement to Bibliography.

Margulies, M.: see *Midrash Wayyikra Rabbah.*

Massekhet Soferim, ed. M. Higger (New York, 1937/5697).

May, H. G.: "Hamath, Entrance of," *IDB,* II, 516–17.

Mechilta de-Rabbi Simeon ben Johai, ed. J. N. Epstein; E. Z. Melamed (Jerusalem, 1955/5715).

Mekilta de-Rabbi Ishmael, edited and translated by J. Z. Lauterbach, 3 volumes (JPS, 1933–35).

Melamed, E. Z.: *"Shnayim She hem Eḥad (hen dià duoîn) Be-Miqra," Tarbiẕ,* 16 (1945/5705), 173–89, 242.

See also under *Mechilta de-Rabbi Simeon ben Johai.*

Menaḥem ben Solomon: see *Sechel Tob.*

Mendelsohn, I.: "Guilds in Ancient Palestine," *BASOR,* 80 (December 1940), 17–21.

———: "Gilds [*sic*] in Babylonia and Assyria," *JAOS,* 60 (1944), 68–72.

———: "On Corvée Labor in Ancient Canaan and Israel," *BASOR,* 167 (October 1962), 31–35.

Meyuḥas ben Elijah: commentary on the Torah (London, 1909).

Midrash Ha-Gadol, on the Pentateuch; a post-Maimonidean Yemenite compilation of older materials.

Midrash Wayyikra Rabbah, ed. M. Margulies, 5 volumes (Jerusalem, 1953/60–5713/20).

Mihelic, J. L.: articles in *IDB* on "Firepan" (II, 270), "Red Sea" (IV, 19–21), and "Snuffers" (IV, 394).

Moffat, J.: *A New Translation of the Bible,* revised edition (1936; frequently reprinted).

Montgomery, J. A.: *A Critical and Exegetical Commentary on the Books of Kings,* ed. H. S. Gehman (*ICC* series; 1951).

Moore, G. F.: "The Vulgate Chapters and Numbered Verses in the Hebrew Bible," *JBL,* 12 (1893), 73–78.

Myers, J. M.: "Brooch," *IDB,* II, 467.

Nachmanides: see Ramban.

Netter, Shlomo Zalman: see *Perush 'al Ibn Ezra.*

Neuman, A. A.: *The Immortality of Man: A Jewish Viewpoint* (Lancaster, Pa., 1949; 26 pp.).

Or Ha-Ḥayyim: a commentary on the Torah by Ḥayyim ben Moses ibn Attar (1696–1743).

Orlinsky, H. M.: "On the Cohortative and Jussive after an Imperative or Interjection in Biblical Hebrew," *JQR,* 31 (1940–41), 371–82; 32 (1941–42), 191–205, 273–77.

———: "Critical Notes on Gen. $39_{14,\ 17}$ Jud. 11_{37}," *JBL,* 61 (1942), 91, n. 8.

———: "On Biblical *TÔP̄EŚ-TÔP̄ŚÊ,*" *JQR,* 34 (1943–44), 281–97.

———: "The Hebrew Root *ŠKB,*" *JBL,* 63 (1944), 19–44.

———: "The New Jewish Version of the Torah: Toward a New Philosophy of Bible Translation," *JBL,* 82 (1963), 249–64.

———: *The Masoretic Text: A Critical Evaluation.* Prolegomenon to KTAV reissue of C. D. Ginsburg's *Introduction to the Massoretico-Critical Edition of the Hebrew Bible* (1966).

See also under Rashi, *The Pentateuch and Rashi's Commentary;* Septuagint.

Perush 'al Ibn Ezra: commentary on Ibn Ezra by R. Shlomo Zalman Netter (in Horeb edition of rabbinic Bible, New York-Berlin, 1928/5688).

Peshitta: ancient Syriac translation of the Bible (1st–2nd centuries C.E.).

Rad, G. von: *Genesis: A Commentary* (Philadelphia, 1961).

Radak (David Kimchi, 1160–1235): his notable commentary on most of the Bible (as well as his grammatical-lexicographical works) has had the widest influence on Bible translations and interpretations.

Ralbag (Levi ben Gershon, Gersonides; Magister Leo Hebraeus; 1288–1344): his commentary on the Torah may be found in the rabbinic Bible.

Rambam (Moses ben Maimon, Maimonides; 1135–1204).

Ramban (Moses ben Naḥman, Nachmanides; 1194–*c.*1270]: his commentary on the Torah may be found in the rabbinic Bible.

Rashbam (Samuel ben Meir, grandson of Rashi; *c.* 1085–1174): his commentary on the Torah may be found in the rabbinic Bible.

Rashi (R. Solomon ben Isaac; 1040–1105): *The Pentateuch and Rashi's Commentary: A Linear Translation into English,* 5 volumes, by A. ben Isaiah; B. Sharfman; H. M. Orlinsky; M. Charner (Brooklyn, N. Y., 1949–1950). The reader may consult with profit such general works as the *Rashi Anniversary Volume* (American Academy for Jewish Research; New York, 1941); H. Hailperin, *Rashi and the Christian Scholars* (University of Pittsburgh Press, 1963); or the popular article by E. Shereshevsky, "The Significance of Rashi's Commentary on the Pentateuch," *JQR,* 54 (1963–64), 58–79.

Reed, W. L.: "Asherah," *IDB,* I, 250–52.

Reggio, Isaac Samuel (1784–1885): author of a rationalistic commentary on the Torah, *Sefer Torath Ha-Elohim* (Wien, 1818).

Revised Standard Version (RSV): *The Holy Bible containing the Old and New Testaments* (1952; frequently reprinted).

Ross, J. F.: "Flour," *IDB,* II, 302; "Strong Drink," *IDB,* I, 448.

Saadia ben Joseph (882–942): *Version Arabe du Pentateuque* (Paris, 1893), in series *Oeuvres Complètes de R. Saadia ben Iosef al-Fayyoûmî,* ed. J. Derenbourg.

Saarisalo, A.: *The Boundary between Issachar and Naphtali* (1927).

La Sainte Bible: French translation of the Bible by the Dominican École Biblique of Jerusalem (Paris, 1956); also known as *La Bible de Jérusalem* (Paris, 1961). See also *Jerusalem Bible.*

Sarna, N.: *Understanding Genesis* (New York, 1966).

Schefftel, S. B.: *Biure Onkelos,* ed. J. Perles (Hebrew; München, 1888).

Sechel Tob: a midrashic compilation on the Torah by Menaḥem ben Solomon (12th century).

Septuagint: for the interested reader, there is now available S. Jellicoe's *The Septuagint and Modern Study* (Oxford, 1968), in conjunction with H. B. Swete's basic work, *An Introduction to the Old Testament in Greek* (KTAV reissue, 1968); H. M. Orlinsky's *The Septuagint: The Oldest Translation of the Bible* (*Union* [of American Hebrew Congegation] *Anniversary Series,* 1949; 20 pp.) is a convenient essay. Data on Theodotion, Aquila, and Symmachus, translators of the Bible into Greek, will be found in these works.

Sforno, Obadiah ben Jacob (1475–1550): his commentary on the Torah may be found in the rabbinic Bible (*Miqra'oth Gedoloth*).

Shadal: see Samuel David Luzzatto.

Sifra (*Torath Kohanim*): a halakhic midrash on Leviticus.

Sifre: a halakhic midrash on Numbers.

Snaith, N. H.: *Leviticus and Numbers* (in new series *The Century Bible,* 1967).

Speiser, E. A.: " 'Coming' and 'Going' at the 'City Gate,' " *BASOR,* 144 (Dec. 1956), 20–23.

———: "Leviticus and the Critics," in *Yehezkel Kaufmann Jubilee Volume,* ed. M. Haran (Jerusalem, 1960), 29–45.

———: " 'People' and 'Nation' of Israel," *JBL,* 79 (1960), 157–63.

———: "The Word *SḤR* in Genesis and Early Hebrew Movements," *BASOR,* 164 (Dec. 1961), 23–28.

———: "Man, Ethnic Divisions of," *IDB,* III, 235–42.

———: *Genesis* (in *The Anchor Bible* series; 1964).

Staples, W. E.: "Bitumen," *IDB,* I, 444.

Tanḥuma: a midrash attributed to Rabbi Tanḥuma bar Abba (4th century).

Targum: for those who wish to go beyond the popular editions in the rabbinic Bibles *(Miqra'oth Gedoloth)*—J. W. Etheridge's English translation of *The Targums of Onkelos and Jonathan ben Uzziel on the Pentateuch with the Fragments of the Jerusalem Targum* (1862–1865) has now been reissued in one volume by KTAV (1968)—there is now available *The Bible in Aramaic,* 4 volumes to date (Onkelos on the Pentateuch, Jonathan on the Nevi'im and Kethubim), ed. A. Sperber (Leiden, 1959–1968).

Tobiah ben Eliezer: see *Leḳaḥ Ṭov.*

Toombs, L. E.: "Lampstand," *IDB,* III, 64–66.

Torah Shelemah, ed. M. Kasher, 22 volumes to date—an extremely full collection of rabbinic, medieval, and modern Jewish interpretations of the Torah.

Torah Temimah: a compilation of rabbinic interpretations of the Bible, by Baruch Halevi Epstein (1904; frequently reprinted).

Trad(itional): while referring specifically to the JPS Bible Translation of 1917, such authorized translations as King James Version, Revised Version, American Standard Version, and Revised Standard Version are by no means excluded, since they frequently exhibit the same translation or interpretation.

Trever, J. C.: articles in *IDB* on "Myrrh" (III, 478–79), "Reed" (IV, 22–23), "Sweet Cane" (IV, 468–69), and "Wheat" (IV, 839–40).

Vulgate: Latin translation of the Bible made by Saint Jerome (Hieronymus) *c.* 390–405; it became the official Bible of the Roman Catholic Church.

Werner, E.: "Musical Instruments," *IDB,* III, 469–76.
Wickwire, C. L.: articles in *IDB* on "Crimson" (I, 744) and "Scarlet" (IV, 233–34).

Yehoash (Solomon Bloomgarden): *Torah, Nevi'im, u-Kethuvim* (several editions); see H. M. Orlinsky, "Yehoash's Yiddish Translation of the Bible," *JBL,* 60 (1941), 173–77.
———: *Notes (He'aros tsum Tanakh)*—see at head of Bibliography.

Zeitlin, S.: "Some Reflections on the Text of the Pentateuch," *JQR,* 51 (1960–61), 321–31; 52 (1961–62), 130.
Zohary, M.: "Flora," *IDB,* II, 290 f. (§A 7 e).

INDEX OF AUTHORS, SUBJECTS, AND WORDS

(See also Bibliography)

"Trad." indicates a traditional rendering that is sometimes rejected; t.=times.

INDEX OF BIBLICAL AND OTHER PASSAGES (apart from those found in their natural chapter-verse sequence in the *Notes*)

For references to Mekilta, Sifra, Sifre, the Midrashim (Bereshith Rabba and Wayyiḳra Rabba, Midrash Ha-Gadol), and the Baraita, see Index of Authors, Subjects, and Words.